First published in 2021 by Agenda Publishing

Agenda Publishing Limited
The Core
Bath Lane
Newcastle Helix
Newcastle upon Tyne
NE4 5TF
www.agendapub.com

ISBN 978-1-78821-420-9

British Library Cataloguing-in-Publication Data
A catalogue record for this book is available from the British Library

Typeset by JS Typesetting Ltd, Porthcawl, Mid Glamorgan
Printed and bound in the UK by CPI Group (UK) Ltd, Croydon, CR0 4YY

Contents

Preface

Until recently, we thought we were pretty clear about money. It was quite simply the notes and coins in our wallets, or our debit and credit cards, or the welcome additions to our bank accounts, appearing as credits on our screens or on our bank statements. We never doubted that a shop would accept cash, or cards, when we pay for goods and services. We transfer money to other people's bank accounts either in the same country or to another, rarely doubting that it will arrive, even if we might consider the process slow and expensive. Most people in developed economies do not give the form of money or the underlying processes which ensure it functions a moment's thought. Their only concern is very likely the need or desire for more money!

The arrival of new forms of "money" – so-called "cryptocurrencies" – has created much interest and considerable controversy. The purpose of this book is to describe, explain and evaluate the attempts to provide these new currencies as alternatives to fiat money, the government-issued currencies. We shall examine in detail these various forms of new currencies and consider whether or not they can really count as "money" and can replace the familiar forms. Concerns about the safety and reliability of digital assets and their impact on fiat money and monetary policy has led to many central banks exploring the possibility of issuing their own digital currency. The book shall also assess the possible emergence of a central bank digital currency and what that might mean for money.

The key theme throughout this book is that these various efforts to replace fiat currency with cryptocurrencies fail because their structures cannot establish trust, which is essential for money to operate as a means of exchange and value. It is ironic that "trust" was a key motivation behind the first "peer-to-peer electronic cash systems", designed in the wake of the global financial crisis when faith in central banks and the global financial system was at its weakest. Satoshi Nakamoto, the developer behind Bitcoin, wrote in one of his posts in February 2009:

> The root problem with conventional currency is all the trust that's required to make it work. The central bank must be trusted not to debase the currency ... Banks must be trusted to hold our money and transfer it electronically, but they lend it out in waves of credit bubbles with barely a fraction in reserve. We have to trust them with our privacy, trust them not to let identity thieves drain our reserves.[1]

The book begins with Bitcoin, by far and away the most well-known cryptocurrency. Chapter 1 outlines the development of Bitcoin and identifies some of the problems with it. The following chapters then examine the broader idea of a digital currency and its development over the ensuing decade or more. Chapter 2 examines attempts to overcome the vulnerabilities of Bitcoin, by introducing new variants of Bitcoin – "altcoins" – and the development of Ethereum, the decentralized, open source blockchain. Chapter 3 looks at "stablecoins", an attempt to overcome the extreme volatility of Bitcoin by linking it to a fiat currency, such as the US dollar or physical assets such as gold or to some kind of algorithm. The characteristics of stablecoins and whether or not they meet the ideal standards are examined. Chapter 4 charts the proliferation of initial coin offerings in the heady years of 2017–18, which led to the introduction of a vast array of stablecoins, many of which did not actually come into existence and others which were used to defraud potential investors.

The era of unregulated ICOs led to increased regulatory attention and the introduction of regulations to cover stablecoins, which are discussed in Chapter 5. The focus on stablecoins and then especially, global stablecoins, was sharpened by the potential introduction of Libra/Diem, the global stablecoin announced by Facebook in 2019. Chapters 6 and 7 considers this significant development and the intense regulatory and political scrutiny the proposals have received from international standard setting bodies.

The potential arrival of Libra (now called Diem) had another, probably unforeseen, effect. Central banks and regulatory authorities began to develop their own proof-of-concept projects to understand the core technology of cryptocurrencies, blockchain and distributed ledger technology (DLT) and how it might be used in clearing and settlement. These were undertaken, partly to understand the use and risks of the technology, and partly to ensure that such developments were under the purview of the central banks. These projects led, perhaps inevitably, to the central banks themselves considering their own central bank digital currency (CBDC), which are considered, alongside the decline in cash, in Chapters 8 and 9. The final chapter returns to the notions of trust and credit and examines the unresolved challenges of privacy and the concentration of economic power that cryptocurrencies, including CBDCs, exhibit.

I would like to express my gratitude to David Black at OakHC/FT for his expertise on technical aspects and also to two anonymous referees. Needless to say, any remaining errors remain my responsibility.

Acronyms

AML/CFT	Anti-Money Laundering and Combating the Financing of Terrorism
BoE	Bank of England
BIS	Bank for International Settlements
CAFF	Cambridge Centre for Alternative Finance
CSA	Canadian Securities Administrators
CBDC	central bank digital currency
CFTC	Commodity Futures Trading Commission
CPMI	Committee on Payments and Market Infrastructure
CPP	central counterparties
CPU	Central Processing Unit
CSD	Central Securities Depository
CSD/SSS	central securities depositories and securities settlement systems
CTPs	cryptoasset trading platforms
DAO	decentralized autonomous organization
DApps	decentralized applications
DTCC	Deposit Trust and Clearing Corporation
DeFi	decentralized finance
DLT	distributed ledger technology
DVP	delivery versus payment
EBA	European Bankers Authority
ECB	European Central Bank

ESMA	European Securities and Markets Authority
FATF	Financial Action Task Force
FIEA	Financial Instruments and Exchange Act (Japan)
FINMA	Financial Markets Supervisory Authority (Switzerland)
FI	Finansinspektionen (Sweden)
Fintrac	Financial Transactions and Reports Analysis Centre of Canada
FPC	Financial Policy Committee (UK)
FSB	Financial Stability Board
GDPR	General Data Protection Regulation
ICO	initial coin offering
IPO	initial public offering
IOSCO	International Organisation of Securities Commissions
JFSA	Japan Financial Services Authority
LN	lightning network
MAS	Monetary Authority of Singapore
MDIA	Malta Digital Innovation Authority
MiCA	Markets in Crypto Assets
MFSA	Maltese Financial Services Authority
MiFID	Markets in Financial Instruments Directive
MiFIR	Markets in Financial Instruments Regulation
MMF	money market funds
NFC	near field communication
NYAG	New York State Attorney General
OECD	Organisation for Economic Co-operation and Development
OTC	over-the-counter
PIP	payment interface provider
PSA	Payment Services Act (Singapore)
PSD	Payment Services Directive
PVP	payment versus payment
QR code	quick response code
SBA	Swedish Banking Association
SEC	Securities and Exchange Commission
SPV	simplified payment verification
VFA	Virtual Financial Assets (Malta)
VPN	virtual private networks

CHAPTER 1

Introduction: Bitcoin beginnings

Satoshi Nakamoto published the paper, "The Peer-to-Peer Electronic Cash System" in October 2008 and in 2009 he mined the first Bitcoin on the Bitcoin blockchain, now known as the Genesis Block. Bitcoin's aim was to replace banks with a new currency without financial intermediaries of any kind. It was launched at a time when trust in the traditional banking system and central banks had been sorely tested after the global financial crisis. This "new" form of money created great excitement. It promised a way forward that escaped the dominance of the central banks over the supply of money, and of transferring value from one person to another person without expensive intermediaries.

The use of the word "coin" is misleading in the case of Bitcoin, as it is completely digital. It does not represent notes, bills or coins. A person who owns Bitcoins has a long series of numbers, the "private" key, which is the key to the place where Bitcoin is stored in the one and only Bitcoin "bank". Using that key, a person can transfer Bitcoin to another person, that is, to the key known to that person. The transactions are recorded in an ever-growing ledger, holding all the Bitcoins ever created and all the transactions which have ever taken place. The many transactions are stored in a block and all the blocks are linked together in a chain, with the first block, the "root block", holding the first Bitcoin ever created. The ever-lengthening chain of transaction-holding blocks, the blockchain, are stored on many computers, all networked, so that even the loss of dozens of computers would not cause a problem. A block is only added to the chain when most of the computers agree that everything about the new transactions in the block is correct, after which all the computers store the newly lengthened chain of blocks. The miners are paid with newly minted Bitcoins in exchange for their work.

Nakamoto announced that his electronic transfer system does not rely on trust in any intermediary. Instead of currency-users having to trust the integrity of the extensive commercial and central banking system, all currency and the equivalent of accounts would be managed by a body of computer software running on an all-volunteer network of computer servers (nodes) that create and maintain the new currency and handle payments between currency holders. The software that the nodes run is termed "mining" software, and the nodes that run it are called "miners". In other words, the term "node" refers to a computer on a network.

The usual process involved in joining a network is that a person downloads a copy of the Bitcoin miner software code, setting it up to run one or more copies of that program. Once the miner is running, it reaches out and connects with other miners, thus becoming another node in the network. A single physical location can have many other nodes, each connecting with each other and with nodes "outside" the physical location. Once established, the system is "secure as long as honest nodes collectively control more CPU (central computing unit) of a computer than any cooperative group of attacker nodes".[1] Then the "honest chain will grow the fastest and outpace any competing chain".[2] Anyone using Bitcoin only has to believe that the honest nodes have most of the central processing unit (CPU) power of the miners. As long as the nodes remain honest, and they have every incentive to do that, according to Nakamoto, then an "electronic payments system based on cryptographic proof instead of trust, allowing any two willing partners to transact directly with each other without the need for a trusted third party" will work. "Money can be secure and transactions effortless".[3] The nodes themselves do not need to be selected or controlled by a central authority. They volunteer and if they are prepared to invest the necessary funds to acquire the computer power, and the required effort to run the miner software, they will be rewarded with Bitcoins.

Nakamoto describes the security as follows:

> ... the network time stamps transactions and hashing them into an ongoing chain of hash-based proof-of-work, it forms a record that cannot be changed without re-doing the proof-of-work. The longest

chain not only serves as proof of the sequence of events witnessed, but proof that it came from the largest pool of CPU power. As long as the majority of CPU power is controlled by nodes that are co-operating to extend the network, they'll generate the longest chain and outpace the attackers.[4]

Miners who choose not to follow the rules, run the right software or do something else in the hopes of getting illicit profits are wasting their time and money. This is because the majority decision is represented by the longest chain, the honest chain, which records all transactions in the order in which they have been received. To alter the past block, an attacker would have to "redo the proof-of-work of the block and all the blocks after it and then catch up with and surpass the work of all the honest nodes".[5] Its basis is cryptography, designed to secure transactions, thus ensuring that people cannot steal from each other or "double-spend" (see below).

HASHING

A Bitcoin is simply a chain of digital signatures, which each owner transfers to another by digitally signing a hash, a kind of code, which keeps Bitcoin's blockchain secure. The "hash" is a short, fixed length of data, which uniquely corresponds to a longer, variable piece of data. It is computed by an algorithm using SHA-256, a variation on the National Security Agency's SHA-2, (a secure hash algorithm) developed in 2001.[6] The hash of a block's header, which must be 256 bits (binary numbers, either 0 or 1), confirms whether the data from which it was derived/computed has been altered. It is usually a quick process to apply the hash algorithm to the data to compute the hash and if the newly-computed hash is not exactly the same as the hash stored with the data, then the data has been altered.

Hashes are used in several places in Bitcoin, always with the same purpose: to see whether the data, which was hashed was altered. For example, when data is stored on a disk or sent on a network, a hash of the data is often included. When the data (and hash) are read from a disk or the network, checking to see if a newly-computed hash of the data as read or received matches the original hash is a reliable way to assure the data is unaltered. Similarly, each transaction and each block (which contains many transactions) are created along with a hash of data.

The hash used to assure the integrity of a block on the blockchain is given special treatment and it is a key component of the novelty of Bitcoin. To prevent a malicious miner from changing transaction data by re-computing hashes to make it appear that nothing had been altered, Nakamoto added the requirement for "proof-of-work" for blocks in the blockchain. One key component of "proof-of-work" is a special 32-bit piece of data, called a nonce added to the block header. These act as essential protections.

The proof-of-work process involves identifying the "block header", a particular hash which is used to identify a particular block on the blockchain. All the miners try to get a conforming hash for a newly proposed block by varying the nonce and recomputing a new hash for the block until a starting-zeros requirement is met. The miner who completes this arduous "proof-of-work" sends the conforming block to all the other miners, who confirm its integrity and add a new block to their copy of the chain. The miners compete in calculating the hash out of 4 billion possible nonce values to select the currently required number of zeros at the start of the 256 bit hash. Although this process is often described as solving a complex mathematical problem, it is nothing of the sort. It is simply a matter of continually searching for one nonce after another until the computer hits upon the right one.

At present, only hashes which meet certain requirements, starting with at least ten consecutive zeros qualify to be added to the blockchain. Adding transactions to the blockchain requires considerable computer processing power. The individuals and computers who process the blocks are the "miners". They are rewarded only if they are they are the first to create a "hash" which meets a certain set of requirements. Naturally the rush to complete the hash is very competitive, because the first to do so, is rewarded with a certain number of Bitcoins. They are searching for a nonce[7] and success in finding the nonce is the "proof-of-work".

The digital signatures link the blocks to each other, making a chain of blocks, each containing a number of transactions. If one of the signatures is altered, then blocks 1 and 2 are no longer chained to each other. The blocks in the chain are publicly available, so that any alteration of the blocks is immediately obvious. However, that only works if the participants agree on a single

4

history of the order in which notification of transactions has been received for which a timestamp server is required. This server works by taking a hash of a block of items to be timestamped and widely publishing the hash, proving the data must have existed at the time. Each timestamp includes the previous one in the hash, forming a chain. As new blocks are added to the chain, anyone wishing to alter a particular block in order to remove a particular transaction, would have to undo all the subsequent blocks, which is an extremely unlikely event. If there is a dispute, the longest chain, representing the most intensive proof-of-work will be considered the valid chain.

This process is called "mining". Miners use their computational power to solve these puzzles by a process of trial and error, that is, by repeatedly changing the nonce and hashing it until they find an eligible signature. Millions of users across the world are engaged in mining so it is assumed that if one attacker wishes to alter a block, they will not have enough computational power to outsmart the rest.[8] The mining process is expensive, so why would anyone take part in the process? The one who solves the puzzle first is rewarded with a transaction fee, paid in Bitcoins. On the Bitcoin chain, all transaction history and wallet balances are made public but the owners remain anonymous.

BUYING AND USING BITCOIN

Bitcoins can be purchased from an increasing number of cryptocurrency exchanges using credit or debit cards or any other traditional means of payment. A "wallet" is used to store the Bitcoins or other cryptos and is often provided by the exchange or it is possible to choose from one of a series of online wallets offered on the internet. The other alternative is to have an online service act as the wallet. The wallet stores the private keys required to access or spend the Bitcoins in an individual's wallet, the record of which is exclusively stored in the Bitcoin's blockchain. But they are not "stored" in the wallet in the same way as cash is. The wallet contains one or more public/private key pairs corresponding to the public keys copied into transactions of Bitcoin (BTC) the owner of the wallet sends or receives. The private key is used to validate ownership of the Bitcoin. The transactions do not take place until the owner uses the private key to validate ownership of the Bitcoin. All transactions are broadcast to the network and are usually confirmed 10 and 20 minutes later in the "mining" process.

Eliminating the "double-spend"

As previously mentioned, a problem with digital money is that transactions can be copied and spent more than once. Nakamoto considered that his solution to the problem eliminated the need for a trusted third-party middleman. Each "block" comprises a file of permanently recorded data, containing all recent transactions and all the nodes on the network maintain a copy of the blockchain ledger. So should someone try to spend a Bitcoin twice, in two separate transactions, by sending the same digital coin to two separate Bitcoin addresses, both transactions would go into the pool of unconfirmed transactions. The first transaction would be approved through the confirmation mechanism and then verified into the subsequent block whereas the second transaction would be recognized as invalid, as it follows the first. Nakamoto writes:

> The earliest transaction is the one that counts, so we don't care about later attempts to double-spend. The only way to confirm the absence of a transaction is to be aware of all transactions ... Transactions must be publicly announced and we need a system for participants to agree on a single history of the order in which they are received. The payee needs proof that at the time of each transaction, the majority of nodes agreed it was the first received.[9]

His solution is the "timestamp server", which works by taking a hash of the transaction and proves that the data existed at the time. Each timestamp includes the previous timestamp in the chain, forming a chain with each additional timestamp reinforcing the ones before it. This cannot be changed without redoing the proof-of-work.[10]

Not all the of the cryptocurrency participants run a full node to verify previous transactions. They rely on "light nodes" or "light wallets", using a simplified verification system (SPV). These SPV nodes connect to one or more full nodes and ask them to include a particular transaction in a block. The SPV

6

wallet then receives confirmation from the full node that the transaction has been included in a block and that block is then included in a chain, the SPV wallets accept the transactions as valid without further checks. Nakamoto himself drew attention to the vulnerability of the SPV verification, noting that it is "reliable as long as honest nodes control the network, but is more vulnerable by an attacker ... the simplified method can be fooled by the attacker's fabricated transactions".[11] What is interesting is, first, that Nakamoto draws attention to a weakness in ensuring that the transactions have actually taken place, and secondly, the implication that this process takes place without any human intervention.

Attacking the blockchain

Nakamoto argues that it is not possible to hack the blockchain underpinning Bitcoin, but it is clear that this is based on the computational power of the attacker. In Section 11 of "Bitcoin: A Peer-to-Peer Electronic Cash System", he analyses the "scenario of an attacker trying to generate an alternate chain faster than the honest chain".[12] This is based on the assumption that the attacker controls less computational power than a majority of such power: as soon as the attacker adds on a block, he finds that the majority have been able to add another so that he never catches up. Nakamoto concludes that it quickly becomes "computationally impractical for an attacker to change (the public record of transactions) if honest nodes control the majority of CPU power".[13] On the other hand, it is acknowledged that with the majority of computational power, such an attack would succeed. If the attacker has more than 50 per cent of the network's computer power then for the time that he maintains this majority he is in control, and could exclude and modify the ordering of transactions. That would enable the majority owner to reverse transactions, to double-spend, prevent transactions from gaining any confirmations, and prevent any other miners from mining any other blocks.

Having the majority enables a majority attacker to solve the computational puzzles faster, and so create the alternative longest chain of transactions replacing the honest chain with the alternative chain at a strategically opportune moment. But there are some limits to the powers of the majority: other people's transactions cannot be reversed without their consent; transactions can not be prevented from being sent at all; the number of coins generated per block cannot be changed. These limitations, however, do not apply to the lightweight nodes, which depend on trusting miners absolutely.

Nevertheless, even an attacker with considerably less power than the majority can undermine the fair distribution of rewards in the system. The assessment of the purpose of such attacks on the blockchain assumes that costs and benefits of launching an attack provide the main motivation. The motivation, however, could be quite different: to undermine and destabilize the consensus integrity.[14] Similarly, given that remuneration for miners is relatively low in comparison with double-spending, bribery is possible, for example, an attacker might pay miners outside the protocol directly or through a negative fee-mining pool or with very high fees only on the attacker's branch.[15] This is just one of the many strategies which can subvert the claims made by Nakamoto, that all that is required is the concept of the "honest" nodes.

Nayak and Kumar have set out the concept of "stubborn" mining as opposed to "selfish" mining:

> Selfish mining undermines incentive compatibility. Nakamoto's blockchain suffers from a so-called selfish mining attack, where even a minority coalition that controls the network delivery that can manage to reap close to twice its fair share of block rewards. If the adversary wields close to half of the computational power, it can reap almost all the rewards … if the adversary controls the network, it can ensure that all honest players receive the adversarial block before the block mined by the honest players, and as such, it effectively 'erases' the honest player's block replacing it with its own blocks.[16]

These strategies illustrate the central importance of the belief that the blockchain ensures the honesty of the nodes and the immutability of the records of the transactions ensures security and reliability of transfers of Bitcoins from one to another. However, the possibility that the blockchain can be manipulated in other ways, especially given the current concentration of computational power in the hands of a small group, suggests that blockchain may not be the model to adopt for clearing and settlement and payment systems.

So does Bitcoin work as a currency that could replace fiat currencies? Let's consider further some of its characteristics and how these might limit its ability to act as a fiat currency: deflationary, integrity, speed, volatility and energy consumption.

Deflationary results

The founders of Bitcoin determined a finite number of Bitcoins. Only 21 million coins will be mined, of which about 18.5 million were mined by May 2020, leaving under 3 million more to be introduced into circulation. It may seem as though the end of Bitcoins is in sight, but that may not be the case, because the amount of the reward the miners receive is being reduced over time. At the beginning the reward was 50 coins, in 2012, it had reduced by half to 25 Bitcoins, then 12.5 in 2016 and in May 2020, to 6.25. It will continue to halve every four years, or every 210,000 blocks added to the blockchain, each verifying and securing Bitcoin transactions, until the final Bitcoin has been mined. Since new Bitcoins are created and added to the current total supply every ten minutes, it is hard to predict when the 30 more halvings will occur and when the final Bitcoin will be issued. The final date when no more Bitcoins are created depends on the speed with which new blocks are added.

Miners earn most of their income through the block reward, but when all 21 million Bitcoins have been mined, miners will not receive a block reward.[17] Without an incentive to produce Bitcoins, the miners may have to continue the work of adding to the decentralized blockchain, otherwise the blockchain will either collapse or become centralized, which would defeat the whole object. The miners may continue to actively participate and validate new transactions, because of the transaction fees they receive and the likelihood that these will increase over time.[18] Nevertheless, the limitation on the number of Bitcoins in existence over time would likely be severely deflationary.

Honesty

Nakamoto considered that he had established a kind of payments system which not only did not require a central authority, but also one which would be able to establish to its own protocols as well as change them, using the same consensus procedures: "They [the nodes who participate in the payments] vote with their CPU power, expressing their acceptances of valid blocks by working on extending them and rejecting invalid blocks by refusing to work on them. Any needed rules and incentives can be enforced with this consensus mechanism".[19]

The advantages Bitcoin claims for itself over a centralized model is that the integrity of the messages is maintained in an extremely secure encryption process in which the miners take part because they receive Bitcoins as their reward. The transaction process is final when the miner submits the block for verification to the network and 51 per cent agree that the transaction is valid. They use open-source software, which can be maintained by a large number of users. As we have seen, in order to prove that payments have taken place and to eliminate double-spending of the same coins, the system consists of a "peer-to-peer network using proof-of-work to record a public history of trans-actions that quickly becomes computationally impractical for an attacker to change if honest nodes control a majority of CPU power".[20] This is Nakamoto's way of validating payments and eliminating double-spending without the need for a third party to check every transaction for double-spending. Nakamoto argued that "what is needed is an electronic payment system based on cryp-tographic proof instead of trust".[21] But "honesty" keeps intruding into Bitcoin. "The system is secure as long as honest nodes collectively control more CPU power than any cooperating group of attacker nodes".[22] This is not just a semantic point. By using the term, "honest" referring to the nodes, Nakamoto may not be attributing any moral characteristic to the nodes, but he is making Bitcoin more acceptable by attributing a moral characteristic to the miners, who are after all acting in their own self-interest by seeking a fee for their work.

Speed

The blocks or ledgers are difficult to manipulate with Bitcoin because the transactions have to be verified by the majority. The result is that Bitcoin can only handle 3.5 transactions per second, with a median confirmation time of about ten minutes with about 300,000 per day.[23] It will never be possi-ble to approve transactions in under a minute, because of the requirements for mining and group approval to prevent double-spending and theft. That is nowhere near the speed at which Visa, for example, can process transactions.

In 2017, they managed over 64,000 transactions per second.[24] Buying a cup of coffee with the transaction taking anything approaching Visa's speed is still a goal for Bitcoin, or, more likely a mirage.

Engineers have designed additional protocols to improve the speed and privacy of Bitcoin transactions. Back in 2014, Joseph Poon and Thaddeus Dryja launched Lightning Network to be grafted on to a cryptocurrency's blockchain with an extra line of code, designed to make more transactions possible, almost instant, reliable and cheap. By 2017, the Lightning Network began to come to life with several successful experiments.

The problem that needs surmounting lies with the design of the blockchain. If a Bitcoin is used to buy or sell anything, that transaction has to be recorded throughout the entire network, some 200,000 computers. The miners have to carry out the procedures described above to place the transaction in a new block, which can take up to ten minutes. The idea behind Lightning is that most payments do not need to be recorded in the Bitcoin ledger but instead they can take place in private channels between users, when two parties open up a private channel and commit funds to it. The code underpinning Lightning enables the user, for a subscription, to use these channels to do business throughout the whole network.

It all sounded so promising, but the Network continues to have major vulnerabilities, none of which have been resolved yet. Two recent articles in Coindesk argue that Bitcoin's secondary network needs more development work before it can support mass deployment, highlighting potential vulnerabilities to "eclipse" and "pinning" attacks, among others. An "eclipse" attack involves crowding out Lightning's full node connections in such a way that the victim is no longer connected to any honest users. A pinning attack interferes in a channel's closing transaction. Both isolate the user from receiving real network data and leave them exposed to theft. Despite these vulnerabilities, Lightning has not yet been hacked. But once these lines of attack have been described, there will be specialists who understand them and will learn how to exploit them: "What we should be reminded of is that each class of vulnerability needs its own solution; there is no silver bullet solving all of them. Eclipse attacks need better network-partition resistance. Pinning attacks require network-partition resistance. Pinning attacks require better fee models. Some of these engineering solutions may be integrated in Bitcoin Core because it's a common factor beyond any LN implementation".[25]

Lightning network may have offered the possibility to speed up payments to those who took the opportunity, although it now appears that users could lose out given the inherent risks in the system. The latest estimates for the speed of transactions show that little has changed. The average confirmation time of Bitcoin transactions stands at 12.74 minutes (as opposed to the median) in October 2020. This, of course, may not be an issue for cryptocurrency speculators but it makes Bitcoin unattractive as a means of exchange, compared with the various versions of speedy international payments systems available, even when using traditional bank accounts.

Energy consumption

The work of the miners is extremely energy intensive, or as headline grabbing claims put it in 2019, Bitcoin consumes more energy than Switzerland, based on estimates made by the Cambridge Bitcoin Electricity Consumption Index. Other estimates, such as the Bitcoin Energy Consumption Index, published by Alex De Vries, compare Bitcoin's use of energy with Visa, which performed 111.2 billion transactions in 2017 and consumed the energy equivalent of 17,000 US households, with a single Bitcoin transaction, which requires several thousand times more energy. The Cambridge Centre for Alternative Finance (CCAF) rejects the comparison, arguing that Bitcoin is designed to function as an open-censorship free transfer system that anyone can access without permission. However, it was also designed to be a "version of electronic cash" and as such, it is perfectly reasonable to compare its speed and energy efficiency with existing means of transferring cash from one person to another electronically. Despite these comments, Bitcoin uses 80 per cent more energy than it did at the beginning of 2020. The Cambridge Centre now estimates the annualized electricity consumption at the beginning of 2020 was 71.07 terawatt hours but on 11 March 2021 it hit 128 terawatt hours, more than the whole of Argentina.

Bitcoin's dependence on China's extensive coal-fired power stations was revealed when a flood in a coal mine in China's Xinjiang region on 18/19 April 2021 shut down 35 per cent of Bitcoin's global mining power, helping to increase the cost of making a payment or transferring a Bitcoin to $52 from $18. It was a power disruption in one of the smallest of Xinjiang's 61 counties.

De Vries told *Fortune* magazine that "we now know for sure that one-third of all production runs on pure coal from a tiny place in China". As significant is the point that a concentration of computing power can facilitate a 51% attack. By 2019, two thirds of blockchain related patents came from Chinese firms or entities, and China held 72 per cent of the mining power for Bitcoin. China was very pro-blockchain technology and the government has positioned itself to dominate the blockchain space in the world.[26]

However, China's dominant position in mining Bitcoin is unlikely to survive as its government cracks down on Bitcoin and mining. The retreat began in May 2021, when the province of Inner Mongolia banned mining and introduced a telephone hotline for reporting suspected operations. Sichuan with its extensive hydrogen power facilities has ordered the 26 largest local mines to stop operating and mining operations in Xinjiang, Yunnan and Qinghai provinces have already announced the closure of mining operations. In an effort to eliminate Bitcoin in China, its central bank ordered some of its largest banks to "investigate and identify" bank accounts which facilitated Bitcoin trading and to block transactions. The central bank is determined to have all its citizens use its own digital currency and thus further extend its control over them.[27] It is not clear at the time of writing which countries will take over Bitcoin mining, but some US states such as Texas appear interested.

The reason for the high level of energy consumption is because the solution to finding all the 64 numbers required to win, is not a solution to a complex mathematical problem, but simply a matter of trying out endless numbers until one of the miners is lucky enough to come up with the right series. It is comparable to standing in front of a slot machine, feeding it with a heap of coins until the right combination comes up.[28] Nakamato took a more relaxed view of energy consumption. He anticipated the use of a personal computer in a home heated by electricity, so the additional cost would be negligible: "Bitcoin generation should end up where it is cheapest. Maybe that will be in cold climates where there's electric heat, where it would be essentially free".[29]

As we have seen, Nakamoto claimed that the rewards of newly minted Bitcoins gave the miners the incentive to be honest, as it is "more profitable to play by the rules, since the rules favor him with more new coins than everyone else combined".[30] In fact, what is really being rewarded is superior computing power and cheap electricity.[31] That is what led to the concentration of nodes in China.

The latest available estimate of the hash rate, the measuring unit of the processing power of the high-performing computers, which make up the Bitcoin network, was published by CCAF in May 2020. The map is limited by the available data, representing only 37 per cent of the total hash rate, and the data is provided by two of the mining pools located in China. The country has dominated Bitcoin mining recently because of their relatively low fee charges, which has attracted many non-Chinese miners. With those limitations, CCAF estimates that China has 67.08 per cent of the network's mining power, with the United States far behind at 7.24 per cent. A further problem arises from the fact that hashers in certain locations use virtual private networks (VPNs) to hide their IP addresses and their locations. Statista, however, in its latest statistics, estimates, on the basis of the hash rate that the world's top mining pools all come from China with five pools being responsible for mining more than half of the Bitcoins in the world in February 2021.[32] This concentration of mining power would indeed create the possibility of a 51 per cent attack.

What is interesting is that despite the rewards for miners, the number of nodes has declined from a peak of 200,000 in January 2018, despite the recent surges in price and mining power. After price crashes, of which there have been several, Bitcoin users "lose interest and stop opening their wallets or running their nodes", or because running the software "just gets too hard with block sizes exceeding the rate of technological improvement".[33] However, according to various surveys, the number of nodes has started to increase again with 11,558 reachable nodes currently active according to Bitnodes.io. Another Bitcoin nodes tracker, Coindance, calculates the number of Bitcoin nodes as 11,631, just above the high of 11,250 set in January 2020. The number could increase further, especially with newer more reliable software such as Bitcoin Core. It is plainly very difficult to calculate the number of nodes remaining fully operational and also to assess the computing power of nodes designed for the purpose.[34]

Volatility

Another limitation of Bitcoin has been its volatility. It is currently the world's largest cryptocurrency by market capitalization, which considering that it initially traded for next to nothing is a considerable achievement. The first price increase occurred in July 2010, when the value increased to $0.08 for a single coin. A couple of the first sales of Bitcoins caught the public's attention: the first by a Finnish developer, who sold 5,050 Bitcoins for $5.02, followed by the famous purchase of two Pappa John's pizzas for 10,000.99 Bitcoins on 22 May 2010 (the 0.99 Bitcoins were the miner's fee). It was not, however, until late 2013 that Bitcoin began to pick up (see Figure 1.1). In October 2013 the price was $196. By the end of December 2016 it was $425. However by 18 December 2017 it had climbed to $15,852 before dropping back down to $3,854 a year later. By May 2020 the price was $9,375. Since then the price has soared, rising to $34,622 in January 2021 and then reaching its peak on 13 April when it topped $63,729, before falling back to $34,213 at the end of June 2021.

The price of Bitcoin in 2021 has been affected by events involving Tesla and Coinbase. The initial public offering (IPO) of the largest US crypto exchange created yet more interest worldwide, and fell again because of speculation about government regulation. A further problem is the rumoured concentration of Bitcoin in a few cryptocurrency holders, the "whales", said to make up 2 per cent of anonymous ownership accounts, whilst owning about 92 per cent of BTC.

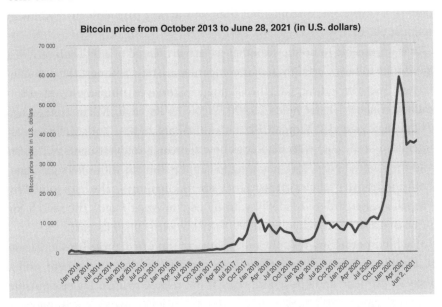

Figure 1.1 Bitcoin price October 2013 to June 2021 (US dollars)

Source: Statista.

15

This gives some idea of the extreme volatility of Bitcoin, but it does not do justice to the variations during the course of a day or a week. The aim was to build an electronic payments system, allowing any two willing partners to transact directly with each other without the need for a trusted third party. But such a volatile cryptocurrency undermines trust in that exchange, since the value of the Bitcoins exchanged in such a transaction can vary considerably from day to day and certainly over a week or so. The volatility in purchasing power makes Bitcoins very risky to accept as a means of exchange. Nor is Bitcoin a reliable store of value, as there is no guarantee that the value will not suddenly drop, not to zero, but enough for Bitcoin holders to lose value, as illustrated by the exchange rate in relation to the US dollar. With such large swings in the price, it is extremely hard to predict how and why the movements in relative prices takes place. If your shop sells certain goods for payment in Bitcoins in the morning, but by the evening, the value of the coins has fallen by 10 or 20 per cent, then the shop's profit has disappeared. That could have happened between 6 and 7 December in 2013, when the value of one Bitcoin fell from $1,200 to $600 in the course of 48 hours. Of course, the shop could have accepted Bitcoins and quickly changed them into dollars, to avoid the volatility, but then why accept payments in Bitcoins in the first place?

It is impossible to predict whether we are at the end of a bull run or it is a good time to buy. Certainly, major companies are now amongst the potential buyers. These include Square, the US financial services company, invested $50 million, Galaxy Digital holds 16,400 Bitcoin in its vault, Microstrategy has 71,000 in its vault, J. P. Morgan, Blackrock and Bank of New York Mellon are all interested in the coin with Blackrock now allowing for investments in Bitcoin and the Bank of New York planning to support Bitcoin with offers to "issue, hold and transfer" the cryptocurrency for its customers. They are joined by Paypal, Mastercard and Fidelity with its Digital Asset Fund. The search for returns at a time of such low interest rates obviously plays its part.

Such corporate interest obviously impacts the price, probably increasing it. But these dramatic changes illustrate that Bitcoin is an investment, and a risky investment, and one whose value is not related to anything else outside it. Its extreme volatility, compared with the US dollar, makes it unsuitable as a currency. We use dollars because we do not expect its value to rise or fall by 14 per cent in a day. The value of Bitcoin regularly fluctuates double digits.

Its value is not linked to the real economy in any way, but only to speculation.

The dark side of Bitcoin, less publicized than the championing and well-known financial institutions, is that it remains the criminals' favourite due to its pseudonymous nature and the ease with which it allows users to instantly send funds anywhere in the world, despite its claims of a transparent and traceable design. According to the Chainalysis Report in 2020, a total of $11.5 billion worth of cryptocurrency in 2019 was associated with criminal activity, including terrorism financing, stolen funds, scams, sanctions, ransomware, darknet markets and child abuse material. Illicit activity, however, nearly doubled from 2018. These estimates are likely to be an underestimate, since the company cannot identify some of the activity related to ransomware, tax evasion and money laundering. CipherTrace's 2021 report, "Cryptocurrency Crime and Anti-Money Laundering Report for 2020" shows that $3.5 billion was sent from criminal BTC addresses in 2020, that US exchanges sent $41.2 million worth of Bitcoin directly to criminally associated addresses, and ominously, over half of 2020 crypto-hacks are from decentralized finance (DeFi) protocols, carrying out "rug pulls" in which some investors liquidate the entire DeFi pool, leaving the remaining token holders with no liquidity, unable to trade, and wiping out the remaining value. But a later report, published by Michael Morrell, a former acting director of the CIA, written for a newly formed Crypto Council for Innovation, claimed that its use for criminal activity is grossly overstated. In fact, for Chainalysis criminal activity fell as a percentage as overall economic activity nearly tripled between 2019 and 2020, giving the percentages as 0.34 per cent. Ciphertrace's report (2021) is more detailed, covering DeFi and exchanges, but also notes a sharp decline in cryptocurrency as a percentage of greatly increased cryptocurrency usage. But Morrell and his co-authors' analysis misses the point. The buyer and the seller of each Bitcoin transaction are identified solely by the public side of the encryption keys controlled by the transactors. The real-world identity of the sender and receiver of the Bitcoins are not recorded or revealed in anyway. That is why criminals use it. The authors even acknowledge that Bitcoin is the currency most often found on the "Dark Net markets", that is, websites, which are not registered in domain name servers, but which translate a website name to its IP address. That is where all kinds of objects and information is sold, such as personal identity information, bank details and social security numbers.

CAN BITCOIN EVER REPLACE FIAT CURRENCIES?

Although it is not entirely clear what Nakamoto's original intentions were for Bitcoin, as things stand now, it would not replace fiat currencies. It is not clear who needed his cryptocurrency and why, apart from his claim that his system would prevent fraud, and it would be widely used to make payments. It would not, however, deal with issues of money laundering or theft as it stands, since the persons engaging in the transactions are anonymous, even though the records of transactions are public.

The proof-of-work concept, designed to ensure achievement of a decentralized consensus has become extremely costly and wasteful, with the reward in terms of the number of Bitcoins, being reduced. The number of Bitcoins was halved in 2012, when the amount miners receive for each block was cut to 25 BTC, then halved again in July 2016 to 12.5 BTC, and then in May 2020, to 6.5 BTC, depending on the price of Bitcoins, the fees per transaction and the number of transactions in a block. In 2020, scarcity has meant that the value of Bitcoin has rapidly increased, in part due to the impact of Covid-19 and the search for returns. The miners' fees for completing transactions continue to increase and the number of transactions has decreased. When Bitcoin transactions are first executed, they wait in a "mempool" of unconfirmed transaction, for approval by miners, who can still only mine one megabyte worth of transactions per block mined every ten minutes. The average number of transactions in a block of this size is 2,000. With spikes in demand for Bitcoins, miners increase their revenue by prioritizing transactions with higher fees, leading other users to offer higher fees to avoid a long wait. (The fees themselves are difficult to estimate, so some websites offer guides to enable users to calculate the fees for their transactions).

As more computer power was added to the network, the puzzle automatically became more difficult, increasing the need for further power. As a result, only a few companies, mainly located in China, have installed the computer power now needed, which leads to a further concentration of market power, and hence to an oligopolistic market, and a danger only likely to increase with the decline in the number of Bitcoins and the rising energy costs of mining.

Scalability

The other problem Bitcoin faces is scalability. It is not just that transactions are slower than other payment systems, such as credit cards, but also that the number of transactions is limited. Worldwide total non-cash transactions in 2019, according to the latest available estimates reached 708.5 billion.[35] The number of cash transactions is obviously very difficult to estimate. Cash in circulation continues to increase in all six continents with its use likely to be concentrated on small transactions under $25 in the United States. Although an increasing number of countries show a decline in cash relative to GDP at a global level the value of ATM withdrawals is increasing, indicating a growing need for cash in day-to-day transactions. The reference to cash here is to indicate that, on top of the number of non-cash payments, billions if not trillions of payments of cash payments would have to be added to the total. And this is why the cryptocurrency is not scalable for the trillions of transactions taking place daily. This is not a matter of concern for most transactions, since goods and services are not priced in Bitcoins. Bitcoin is not and cannot be a unit of account, widely used as a means of payment; shopkeepers do not use Bitcoins in their ledgers. Nothing is priced in Bitcoins, not even a cup of coffee. Even if it was possible to pay for it with a Bitcoin, say, using "Satoshis", fractions of Bitcoins, the coffee would be cold long before the transaction was completed.

SOME CONCLUSIONS

Using the now standard definition of money, as a means of exchange, a unit of measurement and a store of value, it is clear that Bitcoins cannot serve as a substitute for a fiat currency. This is why Nouriel Roubini dismissed cryptocurrencies and not just Bitcoin as "bubbles". In 2017, the price of Bitcoins went up by 20 times, but, according to Roubini it was simply that "suddenly there was a lot of buzz about Bitcoin ... and usually smaller retail investors ... discover the bubble and buy in due to intense FOMO (fear of missing out). When you have insiders selling at inflated prices to outsiders who are clueless, that's the peak of a typical bubble".[36] In his testimony to the US Senate Committee on Banking Housing and Community Affairs, he pointed out,

"Since the invention of money thousands of years ago, there has never been a monetary system with hundreds of different currencies operating alongside each other. The entire point of money is that it allows parties to transact without having to barter".[37] The bubble, however, has yet to bust. People continue to invest in the hopes of making a killing. Jamie Dimon, CEO of J. P. Morgan described Bitcoin as a "fraud, which will eventually blow-up".[38] Paul Krugman famously described Bitcoin as "evil."

As it became clear that Bitcoin was never going to replace fiat currencies, those who still wanted to see cryptocurrencies as an alternative currency began working on the technology and adapting the protocols in the hopes that cryptocurrencies would reach the desired scale and acceptability for that to happen. Those with hopes that Bitcoin can become a currency will be keenly eyeing what happens in El Salvador, following President Bukele's announcement at the Bitcoin 2021 conference in Miami on 5 June, that Bitcoin would become legal tender alongside the US dollar. Four days later the declaration became law and was approved by the country's congress. Just before the announcement, El Salvador broke ties with the International Commission against Impunity, established by the Organisation of American States to propose a series of legal reforms seeking to prevent corruption, guarantee the transparency and accountability of officials and new ways of prosecuting crimes against the state. The media focus has been on Bitcoin and the intention to partner with the digital wallet company, Strike, to build a modern financial infrastructure using Bitcoin technology. In the excitement following the announcement, few looked at the structure of the country's economy. Its GDP per capita was $4,187.25 in 2019 according to the World Bank's latest figures. In the same year, it was estimated that 45.6 per cent of the income generated in the country was held by the richest 20 per cent.[39] It does not look as though many will be able to purchase one Bitcoin in the current range of prices. Perhaps they will be able to afford a few Satoshis, but the incentive for doing so is unclear. A typical business with its margins in the 10–20 per cent range could find its entire profits wiped out, given the weekly volatility in Bitcoin. Despite all these problems, the legislation requires all economic agents to accept Bitcoins as a means of payment, which in view of the extreme fluctuations in the dollar value of Bitcoins might prove to be unpopular with many "economic agents". The dollar remains as the "reference currency" for the Bitcoin price.

In an article in the *Wall Street Journal*, Max Raskin explains that Bitcoin is now legal tender for all debts, public and private. Any economic actor technologically able to accept Bitcoin is required to do so for payments of goods and services. In addition Bitcoin can be used to pay taxes and exempts Bitcoin transactions from capital gains taxes. He then adds that "to deal with Bitcoin's wild price fluctuations, the legislation establishes a free-floating exchange rate determined by the market. If someone immediately transfers his Bitcoins to dollars when he receives them, then it shouldn't matter how volatile the exchange rate is, because he will always have the equivalent in dollars".[40] The government will set up a trust at the Development Bank of El Salvador to enable the automatic conversion of Bitcoins into dollars. The dollar/Bitcoin exchange rate for that day would still apply as far as taxes are concerned. This will produce a temporary increase in the money supply, which may give a temporary boost to economic activity in the short term, but it may bring problems such as inflation further down the line. The Government may make a profit or loss when it subsequently cashes the Bitcoin in dollars.

But perhaps, the president has other possibilities in mind: foreign investors who would then transfer their Bitcoins into dollars on a one-to-one basis. Although volatility is being claimed not to be a problem, the anonymity of Bitcoin transactions surely would be a problem for a government, since with such transactions, it is not possible to know how much anyone has earned and hence how much tax is due. Others have speculated that the president has other considerations in mind: El Salvador is looking for $1 billion loan from the IMF, which became more complicated when Bukele sacked its five Supreme Court judges in May. If international Bitcoin holders purchase goods and services from El Salvador in Bitcoin, and refunds have to be in dollars, then merchants will immediately sell their Bitcoins for dollars on the exchange, thus creating a form of indirect dollar funding for the country.[41] It is an intriguing prospect but it is entirely possible that the president was not that far-seeing. It will be interesting to see how long the experiment lasts, its effects on the economy and whether or not Bitcoin can really function as a currency in an economy. The World Bank and the IMF with whom El Salvador is negotiating its loan, have both stated that they will not assist the country in the implementation because of environmental and transparency drawbacks, and for the IMF, economic and legal concerns.

Perhaps Nakamoto never intended Bitcoin to be more than a peer-to-peer version of electronic cash that would allow online payments to be sent from one party to another without going through a financial institution, but only for the few. The unbreakable record of transactions is the substitute for the trusted third party, the financial institution. Users are dependent on "miners" and the confirmation of a transactions on the "nodes" whose location and identity can be hidden from view. Nakamoto assumes that the nodes are honest, but that cannot be known prior to their inclusion in the blockchain and requires trust in them without knowing or being able to know anything about them.

The limit placed on the number of Bitcoins produced means that Bitcoins could not replace the domestic dollar payments that run into trillions, taking into account all forms of payment, in a single year. The limit of 21 million Bitcoins is never explained. Nakamoto writes,

> Imagine if the population were to discover, through real life experiences, what it is to conduct their lives with a currency that does not lose its value, but in reality gains in value. As our economy grows and as our manufacturing capabilities increase, prices go down. The only reason prices are not going down today – except in products where improvements are very rapid (e.g. computers) – is because of government-caused currency inflation.[42]

This is one of his main reasons for the introduction of Bitcoin: central banks are not to be trusted and can now been replaced with another way of ensuring trust in a currency.

Satoshi Nakamato disappeared from public view in December 2010 after his final bit-cointalk.org communication. Only one person is known to have received an email from him after that date, the software developer Gavin Andresen in April 2011, in which he said, "I wish you wouldn't keep talking about me as a mysterious shadowy figure, the press just turns into a pirate currency angle".[43] Despite Andresen's claim that Craig Wright was Nakamoto at Coindesk's Consensus conference in 2016, he later withdrew that claim, which was greeted with considerable scepticism at the time. Andresen had worked closely with Nakamoto and after the latter disappeared from view, he redesigned the code, renamed Bitcoin Core. He is currently working on a project called Graphene, a protocol for the propagation of information by nodes

Bitcoin. As for Satoshi Nakamoto, no one knows where he is or who he was. His net worth depends on the value of his coins which have remained unspent since mid-January 2009. Whatever the mystery surrounding Nakamoto, Bitcoin has certainly given rise to the search for alternative currencies.

One of the central difficulties with Nakamoto's manifesto is the constant reference to the "honest" node. Honesty cannot apply to a computer or to a particular program, but only to the person or company setting up a particular program. Possible misuses of the program have already been outlined here. They may or may not be feasible, but the intent to misuse a program is what matters. Nakamoto only considers one possible misuse of the blockchain: eliminating the possibility of a double-spend. This, however, is not the only misuse of blockchain to be considered. Anonymity and freedom from a central bank are what blockchain offered and which Nakamoto valued. Bitcoin are transferred directly from person to person and cannot be hindered, restricted, frozen, stopped, confiscated or reversed. Bitcoin is decentralized and extremely difficult to control. Transactions and accounts are not connected to real-world identities. The software can be downloaded by anyone. Payments and transfers made with cryptocurrencies are beyond the control of banks and governments and the limit of monetary policy. Small wonder that criminals descended upon cryptocurrencies with glee. It was only slowly during the decade that regulators understood how to ensure some degree of "honesty" to cryptocurrencies.

In the next chapter, we will examine the "improvements" to Bitcoin and the reasons for them. These improvements involve architecture, speed and scalability and herald the introduction of "altcoins", cryptocurrencies other than Bitcoin. These developments go to the heart of what cryptocurrencies really are. Are they really viable methods of payment, or a new commodity, or a security? Can any of them really be "money", given that they are not linked to the real economy and if not money, why not?

CHAPTER 2

New cryptocurrencies and new developments

This chapter examines some of the major cryptocurrencies that have sprung into existence following Bitcoin. Bitcoin continues to dominate this landscape but it did not remain alone for long, as many sought to improve on Bitcoin, whilst others saw opportunities for making a quick profit by offering new altcoins (alternatives to Bitcoins). Investors poured money into the various offerings, selling real-world assets, dreaming of becoming millionaires overnight. We shall consider the top altcoins in terms of market capitalization and examine how their structures differ, the impact of hard and soft forks and their defences against hacking. We shall see that Nakamoto's dream of "honest" nodes working together to record transactions in an immutable and transparent blockchain did not last very long, even for Bitcoin.

BITCOIN, SPEED AND HARD FORKS

The slow and expensive process of transferring Bitcoins from one person to another led to technical changes that sought to address Bitcoin's transaction processing capacity. One such development adopted by mining pools and companies was a soft-forking change, "segregated witness" (SegWit) the process by which the blockchain limit on a blockchain is increased by removing the signature data from transactions in order to provide more capacity so that more transactions can be added to the chain. The plan to further upgrade the Network to SegWit2x (a hard fork) was presented at the 2017 Consensus conference in New York, and was expected to be introduced in November by the Digital Currency Group with the support of some 58 companies, including wallet providers, exchanges, other businesses providing goods or services providing goods or services in the cryptocurrency space (but only seven miners). But by mid-November, a number of companies began to withdraw from the agreement in order to focus their resources on Bitcoin cash, but none of the miners formally withdrew from the agreement. Some thought it was too soon to upgrade the Bitcoin Network up to SegWit2x three months after it had been upgraded to SegWit.

Despite the adoption of SegWit Bitcoin was still experiencing congestion problems for transactions, which led to high transaction fees and slow confirmation. SegWit2x proposed to increase the size of the block from 1 megabyte to 2 megabytes. Those arguing in favour of the increase in the block size hoped that this would not only increase the number of transactions in the block but also lower the fees paid by users to the miners for the transactions. Increasing the block sizes, however, would add to the burdens of the node operators, who would then have to store more data. An article in Forbes pointed out that 2017 was the "year when everyone (finally) learned that Bitcoin isn't controlled by miners".[1] According to the Blockstream CEO, Adam Black, people come to realize that "miners are just service providers who provide a security service ... and the users and investors create the value for the supply and demand for the coin ... miners just follow the profit".[2]

Cointelegraph reported that when SegWit2x was cancelled, the effect was a drop in the price of Bitcoin, from $7,800 to $6,400, since many investors believed that a "hard fork" was free money. They did not understand the "existential split that a chain split between legacy Bitcoin and Bitcoin 2x could have brought about". However, since the split did not occur, "the network was more unified in terms of hash power and cooperative nodes, both of which play a vital part in the Bitcoin economy".[3] The point here is that this was a serious attempt to correct one of the key failings of Bitcoin: its lack of scalability. That effort failed. It was, however, one of many hard and soft forks, which Bitcoin has spawned, all of which are aimed at making Bitcoin work as a currency, whilst at the same time making the cryptocurrency ever more complicated.

BITCOIN CASH AND BITCOIN SV

Bitcoin Cash and Bitcoin SV also arose out of concerns with Bitcoin's scaleability. Developed by miners with reservations about SegWit's solution to scaleability, they created a new currency, based on a "hard fork". When a developer adds a new rule to the code, it creates a fork in the chain: one path follows the new upgraded blockchain and the other nodes continue on the old path. All of the miners need to agree on the new rules and about what comprises a new valid block in the chain. This is how Bitcoin Cash emerged. Bitcoin Cash (BCH) increased the block size to 8 megabytes, which speeds up the verification process, so that Bitcoin Cash can handle many more transactions per second than the Bitcoin network can. A year later, in 2018, the Bitcoin Cash blockchain was hard forked, creating a second new currency, Bitcoin SV (SV: Satoshi's Vision), an attempt to stay closer to Nakamoto's White Paper, whilst speeding up transactions and allowing for scalability. Both are still trading, but in both cases their value is far below Bitcoin's, although Bitcoin Cash is the most successful, with a market cap of $11.4 billion (4 April 2021).

ETHEREUM AND ETHER

Ethereum came into being in 2015, launched by Vitalik Buterin, funded by an online crowd sale in 2014, with 11.9 million coins already mined. It is an "open-sourced, block-chain based, decentralized software platform",[4] used for its own cryptocurrency, ether. "Open-sourced" simply means that the source code of the software is released under license, allowing the lessee to use and distribute the software to anyone for any purpose. It is decentralized, just because there is no centralized data storage mechanism, only nodes. The nodes are run by volunteers across the globe, forming a "world computer". It uses blockchain technology to create and run "decentralized digital applications" so that users can make agreements and conduct transactions directly with each other to buy, sell and trade goods and services without an intermediary. The applications are accessible anywhere in the world, so that users can bypass banks to transfer money, for example.

Ethereum's global network of computers assembles and runs smart contracts, independently of any third-party interference or censorship. Smart contracts work out exactly as they are programmed, thus reducing the risk of fraud, and are self-executing. Once certain conditions have been met, such as the transfer of a payment, then the merchandise is conveyed or made accessible to the buyer. All the data concerning the transaction are stored in individual blockchain ledgers. Whether or not smart contracts can fulfil all the roles ascribed to them is a significant issue, which will be examined in further detail later. Ethereum will make frequent appearances in the following two chapters as it is widely used by other issuers.[5]

Like any other blockchain Ethereum needs several thousand people running software on their computers to power the network. Every node in the network runs the Ethereum Virtual Machine, which executes the software, the smart contracts, which are recorded on the blockchain. The cost of the smart contract, covering memory, storage, computation and electricity is called "gas". This is converted to Ether, which is not just a cryptocurrency to be traded, but a coin primarily used to pay for Gas, the use of the distributed world computer.

Ethereum suffered its first setback in 2016 when its decentralized autonomous organization (DAO), which was meant to be a kind of venture capital fund for cryptocurrencies was hacked. Setting up the fund was seen as a great success at first, gathering 12.7 million Ether worth about $150 million at the time. Investors could decide to withdraw from the DAO if they changed their minds through a kind of exit door, known as a "split function". The hacker spotted this weakness and within a few hours on 18 June, stole 3.6 million Ether, worth about $70 million. This highlighted a problem with Ethereum. If the network fails, Ether also fails.

The problem then was to find a way to handle those losses. The proposal took the form of a "hard fork" that return all the Ether taken from the DAO to a refund smart contract, refunding all the original investors but leaving the hacker with what had been taken. Most of the Ether holders voted to accept the proposal but it entailed splitting the Ethereum blockchain into two: Ethereum Classic, the original form of Ethereum, and Ethereum became the newer version

That is not Ethereum's only fork. A soft fork, Ether Zero aims to improve the transaction rate and to make them completely free. That has not happened yet, but would be a significant change. There were also two other hard forks: Metropolis and Serenity. The first refers to a transition to "proof-of-stake" consensus mechanism as opposed to a proof-of-work one and Serenity refers to the completion of the move to proof-of-stake, that is, an individual can mine or validate block transactions according to the number of coins that individual owns. That puts it simply, but it is in fact a pseudo-random election process to select a node to be the validator of the next block, based on various factors including the staking age and the node's wealth. In this context, blocks are "forged" rather than mined and the rewards are fees for transactions rather than for mining. The rules for a random selection can vary from one crypto-currency to another.

RIPPLE (XRP)

Ripple, established in 2012, is a privately held company, which aims to create and enable a global network of financial institutions and banks in order to reduce the cost of international payments. It does so by using the RippleNet blockchain, which Ripple calls the "Internet of Value". Its website claims that it is the only enterprise blockchain company with products in commercial use. Its global payments network includes over 300 customers across 40 countries and six continents. Those who use their digital asset, XRP, to source liquidity can do so in seconds. Several banks run on Ripple at present, including American Express, Santander, Standard Chartered Bank, Banco Santander, BBVA and Siam Commercial Bank. Banks alone can become "transaction validators". Ripple possesses a semi-permissioned blockchain, as all the banks which are part of its network can use its ledger, which speeds up its performance. When a user sends XRP coins to another person, it takes only 4 seconds for transaction validation.

Companies, governments and financial institutions pay to join the network, RippleNet via a digital portal, Ripple Transaction Portal (RXTP). Once an institution joins RippleNet, it can transact with other gateways more quickly and at a much lower cost, using any fiat currency or cryptocurrency. It also functions as a currency exchange between a range of fiat currencies via XRP, in order to provide liquidity. XRP is the ledger's native cryptocurrency and digital asset provides source liquidity to banks, market makers and payment providers.

Ripple offers three products: xCurrent, the platform's primary product, intended for banks and does not require XRP; xVia, a payment interface and suite of APIs, usable without XRPs; and xRapid, which is the only product to uses XRPs. None of these methods of payment are designed for the retail sector. Ripple can handle 1,500 transactions per second. As part of its aim for speed and efficiency, XRP has been created with a total supply of 100 billion. In May 2017, Ripple announced its plans to release 55 billion of its XRP in escrow to ensure certainty regarding its total supply. By May 2020, Ripple had released 500 million XRP, worth over $101 million, from their escrow wallet.[6]

It is not entirely clear whether Ripple XRP is a centralized or decentralized currency. The founder and CEO of Ripple, Brad Garlinghouse, takes the view that it is not, "because if the Ripple blockchain disappeared, then XRP would continue to function. To me that is the most important measure of whether something is decentralized".[7] In May 2017, Ripple announced their decentralized strategy, which consisted of diversifying the validators on XRP ledger and expanding them to 55 validator nodes in July 2017. They also indicated that they wished to add third-party validating nodes by removing one Ripple-operated validating node for every two third-party nodes, until there is no single entity operating a majority of the trusted nodes on the XRP ledger. In 2020, Ripple currently has 26 unique default validating nodes, of which Ripple operates only seven. This move means that 73 per cent of the nodes are controlled by outside parties.

At the time of writing, Ripple faces a lawsuit, alleging that XRP is an unregistered security, yet to be considered, after a ruling by Judge Phyllis Hamilton in the court of the Northern District of California on 26 February 2020. If the plaintiff's motion was successful and Ripple was judged to be an unregistered security, then, according to Ripple, "it would not only threaten to eliminate XRP's utility as a currency, but it would upend and threaten to destroy the established XRP market more broadly ... potentially wiping out the value held by the alleged thousands of individual XRP holders around the world".[8] On 1 April 2020 the same investors added further claims concerning Ripple's business practices, such as false advertising and taking issue with statements made by Ripple and Garlinghouse about XRP being a utility token essential for international payments and that sales are made primarily to market makers. That lawsuit is still under way.

Since then, Garlinghouse has taken a more optimistic view of the implications of XRP being declared a security by the US Securities and Exchange Commission (SEC). He acknowledged that "it's very hard to look at XRP as a security," but added that "if XRP were deemed a security here in the United States that, you know, we have other G20 markets that have taken a different view. I'm not aware of any market globally that thinks that XRP is a security". He also added that "more than 90% of RippleNet customers are out of the United States", suggesting that a securities designation would not necessarily hinder the company's underlying business.[9]

Such optimism might well prove to be ill-founded. On 22 December 2020, the SEC filed its Complaint against Ripple Labs, Inc, Bradley Garlinghouse and Christian Larsen. The details are significant, so they are recorded here with the caveat that the case has yet to be heard. The summary states that from 2013, the "Defendants sold over 14.6 bn units of a digital asset security worth over $1.3 bn to fund Ripple's operations and enrich Larsen and Garlinghouse. Defendants undertook this distribution without registering their offers and sales of XRP with the SEC as required by the federal securities laws, and no exemption from this requirement applied".[10] Garlinghouse and Larsen did consult a leading law firm in 2012 that under certain circumstances XRP could be considered an "investment contract" and therefore a security under federal securities laws. An "investment contract" is "an instrument through which a person invests money in a common enterprise and reasonably expects profits or returns derived from the entrepreneurial or managerial efforts of others".[11]

Ripple undertook not to file a motion to dismiss the complaint and based on recent filings it appears that a pre-trial settlement is likely. At the time of writing, this case has not yet been settled, but the issues raised are extremely important and will be discussed further.

The application to those using distributed ledger or blockchain-enabled means for capital raising had already been made clear following the publication of the SEC's investigation of the Decentralized Autonomous Organization (DAO) in July 2017. Although the case was not pursued in this instance, it was published to "ensure that all market participants have concurrent and equal access to the information contained in DAO's White Paper or elsewhere".[12]

Without registration, Ripple was able to raise at least $1.38 billion without providing the usual financial and managerial information and used this money without disclosing how the money was spent or the full extent of its payment to others to develop a "use" for XRP and to maintain the secondary trading markets. Larsen and Garlinghouse orchestrated these "unlawful sales" and profited to the extent of $600 million from their unregistered sales. Garlinghouse did so whilst repeatedly touting that his own investment in XRP was "very long", meaning that he held a significant position he expected to rise in value without disclosing his sales of XRP. The defendants continue to hold substantial amounts of XRP while using the information asymmetry they created in the market for their own gain, creating substantial risks to investors. Cointelegraph reports that the immediate reaction was that the price of XRP fell by almost 25 per cent but that this still leaves it with a total market cap of $10.5 billion.[13] The lack of registration is not a light matter. It determines the financial and company information that investors have a right to know and which provides the basis on which potential investors can decide whether or not to invest.

LITECOIN (LTC)

Litecoin was an early Bitcoin spin-off, starting in October 2011, but the open-source project was not released until 2017. It is a peer-to-peer internet currency, an open-source, global payment network, that is fully decentralized, enabling instant near zero cost payments to be made anywhere in the world. According to its website, "mathematics secures the network and empowers individuals to control their own finances".[14] Wallet encryption allows the individual to secure their wallets, but they must use a password before spending Litecoins. Miners are rewarded with 25 new Litecoins, an amount which gets halved every four years, so about 84 million Litecoins are scheduled to be produced. There are similarities to Bitcoin – both use proof-of-work processes – but adding a new block to Litecoin takes 2.5 minutes as against 10 for Bitcoin. The script or algorithm used in its proof-of-work process makes it possible for regular PC users to mine new blocks, and it was one of the first cryptocurrencies to adopt SegWit. It was for a time one of the most popular altcoins to Bitcoin. Like Bitcoin, prices have been subject to dramatic volatility. In March 2021, Litecoin was the sixth largest by market cap at $12.16 billion but fell back to twelfth place in June 2021 at $11.3 billion.

Table 2.1 Market capitalization of top 10 cryptocurrencies, 17 June 2021

	Unit price	Market cap (billions)
Bitcoin	$38,024.66	$712.9
Ethereum	$2,365.18	$275.3
Ethereum 2	$2,365.18	$275.3
Tether	$1.00	$62.5
Binance Coin	$353.60	$54.2
Cardano	$1.48	$47.2
Dogecoin	$0.31	$40.08
XRP	$0.84	$38.8
USD Coin	$1.00	$23.8
Polkadot	$22.44	$21.4

BINANCE COIN (BNB)

Binance Coin (BNB) was launched in China in 2017 by Changpeng Zhao, with a strict limit of 200 million coins, initially running on the Ethereum network. Binance itself is a currency exchange, which will match "buy and sell" crypto-currency orders with those of other users for the relevant fees. Binance uses the BNB coin to make the platform more attractive for those who already hold the coin. The most important role of BNB is to provide the funds for the services the exchange offers to its customers.

The users of the exchange can use the coin to pay for the trading fees and then they get a discount provided they hold BNB coins in their wallets. The amount ranges from 50 per cent in the first year, 25 per cent in the second and 12.5 per cent in the third. Even when the discount drops to zero in the fifth year, the coin will still be used to manage the fee payment for the Binance platform. To prevent depreciation and maintain a stable price for BNB, its creators are committed to destroying (burning) some of these coins to reduce the supply until 50 per cent of the total BNB supply (100 million) is burned. In July 2020, the cryptocurrency exchange announced its largest ever coin burn, removing $60.5 million from circulation. It uses 20 per cent of its profits to buy BNB on the open market and burn them up to a maximum of 50 per cent of its supply. It did not succeed in raising the price. Although BNB is closely tied to the Binance Exchange, it is being traded on other exchanges such as CoinSwitch and Lbank. In April 2019 Binance launched Binance Chain as a public blockchain, and BNB was moved from the Ethereum blockchain to the Binance platform.

At the same time, it unveiled its digital currency debit card in Europe and the UK, allowing users to pay with crypto directly at over 60 million merchants across 200 regions. The Binance Card is powered by a multi-asset wallet and the Visa debit card platform, Swipe. However, it turns out that the card users are not really paying with crypto at all nor are they making purchases on the blockchain: they are converting the crypto into fiat currency before sending the payment to the merchants. The lack of transparency about the process also means that, unlike payments using a credit card drawing on an account in one currency and paying in another fiat currency, the customer does not have any idea what the rate of exchange is.

Binance moved its servers and headquarters out of China to Tokyo in advance of the Chinese government ban on cryptocurrency trading in 2017. But on 23 March 2018, Japan's Financial Services Authority ordered the company to suspend its services to Japanese residents with immediate effect. Binance was warned that it was operating the virtual currency exchange business without proper registration in violation of the Payment Services Act. Binance then gradually stopped serving Japanese residents on its main platform, but has partnered with Z corporation, a subsidiary of Yahoo and TaoTao, a licensed Japanese crypto exchange, to operate in Tokyo since 2020.

In September 2018, the then prime minister of Malta, Joseph Muscat, announced that Malta would become the "blockchain island" in a speech at the UN General Assembly. The island had already approved three new pieces of legislation, the Digital Innovation Authority Act, Innovative Technological Arrangement and Services Act, and the Virtual Financial Asset Act, and now the prime minister welcomed Binance to Malta. Changpeng Zhao responded that Malta's invitation "came at a time when regulatory clarity was very much needed"[15] and announced that it was opening an office in Malta in March 2018 and then in September, the company said that it would work with the Malta Stock Exchange to begin to offer security token trading.

However, following Muscat's resignation in December 2019 in the wake of the ongoing investigation into the assassination of Daphne Caruana Galizia, an investigative journalist, who had accused the prime minister and two of his closest aides of corruption, the political fall-out meant that Binance had lost its political supporters and would have to find new friends in the new administration led by Prime Minister Robert Abela.

Either Binance failed in its attempt to register under the new legislation or did not apply. The only clarification came from a statement issued by the Malta Financial Services Authority:

> The MFSA reiterates that Binance is not authorized by the MFSA to operate in the cryptocurrency sphere and is therefore not subject to regulatory oversight by the MFSA. The Authority is however assessing if Binance has any activities in Malta which may not fall within the realm of regulatory oversight. Admission of virtual financial assets to trading and/or for offering virtual financial assets to the public in and from Malta requires an MFSA license in terms of the Virtual Financial Assets Act, of 2018.[16]

In May 2019, Binance faced losses of $40 million in a large-scale security breach in which hackers stole 7,000 Bitcoins as well as some user two-factor authentication codes and API tokens. In his blog, Binance's CEO, Changpeng Zhao explained that the hackers used a variety of techniques, including phishing and malware and used well-orchestrated actions through multiple seemingly independent accounts. It seems that the hackers were able to compromise several high net worth accounts from Binance's hot wallets, directly connected to the internet. In this instance, the coins were only 2 per cent of the company's overall Bitcoin holdings and Binance undertook to repay them out of its Secure Asset Fund for Users, whilst insisting that crypto exchanges are safer to use than one's own private keys, a view which many dispute.

It appears that it is now impossible to find out where Binance's headquarters is located. In an interview with Coindesk in May 2020, it became clear that this may be partly because Binance has an incentive to keep its newly acquired CoinMarketCap independent from the exchange. In response to the journalist's question, Zhao stated, "Well I think that's the beauty of blockchain ... you don't have to ask ... like where is Bitcoin's office, because Bitcoin does not have an office". Binance has "loads of offices with staff in 50 countries. It is a new kind of organization that doesn't need bank accounts and postal addresses".[17] This is an interesting approach. One can see what he means, but then a virtual currency cannot be regulated, supervised or held accountable by regulators or their clients and customers, if its headquarters is not located anywhere. It is very convenient for the company.

Then on 26 June 2021, the UK's Financial Conduct Authority announced that Binance Markets Ltd, part of the Binance Group is not allowed to undertake any regulated activity in the UK, without the prior written consent of the FCA. The company had until 30 June to comply. No other entity in the Binance Group holds any form of UK authorization, registration or licence to conduct regulated activity in the UK, but the Binance Group appears to be offering a range of products and services in the UK. The FCA does not regulate cryptoassets, such as Bitcoin and Ether, but does regulate crypto asset derivatives such as futures contracts, contracts for difference and options and those cryptoassets, which are defined as securities. The requirement for all businesses offering such services to the public is that they must be authorized to do so. Binance was not. Binance cannot advertise in the UK and it was given until the end of June to confirm that it has stored records of all its customers, so that these can be handed over, if required. The FCA is not alone in taking action. On 25 June 2021, Japan's Financial Services Agency warned Binance that it was operating in Japan without permission for the second time in three years. On 26 June, Binance announced that it was pulling out of Ontario, after the Ontario Securities Commission accused it and several other trading platforms of failing to comply with regulations. Once again, the same principle applies: same business, same risks, same rules. It is not a question of targeting cryptoassets for the sake of it, but they are increasingly expected to be subject to the same rules as others offering the same goods and services with the same risks.

EOS AND EOS.IO

The EOS ecosystem, which was formally launched by Block.one in 2017, consists of two elements, EOS.IO and EOS tokens. EOS.IO manages and controls the EOS blockchain network and the token is the cryptocurrency of the EOS network. A customer/developer has to buy tokens or EOS coins on the open market, to fund the development of their own programs or distributed apps using the EOS blockchain network. The advantage is assumed to be that the blockchain networks will create a high speed, high security format for accessing storage and computing power. EOS offered new, technical scalability solutions, helping to overcome bottlenecks, even to the extent of millions of transactions per second. With its original White Paper, EOS held the record in raising funds with its initial coin offering gathering about $4.1 billion in investments.

EOS is based on a delegated proof-of-stake model, which means that the network of computers that make up the EOS blockchain are organized according to the number of tokens each participant holds. The absence of transaction fees, which makes this model stand out from all the other blockchain projects, is a significant advantage. The other is that EOS does not require a hard fork to make major changes in the network, since all decisions can be made by supermajority without polling all the members in the network. Investors are rewarded with voting power and the ability to decide who can mine the EOS blockchain.

However, EOS's governance model has been subject to sustained criticism in the crypto press over recent years. Its ecosystem is overseen by the EOS Core Arbitration Forum and the Block Producers (BPs). The BPs earn tokens by maintaining the system, with the biggest BPs earning up to 1000 a day. They are elected by a constant voting process with their number being capped at 21.

Cointelegraph describes a case where transactions which had already taken place were reversed by the arbitrators. This example illustrates that a blockchain may not be as immutable as it has been presented, or at least, in certain circumstances. One particular user in a dispute allegedly involving a phished EOS account was referred to one of the platform's "arbitrators," Ben Gates, who decided to reverse transactions, which had taken place without the owner's permission, but this involved undoing transactions which had already been confirmed by the network. Most cryptocurrencies would require a hard fork for that. Cointelegraph quotes the arbitrator as follows: "Under the powers afforded to me as arbitrator under Article 6 of the Rules of Dispute Resolution, I, Ben Gates, rule that the EOS account in dispute should be returned to the claimant with immediate effect and that the freeze over the assets within the said amount is removed."

What is even more interesting for our discussion, is one of the most popular comments on the whole issue was as follows: "Why would anyone use this over a bank account and a traditional legal system? These guys raised ($4 billion) to recreate the legal system using a token that is neither censorship resistant, nor immutable." Similar complaints persisted throughout the rest of 2018. Daniel Larimer, the founder of EOS, commented that "Decentralization is not what we are after. What we're after is anti-censorship and robustness against being shut-down", adding that EOS was "still more decentralized than Bitcoin and Ethereum, because it takes 11 block producers to control the majority of the EOS network and while Bitcoin and Ethereum rely on 4 and 3 pools respectively".[18]

Further and more complex criticisms emerged in September 2019. One of the earliest supporters of EOS, EOS Tribe withdrew from EOS because it was no longer possible to earn funds for maintaining the blockchain without support from the "whales", that is those with very large token holdings. The "whales" are, it is claimed, primarily supporting the concentration of block producers located in China. As noted above, 21 nodes, chosen by the token holders, who stake EOS coins in a vote for up to thirty block producers, have power over all the chain.

According to Coindesk, concerns about EOS persisted in 2018, ranging from the number of block producers failing to qualify for rewards as standby BPs, having put their efforts into developing the chain, or agreeing the draft constitution which had been proposed and then jettisoned. The original idea was that the block producers would use inflation rewards to fund new tools, code improvements and decentralized applications (DApps) to improve the ecosystem. Without an agreement as to the way in which funds would be distributed, all 34 million EOS were burnt (destroyed) on 8 May 2019 and no improvements were made.[19]

The difficulties with decentralization and EOS's corporate governance continued into 2020, according to a report by Binance Research. The initial "constitution" was replaced by an EOS User Agreement, introduced after a somewhat chaotic process. Binance set out a number of tests of the extent to which EOS is in fact decentralized. At this point, the issue of decentralization is less important than what the outcome of the tests tell us about the way in which EOS operates.

A key test is collusion resistance. It appears from the way in which EOS now operates that the decision to end the community pool of funds and to reduce the inflation to 1 per cent to reward the block producers and standby block producer spots, is a move that will consolidate the control of BPs, as it increases their revenue. Since one token accounts for 30 votes, the ability to vote for 30 block producers with a single token facilitates vote sharing and vote trading for the largest BPs. It also makes the whole system open to "Sybil attacks", whereby a single actor may register multiple block producer accounts and multiply their voting weight at a low cost. The role of proxies, entrusted to vote for BPs on behalf of community contributors, allow the BPs to gain control of their votes for a monetary reward. It is to the financial advantage of BPs to do so. The top 21 BPs earn almost seven times as much as other highly placed BP candidates. Another test is that of resistance to attacks. Decentralized systems are supposedly more resistant to attacks simply because of their lack of central points of failure. However, since there appears to be increasing consolidation of the EOS network, it is more vulnerable to cyber-attacks.

CARDANO

Co-founded by Charles Hoskinson, one of the founding members of Ethereum, Cardano is a smart contract platform which seeks to deliver more advanced features than any protocol previously developed, being the first blockchain platform to evolve out of a scientific philosophy and a research driven approach. Hoskinson sees Crypto as a political movement: "Crypto is about as political as it gets, always. We're going to reinvent the concept of money and take it out of government's hands and control it ourselves ... what are the actual consequences of these systems getting adopted? You start realizing everything has to change; trade changes, property rights change, business changes. Business changes, the business structure changes, laws change."[20]

Launched in September 2017, Cardano did not attract much attention at first. The non-profit foundation which runs Cardano is partnered with a number of universities, such as the University of Lancaster, engaged in the process of developing a "reference treasury model" as a means of finding a sustainable way of funding the future development of Cardano's blockchain. By setting aside a small part of every transaction, the project is providing itself with a continuous stream of income in order to attract high quality developers, knowing they will be paid.

There are three problems with cryptocurrency platforms that Cardano hopes to solve: scalability, interoperability and sustainability. The first problem is now a familiar one, namely, the slow speed of networks and high fees due to increasing transaction volumes. Cardano has developed a new algorithm, called Ouroboros as a possible solution to scaling problems. This uses a proof-of-stake approach as a means of lowering energy costs. Instead of having a copy of individual blockchains on each node, Cardano's blockchain reduces the number of networks in a node by appointing a leader responsible for verifying and validating a transaction from a collection of nodes, which the leader then transfers to the main network.

Cardano has also adopted a new computer network architecture, what is called "recursive internetworked" to scale its network. At present, there is no way to carry out cross-chain transactions between cryptocurrencies nor is it possible to transfer cryptocurrencies into the global financial system. Exchanges, which have been known to crash or charge extremely high fees, are the only intermediaries. Cardano wants to become the "internet of blockchain," making it possible for all cryptocurrencies to exist side by side and be converted from one to another without intermediaries. This would enable the use of cryptocurrencies for trading and daily transactions. Cardano would also allow users to attach metadata if they wished, to make the network friendlier to banks and governments. This is but one of a series of announcements of his dreams for the future of the internet, which Hoskinson releases through Cointelegraph.

In addition, Cardano wishes to establish governance structures by providing incentives both to miners *and* other stakeholders. These will govern the development of a self-sustaining economic model for the cryptocurrency. They want a "constitution of protocols" to be baked into the blockchains and the applications using the protocol, such as wallets and online exchanges. Cardano has only just begun its phased development project, the first stage of which, the "Byron" stage saw its proof-of-stake blockchain rebooted, separating out the ledger, consensus and network components of the node, allowing any one of them to be changed, tweaked and upgraded without affecting the others.

The second stage, "Shelley" was completed in July 2020 which saw it move from a federated system to a decentralized network in which the nodes will move away from being governed by the foundation, where the majority of the nodes will be run by the network participants. Shelley also involved the intro-duction of a delegation and incentives scheme. As a proof-of-stake network, users stake their Ada, Cardano's coins, to participate in the network, prefera-bly to stake-pools always on community run network nodes, and be rewarded for "honest participation in the network".[21] That phase has only just begun. The most significant change is the decentralization of the Cardano blockchain. It will be the most decentralized blockchain, 50–100 times more decentralized than other leading blockchain networks with up to 1,000 staking pools taking an active role in consensus and governance, finally pushing voting power into the hands of the community. Holders of Ada will be able to delegate their stake in the pool for the first time, earning passive rewards for taking part in the consensus of the Cardano blockchain – hence the term "proof-of-stake". The Cardano project is a very ambitious project, but it has a long way to go before it is completed.[22]

Cardona is the latest proof-of-stake smart contract blockchain platform aiming to replace Ethereum's space. The idea of community governance sounds attractive in theory but the separation of the settlement layer and the computational layer allows users and nodes the power only to include the transactions of use cases with which they agree. In other words, holders of Ada may find that the use of their own coins is subject to the approval of others. Their use of their coins would be subject to censorship, unlike fiat currency, where only criminal uses are banned.

However, whatever disadvantages Cardona (Ada) may have, it suddenly shot up in value in the first three months of 2021, when Ada traded at about $1.02. By March 2021 it reached a market cap of about $35 billion, making it the fifth largest cryptocurrency by that measure, according to CoinMarketCap. Analysts are at a loss to explain why, apart from the fact that Ethereum is considered to be too costly, but that it uses proof-of-stake, that it can be used as cash and also has voting rights, enabling holders of coins to have a say in development of the cryptocurrency, have significance. Cardona has recently made it possible for users to be able to create unique tokens and non-fungible tokens, which represent ownership of a certain asset. In the search for returns and security during the pandemic, this is not perhaps surprising.[23]

Figure 2.1 shows the top ten cryptocurrencies by market capitalization in January 2021 according to CoinMarketCap. The market capitalizations are huge. However, what has to be kept in mind is that the whole cryptocurrency market is in a constant state of flux, with hard and soft forks, together with scandals, leading to rapid and significant changes in the market.

HACKING CRYPTOCURRENCIES

Mt Gox

The cryptocurrency industry has argued that the advantages of blockchain and smart contracts are that they cannot be changed, that they are transparent and that they can be used to prevent double-spending. All this began to change after 2014 when Mt Gox, then the world's largest Bitcoin exchange, at its peak handling between 70–80 per cent of the trading volume, was hacked. In February 2014, the exchange suspended withdrawals and claimed it was insolvent. Mt Gox declared the loss of 850,000 Bitcoins, 6 per cent of the coins in circulation at the time. The company was later able to recover 200,000 coins, but the remaining 650,000 have yet to be found. The missing coins were valued at over $450 million. It appeared that a hacker had been changing transaction identifiers to steal funds from the exchange's own hot wallet, which the exchange owners were unwittingly refilling, and that this had likely been going on since 2011. The company had to file for bankruptcy in Tokyo in April 2014. Its liquidation was ordered in the same month. Mt Gox's assets, consisting of 200,000 Bitcoins and Bitcoin Cash, valued at $3.5 billion in 2017, were placed in a trust. The trustee, Nobauki Kobayashi, has been selling off Mt Gox Bitcoins to repay creditors, having extended the deadline for submitting claims until the end of March 2020.

Even before 2014, Mt Gox had run into trouble with the US Department of Homeland Securities, having failed to register with the Financial Crimes Enforcement Network (FinCEN), a requirement for money services in the United States. In order to accept funds in dollars, Mt Gox had opened a business account at Wells Fargo for Mutum Sigillum LLC, its US subsidiary. The Department of Homeland Security issued a seizure warrant to Dwolla, a online payment service that transferred funds to Mt Gox, for Mt Gox's Dwolla account. Dwolla had no option but to comply.

Ethereum Classic

Ethereum Classic's blockchain was hacked, using a rare 51 per cent attack on 5 January 2019. One hacker was able to gain control of 60 per cent of the mining power, creating a longer blockchain, which enabled a double-spend. The initial fraud was assessed as $460,000 but was later discovered to be $1 million. From this it became clear that in terms of energy resources, it is much cheaper to launch a 51 per cent attack than had been previously argued. Transactions are supposed to be enforced through a distributed ledger by miners working collectively. In this case, the attackers sold Ethereum Classic coins for cash, then rewrote the blockchain so that they ended up with cash and coins. Transactions can be written out of the ledger, provided the blockchain is split at the right moment, and only the version that excludes the unwanted transaction is built on. The attach works as long as the attacker has enough mining power to overwhelm the rest of the pool. The feasibility of an attack therefore depends solely on the availability and the costs of the mining equipment. Protection against such attacks was under consideration with the possibility of a new method of consensus being developed.

In June 2016 the "decentralized autonomous organization" (DAO), built on the Ethereum network was hacked. The hacker had found a weakness in the DAO source code and was able to use that vulnerability to drain Ether into another DAO. Ethereum developers were able to lock the hackers "child" DAO for 28 days which gave them time to consider what action to take, but it seems that few options were open to them. An open letter from the hacker was published in "Paste Bin". He claimed that he had carefully examined the code of the DAO and

> decided to participate after finding the feature where splitting is rewarded with additional ether ... and have rightfully claimed 3,641,694 ether (about $50 million at the time) and would like to thank the DAO for this reward ... A soft or hard fork would amount to seizure of my legitimate and rightful ether, claimed legally through the terms of the smart contract. Such a fork would permanently and irrevocably ruin all confidence not only in Ethereum but also in the field of smart contracts and blockchain.[24]

However, because the DAO smart contract stated that funds had to be placed in a 28-day holding account, the hacker could not actually get away with the funds and the community could vote on how best to deal with the hack. With 89 per cent of the Ethereum community voting in its favour, the blockchain was hard forked enabling the hacked funds to be sent to an account available to the original owners. The Ethereum blockchain became two chains: Ethereum Classic, the original blockchain, which did not introduce the new consensus rules and did not bring about the transfer, and Ethereum, the forked chain, which did. Either way, it was the end of the DAO, with two exchanges delisting DAO tokens in September and December 2016.

Bitpoint exchange

In July 2019, cryptocurrency exchange, Bitpoint announced that about 55,000 users ($27.9 million) had been affected by an attack through the exchange's "hot" wallet, which is used for transactions. A hot wallet is held on a computer linked to the internet and is therefore vulnerable. The hack was due to unauthorized access to the private keys of its hot wallet. The company said that its cold wallet and cash holdings were not affected. Bitpoint's software was also used to steal another $2.3 million from overseas exchanges.

The company itself is owned by Remixpoint, listed on the second section of the Tokyo Stock Exchange. The founder and CEO of the company, Genki Oda, stated that $19 million of the amount stolen belonged to customers and the remaining $8.9 million belonged to BITPoint, Japan. As a result, the company had to suspend all deposits and withdrawals of their cryptoassets. Oda stated he was in touch with other exchanges, Binance and Houbi, regarding a freeze of the stolen funds which had apparently ended up in their hot wallets. This method is commonly used to prevent fraudsters from gaining access to their cryptocurrencies. The plan is to compensate its users in cryptocurrency rather than in their equivalent fiat value, although no specific timeframe was given.

Each of these cases shows the vulnerability of cryptocurrencies to hacking and the possibilities for changing the contents of the blockchain through hard and soft forks. The impregnability of the blockchain had previously been considered as one of its key virtues.

The cryptocurrency annual anti-money laundering report (AML), published by Ciphertrace includes updates on cryptocurrency related crime, including insider fraud. The 2019 report stated that total cryptocurrency fraud and theft had reached $4.5 billion. The report estimates that $370.7 million was lost in exchange thefts and hacks and a further $4.1 billion lost from fraud and the misappropriation of funds. The losses obviously affect consumers and not just the companies concerned. The "cryptocurrency community" did not anticipate that such issues would arise. The whole enterprise was founded on the notion that the cryptocurrency would, in effect, be self-policing.

MATTERS FOR CONCERN: RESILIENCE AND DECENTRALIZATION

The first concern is the resilience of the blockchain. Since the blockchain design produces multiple shared copies of the ledger data, it is thought to be more resistant to cyber-attacks than centralized networks, because there is no single point of attack and also because the built-in consensus mechanism can easily recognize malicious attacks and isolate them. But blockchains are subject to a different kind of attack. They are informally dominated by coalitions of powerful players in the cryptocurrency ecosystem, who can break the basic rules of the blockchain community and no one can stop them or hold them to account.

Most cryptocurrency users rely on individual nodes, although they may not realize that is what they are doing. Many cryptocurrency users rely on "light" nodes or wallets using a simplified verification system. These nodes connect with one or more full nodes and ask for the transaction to be confirmed by the full node and transferred to the block, which will then be incorporated into a chain. The light nodes rely on the full nodes to verify the transaction, but this means that the light node is entirely dependent on the full node. In July 2015, this was highlighted when not all full nodes had adopted a new protocol so these blocks were not accepted into the valid chain. Some miners on the Bitcoin blockchains were creating invalid blocks. Some software could detect which blocks were invalid and others could not, so showing confirmations that are not real. This particularly applied to lightweight (SPV) wallet users, who were advised to wait for an additional 30 confirmations more than they normally would. Users had to wait until it became clear which chain was going to become the longer and therefore the valid chain. In other words, the SPV verification only works if honest nodes control the whole network.[25]

Various ways have already been shown in which miners can game the system either to allow double-spending or to increase their share of the mining rewards at the expense of other miners. These need not involve a 51 per cent attack, the kind that Nakamoto thought would be unlikely. But they have happened not only with Bitcoin, but also with Ethereum, which has had a series of hard forks, with DAO in 2016, as already mentioned, but also with St Petersburg in 2019, and Istanbul in December 2019. In the case of Bitcoin, not only did it lead to the creation of Bitcoin Cash, but it was a particularly contentious one leading to accusations of bad faith.

The second concern is decentralization. The ideal was set out by Nakamoto. The first step in establishing Bitcoin was to identify the honest nodes, although how these would be selected was unclear. New transactions are broadcast to all the nodes, and are only accepted if all the transactions in it are valid and not already spent. This guarantees that the transaction which is recorded on the block is valid. To ensure the validity of the transactions and the order in which they are received *without a trusted third party*, they must all be publicly announced. The majority decision concerning transactions is represented by the longest chain, which has the greatest proof-of-work invested in it: "If a majority of CPU (computer power) is controlled by honest nodes, the honest chain will grow the fastest and outpace any competing chains".[26] Nakamoto believed that honesty was assured, not by a central authority, but by the honest nodes and that any attacker wishing to defraud the system would have expend so much computer power that it would not be worth it.

Unfortunately, the development of Bitcoin has not conformed to his ideals. They rested on an insecure foundation to begin with, since the production of Bitcoins and the record of transactions in the blockchain involves identifying "honest" nodes to embark on the whole enterprise. Bitcoin certainly starts off as a decentralized "currency" but it inevitably involves taking on trust the honesty of the nodes (i.e. computers plus human beings), a trust in total strangers scattered across the world. Given the amount of energy and computer power involved in the production of Bitcoins, large mining pools, unsurprisingly have developed in countries where there are low energy costs. As a result the control of such currencies becomes centralized, and it is then exposed to the

51 per cent problem: if one node or a cluster of nodes owns more than 51 per cent of the mining operations, it could, in theory at least, change the protocols surrounding Bitcoin at any time. Users of the currency would not have any prior warning of that, and may never know, until something goes wrong. The whole point of decentralization is that it is peer-to-peer, without censorship and without intermediaries, and without the dominance of any one party. But at best, blockchain only confirms and enforces the safe transfer of money between verified recipients, and even that is less certain than it was originally thought to be.

The reason for the rift between the decentralization ideologues and the centralized versions of cryptocurrencies is not just that the latter ecosystems depart from the ideals. It is also because the supposedly trustless ecosystems have failed. Furthermore, new cryptocurrencies find that they need intermediaries for users. That is already clear from the descriptions of some of the major cryptocurrencies outlined earlier. Transfers take place through exchanges and wallets. Taking security a stage further, some cryptocurrencies use custodians, provided by banks and some, like Ripple are linked to banks. This is clearly much more than an ideological dispute. It goes to the issue of whether or not a cryptocurrency can be a currency and whether such a currency can actually be trustless and function as money.

If the trust and willingness of market participants to exchange fiat currency for Bitcoins fade, then this will result in the total loss of value of Bitcoin. That has not happened so far, but that is because Bitcoin, in particular, and some of the other currencies are used as speculative investments. The continued interest in Bitcoin is not because it is a medium of exchange but investors see the chance of huge speculative gains.

SOME CONCLUSIONS

In this chapter, I have set out just a few examples of hard and soft forks, of which there are many more, as well as some examples of significant hacks that have resulted in the loss of millions of dollars. These events underline the currencies lack of scalability, but also that they lack the most important element of all, namely trust. The frequent failures of altcoins and the gaps in their ecosystems as well as their volatility, makes it unlikely that any of them will replace fiat currencies as money.

Although their developers continue to try to overcome these obstacles, it is not easy for these cryptocurrencies to retain a reasonably stable value, especially when retail customers move into the market. Certain currencies become fashionable, or catch the attention of the authors on various websites, and go up in price. Then the mood may change and the price falls back again. The moves towards centralization of decision-making are part of that process, but they are a departure from the original ideals. Some regard this as a necessary development in order to make their ecosystems more secure for the protection of their users.

Perhaps the most important development over recent years has been the introduction of "stablecoins" that seek to counter at least one of the problems of cryptocurrencies, namely their extreme volatility. A stablecoin is linked to another asset, such as gold or another precious metal, or more often, a fiat currency, such as the US dollar or the euro. In the next chapter, the nature of stablecoins will be discussed and the risks considered. While this was happening, regulatory authorities were examining ways in which the cryptocurrencies work in order to ensure that they were properly regulated. The next stage in a decade or more of cryptocurrencies involves both the developers and the regulators.

CHAPTER 3

Stablecoins: the search for stability

The short turbulent history of cryptocurrencies demonstrated several key issues, central among them the lack of trust and extreme volatility. These made Bitcoin and other cryptocurrencies only useful for speculative investment and not as a means of payment. There were two periods of boom and bust with Bitcoin: the first in late 2013/early 2014, that ended with the high-profile hack of the Mt Gox exchange and the second in late 2017/early 2018, when the market capitalization of Bitcoin, Ether and other cryptoassets peaked at $830 billion before crashing. It became clear that the extreme volatility of existing cryptocurrencies meant that they could not be used as a means of payment, a store of value, or a unit of account. The introduction of stablecoins directly addressed the need to reduce volatility by tying digital assets to more reliable, that is, more stable assets such as the US dollar, gold and oil. They were intended to offer the best of both worlds: instant processing, security and privacy of payments and the stable valuations of fiat currencies.

We can breakdown stablecoins into three main types based on how they work: collateralized, crypto-collateralized and non-collateralized. Collateralized stablecoins are linked to a fiat currency, such as the US dollar. Other forms of collateral can include precious metals, or commodities such as oil. Most in fact are linked to US dollars on a one-to-one basis. The reserves are supposedly maintained by custodians and are regularly audited. Crypto-collateralized stablecoins are backed by other cryptocurrencies. Since the reserve currency is very likely to be prone to volatility, these stablecoins are over-collateralized by maintaining a much larger number of cryptocurrencies as a reserve for issuing a lower number of stablecoins. For example, $2,000 worth of Ether may be held as a reserve for issuing $1,000 worth of crypto-backed stablecoins, allowing for 50 per cent swings in the reserve currency. They are supposed to have more frequent audits and monitoring to ensure price stability. Most of these stablecoins use an approach called collateralized debt positions (CDP), a complicated approach that involves the user of the stablecoin opening a CDP by depositing digital assets into a service provider's smart contract, such as Zig. Borrowers can then either convert their Zigs into fiat currencies or buy more digital assets. Non-collateralized stablecoins do not depend on a reserve, but on algorithms to maintain a stable value; for example, the dollar-pegged base coin uses a consensus mechanism to increase or decrease the supply of tokens as required. Typically, they rely on a combination of collateralized positions, with automatic supply balancing techniques. These are the least popular stablecoins.

THE STABLECOIN ECOSYSTEM

Cointelegraph published an article in April 2020 listing the characteristics of the ideal stablecoin, arguably rather late in the day considering the first stablecoins appeared in 2014. Nevertheless it provides a useful checklist for assessing at least the major stablecoins currently in existence. The article's author, Gregory Klumov listed the following requirements for the perfect financial instrument: a convenient payment instrument; can serve as a value measure; can accumulate value; can withstand significant market volatility; can maintain low support costs; can provide decent scalability; can support privacy and decentralization; can be flexible enough to adapt to changing global and local regulations; and can provide transparency for trading and arbitrage transaction.[1]

The ecosystem of the stablecoin should also be flexible enough to adapt to changing global and local regulations. The G7 Working Group on Stablecoins reported that,

50

Private sector entities that design stablecoin arrangements are expected to address a wide array of legal, regulatory and oversight challenges and risks ... such arrangements will need to adhere to necessary standards and requirements and comply with relevant laws and regulations of the various jurisdictions in which they will operate. They will also need to incorporate sound governance and appropriate end-to-end risk management to address risks before they materialize. The G7 believes that no global stablecoin project should begin operations until all of these are addressed.[2]

The "ecosystem" is a term that is increasingly used to describe the way in which a stablecoin operates. This consists of three elements. The first concerns the way in which the stablecoin is issued and redeemed, and how its value is maintained. The second element is how the coins are transferred from one user to another. The third concerns the provision of the access point for users of the coins. The "ecosystem" involves all the elements we are familiar with when we use fiat currencies.

The challenges facing a stablecoin ecosystem are many. First of all, there is the issue of governance. A central agent or a group of agents must design and set the rules for the way in which the value of a stablecoin will be maintained. Those rules will apply to those who are managing the underlying assets or those issuing the stablecoins to make sure that the stablecoin hits the agreed target all the time. The management entities control the redemption of the stablecoins, the custody of the reserves, such as US dollars, commodities or other financial assets. They have to make sure, for example, that they have enough US dollars in reserve so that they can meet the demand of the stablecoin holders to redeem their coins for actual US dollars at any time. Sometimes, third parties can be used to carry out some of the management roles, such as a bank acting as custodian for the reserves.

Stablecoins can be transferred from one person to another without using any of the existing payment systems. Indeed, that is the point. They are distributed using the distributed ledger (DLT) protocols or rules, which govern how transactions are validated, who has access to the stablecoin, what the access conditions are, what roles exist within the system, and who can participate in each role. The ledger can be permissionless, so that anyone can validate the transaction, or permissioned, in which only selected entities can validate transactions. They can be public, so that anyone can use DLT for transactions, or only selected entities can initiate transactions. Sometimes, anyone can see the full version of the ledger, other blockchains only allow designated entities to have full access. Some are open source, allowing anyone to use/modify the original design, preferably in a collaborative way.

Stablecoin ecosystems require a way of providing an access point for consumers. At one level, the access consists of client software that connects the DLT network to a computer terminal or a platform. Some use wallets and websites, which also provide further services such as a store for cryptographic keys, a gateway to initiate transactions, or a place to view balance and transaction histories. In other cases, the user interface consists of trading platforms with links to bank accounts or credit cards, so that the user can buy and sell the stablecoin with fiat currency. All of this may seem irrelevant, but it is vitally important to know whether or not all the elements of the ecosystem are in place and functioning. This is especially important when users need to be sure that their stablecoins are in their wallets, that the custodian really holds all the necessary reserves and that the protocols covering the ownership of the stablecoins is clear. It is crucial to know whether or not the coin depends on a central agency or, if it is decentralized, whether and how it depends on the consensus established by the nodes.

Before going further into Ethereum's blockchain it will be useful to explain two of the key features of the stablecoin ecosystem: wallets and public/private keys. Reference has already been made to "wallets", a familiar term, but digital wallets do not resemble the wallets so many of us use. A software wallet is a computer programme in which Bitcoins or other cryptocurrencies are stored. It consists of a private key corresponding to the Bitcoin address of that wallet, allowing the individual to hold and trade those Bitcoins or other cryptocurrencies; indeed, to trade at all, the trader must have a wallet. The programme is stored on the individual's computer, functioning as an address for the user to receive and deposit digital coins and allow the user to store private keys. The disadvantage of this kind is that they are more susceptible to hacker attacks as they are remotely connected with the internet. Online wallets are very risky since the access to the user's private keys remains in the hands of third parties. Hardware wallets are a separate, secure hardware device, the most secure kind. Some of the best-known wallets include Bitcoin Core, Multibit, Amory,

Electrum, Trezor and Ledger Nano. Mobile wallets (e.g. Bitcoin wallet, Hive Android, Mycelium Bitcoin) perform the same function as a desktop wallet, facilitating payments in stores via "touch-to-pay" and near field communication (NFC) scanning of a QR code. Web wallets facilitate access to digital coins on any browser or mobile device. Since Bitcoin first came on the scene, hardware wallets can hold multiple cryptocurrencies; Nano X, for example, can support over 700 digital currencies and tokens. The cryptocurrencies in the wallet are stored offline, so it is almost impossible to hack the wallet. These devices can also be stored on all major operating systems.

When dealing with cryptocurrency, including stablecoins, a user is usually given a public address and a private key to access their cryptocurrency. The public address is where funds are received and deposited. The core technology enabling public key infrastructure is public key cryptography, relying on a public and a private key, where the two keys are used together to encrypt and decrypt a message. The public key is created from the private key through a complicated mathematical algorithm, which can take various forms, usually depicted as a long series of random numbers, which can only be read by using the associated private key, which is also a long series of random numbers known only to the recipient. The key pair is mathematically related so that whatever is encrypted can only be decrypted by its corresponding counterpart. This kind of public key encryption is not limited to blockchain, but is quite widely used by organizations. There are two features which make this extremely useful for the issuance of cryptocurrencies and stablecoins: the public key cryptography is so scalable that it is able to secure billions of messages exchanged daily over the internet and over an organization's own network. What enables this is that the public keys can be distributed widely and openly without malicious actors being able to discover the private keys required to decrypt the message.

The digital wallet stores the private key of the user and the only person who can retrieve the content of the wallet is the person with the private key. When a transaction is initiated, the wallet software creates a digital signature by processing the transaction with the private key. This is the element of security since the only way to generate a valid signature for any transaction is to use the private key. The signature is used to confirm that the transaction has come from a specific user and ensures that the transaction cannot be changed once it is confirmed on the blockchain.

The private keys can be stored in a particular section of the wallet, an offline partition for their storage and an online partition for the public keys. With this type of software wallet, a new transaction is moved offline to be signed digitally and then moved back online to be added to the blockchain so that it is available to the whole network. This type of wallet is called "cold storage," which is considered to be secure, whereas the "hot wallet" stores private keys on devices or systems, which are connected to the internet and therefore open to being hacked.

The only problem users face is losing the private key. That can be a disaster as the story of an Irish drug dealer, who lost his private keys which he had hidden in the aluminium cap of a fishing rod case, shows. His "wallet" contained a €53.6 million Bitcoin fortune. The fishing rod was stored in a house he rented in Galway, but when he was arrested in 2017 for cannabis trafficking, the landlord gained permission to clear the house. The garbage removal men confirmed that they had seen the fishing rod, but the dumped material was later sent to Germany and China and the keys for his Bitcoins have ostensibly never been found. The drug dealer, Collins has taken the loss in his stride, saying it was a punishment for his own stupidity. But he is not the loser. The Irish Criminal Assets Bureau has not been able to retrieve the largest seizure of assets in 25 years.[3]

Stories about the loss of private keys abound. A Welsh IT worker had 7,500 lost Bitcoins, worth about $56m today. He stopped using the old computer, sold off the parts but kept the hard drive, but when cleaning the house, he threw the wrong hard drive away. It ended up in a vast landfill site, where it remains buried as the local authority refused to dig up 350,000 tons of waste to find it. Another invested $2 million in XRP, but died suddenly at the age of 54. Unfortunately, he stored his private keys in cold wallets that were stored in various banks across the country but did not tell anyone where they were. By 2019, there were still no reports of the wallets or the keys being located.

Maybe people should keep their private keys locked in a safe in their own homes. There is, of course a sense in which the private keys are too clever. Most people will not realize that the two sets of keys are mathematically related: they will just be a long sequence of random numbers, too long to be easily remembered, unlike telephone numbers, for example.[4]

At least the co-founder of Ethereum is aware that what is needed is "user-friendly" wallets. He commented at a recent conference, that "it is still much easier than it should be to lose $200,000 if your wallet breaks. I have a theory that we don't talk about the problem enough because no one is willing to admit that they lost $200,000 ... Because you look like an idiot. I think the reality is that even if you are a super genius or capable of being really careful, the reality is a system that requires you to spend less effort on not losing your stuff is a better system".[5]

THE GROWTH OF STABLECOINS AND ETHEREUM

As we have seen the overall instability of cryptocurrencies is the key obstacle to the development of blockchain as an ecosystem. High volatility has made the use of cryptocurrencies as currencies unattractive, as well as making costs and the miners' incentives unpredictable. Because stablecoins are linked to stable and liquid assets, it is hoped that they can take on some of the same qualities as the assets to which they are pegged, that is most of the characteristics of the ideal financial instrument outlined above.

The majority of stablecoins run on the Ethereum blockchain protocol, because it can provide immediate access to an infrastructure, which can accept a newly issued stablecoin, saving the stablecoin from building a whole new infrastructure of its own. This will undoubtedly facilitate the future development of stablecoins. The Ethereum platform has flexible token standards that allow for easy issuance and interoperability, that is, it can exchange data with different blockchains as if there are no boundaries. (Think of Mastercard or Visa cards which can be used to pay merchants or be used in ATMs across the world, and then you can see why stablecoins need an interoperable network.) Ethereum plans to invest in scalability over the next five to ten years, increasing the speed and efficiency of transactions, which could mean that it comes to rival Visa's current speed of some 65,000 transactions per second, although the major credit cards are already scaled to a much larger capacity.

Other "second generation" applications have already been built on the Ethereum blockchain protocol, including the way in which "wallets" operate, with potential benefits for e-commerce. Ethereum itself is based on the use of tokens, which can be bought, sold or traded. Tokens represent a wide variety of digital assets, such as vouchers, IOUs, and even real-world tangible assets.

Ethereum introduced ERC-20 in November 2015, which is now the technical standard API for all smart contracts on the Ethereum blockchain for token implementation. It provides a set of rules that apply to all Ethereum tokens, that is, smart contract tokens on the Ethereum blockchain. With its help, essential information such as the number of tokens, the balance of tokens in each owner's account, transactions to be executed, transfer of tokens, and finding out if the user has the minimum number of tokens to execute a transaction can be discovered. People can exchange these tokens on the Ethereum blockchain, store them in Ethereum wallets, or send them to other Ethereum wallets. These rules assist developers in that they can predict how new tokens will function in the Ethereum system. Compliance with the rules is essential as it ensures compatibility between the many different tokens issued on Ethereum. At present, about 93 per cent of all stablecoin transactions take place on Ethereum.

Finextra summarises the rules governing the ECR-20 tokens. First of all, the coins based on the Ethereum blockchain are designed to represent a developed project or technology. This financial asset is created with the help of smart contracts. A company conducts an initial coin offering (ICO) and issues a token for sale to investors and an initial offering, which is to raise capital to launch and develop the project.

The standard token on the Ethereum blockchain has the following properties: makes assets interchangeable; can be used on compatible platforms, projects and exchanges; ensures operation with compatible decentralized applications (DApps); simplifies transactions with the receipt and sending of coins; and interacts with other currencies and smart contracts. ERC-20 requires certain protocol functions when creating a token and building a smart contract. These are obligatory and include control of the initial number of coins and issue; assignment of the initial quantity to the company's address and to the owner of the ICO; sending assets to investors, recording the balance; distribution of coins among users for transactions and verification of their movement; checking the remaining balance; and controlling the adequacy of the currency at the address for transmission.[6]

Although Ethereum's regulatory standards for the acceptance or rejection of tokens on its open-source, blockchain-based, decentralized software platform, used for its own cryptocurrency, Ether enables smart contracts and DApps to be built and run without any downtime, fraud, control or interference from a third party, the standards are primarily technical standards governing the ways in which the tokens can use its platform, without having to build their own. It should be noted that they are not concerned with establishing rights of ownership, custody of assets backing the stablecoin or with anti-money-laundering requirements or any other relevant issues governing the use of stablecoins as a currency.

Ethereum's upgrade to its blockchain began in December 2020. Ethereum 2.0 (Eth2) is designed to address the network's scalability and security through a number of changes to its infrastructure, notably from a proof-of-work (as with Bitcoin) to a proof-of-stake consensus model. Proof-of-stake validation depends on ownership of cryptos: validators' stake gives them the right to verify a transaction, based on how much crypto they hold and the length of time they have held it. Other validators can attest they have seen the block, and when there are enough attestations, the block can be added to the blockchain. Validators are then rewarded for the successful block propositions, a process known as "forging" or "minting". The validators are rewarded by earning annualized interest on their locked-in Ether. This includes the implementation of the "Beacon Chain", which stores and manages the registry of validators as well as deploying the proof-of-stake consensus mechanism for Ethereum 2.0.

The launch of this chain saw over 27,000 validators from around the world taking part in the new consensus model. Each validator had to make a 32ETH deposit in order to take part (about $23,754.00). Eth2 is expected to reach 100,000 transactions per second as the system develops. This kind of scalability means greater use and greater demand, which should push up the price of ETH and will mean "a completely seamless experience for the next billion people," according to Jamie Anson, organizer of Ethereum, London.

It sounds too good to be true: an open-sourced platform for anyone to use. That part is true but there are costs involved. Firstly, a user has to purchase Ether, Ethereum's currency in order to buy "Gas" to use the blockchain. The stablecoin provider Tether paid $2.6 million in Ether gas fees in May 2020 even though the number of transactions was not at an all-time high.

TETHER

The first stablecoins were issued in 2014. BitUSD was launched in July and NuBits in September. Both were collateralized through other cryptocurrencies.

BitUSD was issued as a token on BitShares blockchain, having been developed by Dan Larimer (later of EOS) and Charles Hoskinson (now of Cardano). It was backed by BitShares core token (BTS) under the terms of a smart contract. NuBits was one of the non-collateralized stablecoins, but one which used "seigniorage shares" instead. This is a cryptocurrency concept according to which the issuer algorithmically changes the volume of the coins so that they maintain their price. In 2018, BitUSD lost its parity to the dollar and was heavily criticized as a result. Now it trades at about 80 cents to the dollar. NuBits failed miserably. It had two serious crashes, in 2016 and again in 2018 and now trades at 0.6 cents against the dollar.

It was the stablecoin Tether, launched in November 2014 and listed on the crypto exchange Bitfinex a year later, that has had the most tempestuous history since its inception. The coin is linked to the US dollar at a 1:1 ratio, so every Tether token minted had to be backed by a US dollar. One of the issues which quickly emerged was its link to Bitfinex, the exchange responsible for issuing the tokens. Tether coins can be purchased on the Bitfinex exchange, which is registered in the British Virgin Islands, and were designed to allow traders to cash in and out of Bitcoin quickly by transferring proceeds to other exchanges or digital wallets, bypassing lengthy processes involving the banking system. But by 2018, Tether's commitment to its dollar backing was called into question. Rumours questioning Tether's reserves began to surface in late 2018 and on 15 October, the Tether token dropped below the $1 mark apparently due to a sell-off amid a wave of negative sentiment. Cointelegraph reported that this could have been influenced by rumours that both Tether and Bitfinex had ended their relationship with Noble Bank in Puerto Rico. Bitfinex then suspended fiat wire deposits without any explanation.[7]

The Office of the Attorney General in New York began its investigation into Bitfinex and Tether in November 2018. Although Bitfinex is based in the British Virgin Islands, it deals with clients based in New York, and was not licensed by the New York Department of Financial Services to engage in virtual currency business there, which was a requirement. The investigation disclosed many issues of concern about Bitfinex and Tether: it alleged that Bitfinex had never publicly disclosed its relationship with a Panama-based firm, Crypto Capital Corps. The operators of Crypto Capital were indicted in 2019, including the former owner of the Minnesota Vikings, Reginald Fowler accused of stashing funds over a global network of accounts at 56 different banks. Earlier, in 2016, the famous Paradise Papers had revealed that Tether and Bitfinex shared the same CEO, Jan Ludovicus van der Velde, and the Bitfinex, CFO, Giancarlo Devansini had registered Tether back in 2014.

The most serious allegation made by the investigation was that there was a rumoured $850 million funding gap in Bitfinex reserves designed to back Tether. Tether Holdings had stated that it was a stablecoin fully backed by US dollar reserves. However, from about 4 March 2019 its website statement claimed only that Tether was backed by Tether Holdings "reserves", which include unspecified currency, "cash equivalents" and "other assets and receivables from loans made by Tether Holdings to third parties, including affiliated entities." The investigation found that "a third party foreign entity, which processed customer deposits and withdrawals for iFinex had refused to provide iFinex with nearly '$1bn of their commingled client and corporate funds;' Tether Holdings had transferred $625m to iFinex and iFinex took a $900m line of credit from Tether Holdings (despite NYAG's expressed concerns)".[8]

The investigation was taken under the Martin Act and is significant. The Appellate Division of the Supreme Court of New York, First Department decision confirmed the broad authority of the New York State Attorney General (NYAG) to investigate potential fraud and it was the first appellate decision to apply the Martin Act's expansive powers to an NYAG investigation of foreign entities in the cryptocurrency industry. What is also interesting is that the First Department held that the Martin Act applies to virtual currencies because they are clearly covered by its broad definition of currencies, stating that "Martin's Act's definition of commodities as 'including any foreign currency, any other good or article or material' is broad enough to encompass Tether".[9] The First Department explained that "federal courts and the Commodities Futures Trading Commission have found that virtual currencies are commodities under the Commodities Exchange Act, which defines the term more narrowly than the Martin Act".[10] During 2019, both Bitfinex and Tether were in denial, claiming that the funds were in safe-keeping. On 11 December 2020 the NYAG barred Tether from lending any funds to Bitfinex before 15 January 2021 and that by then the NYAG expects to receive all requested documents from both firms. Until then, none of these allegations can be proved.

Earlier, in September 2017, Tether had hired Friedman LLC to assess whether or not it had sufficient reserves, and which was confirmed in a preliminary report that stated that Tether had 442.9 million in US dollars exactly the same number as Tether in circulation then. But this was only a superficial report, which was never completed as Tether terminated the relationship in January 2018. Another law firm, Freed, Sporkin, and Sullivan LLP was hired and published a report claiming that the organization's tokens are fully backed with US dollars, but again this was not an audit and was subject to a number of caveats. That was the case in January 2020 and by the end of November 2020, Tether had still not produced a full audit of its bank accounts, according to Cointelegraph.

However, despite the unresolved issues concerning the past record of both Bitfinex and Tether, both appear to be flourishing, even moving into new ventures. Bitfinex unveiled a new lending service, Bitfinex Borrow, a borrowing platform, which acts as a way for Bitfinex to offer loans to its customers. Customers put up cryptoassets in exchange for a loan, Bitfinex then allocates those assets to different customers via other Bitfinex products all using the same underlying pool of funding.[11] Customers can receive US dollars or Tether in return for their cryptoassets, which Bitfinex holds until the loan is paid back, but, what if, for example, those cryptoassets were Bitcoins, what would their value be when returned, as opposed to when they were handed over as part of the collateral for the loan? So there are questions to be considered. Similarly, since the cryptocurrency is effectively held by software, there is a risk that hackers will find vulnerabilities in the code and steal the funds. The interest rate charges for the loans vary widely, from 5.5 per cent to 18.25 per cent depending on a range of factors, including the length of the loan. Longer-term loans incur higher interest rates, although loans are only available for 120 days.[12] Given the number of entities involved in the service, using one's credit card or a personal loan from one's bank sounds a much simpler and more reliable proposition. As for Tether, its market cap has continued to grow and stood at $20.815 billion on 29 December 2020, third in line behind Bitcoin and Ethereum ETH. Although its market cap began to rise back in January 2018, the sharper increase began in January 2020, possibly because action had not yet been taken against Tether and because of the peg to the US dollar, during the pandemic.

The NYAG case was finally settled in February 2021. The settlement requires Bitfinex and Tether to pay a fine of $18.5 million and to provide quarterly reports describing the composition of Tether's reserves for the next two years, which have to match the information Tether has already provided the NYAG about its reserves. The NYAG stated that "Bitfinex and Tether recklessly and unlawfully covered up massive financial losses to keep their scheme going and to protect their bottom lines. Tether's claims that its virtual currency was fully backed at all times by US dollars was a lie". Coindesk welcomed the transparency requirement, as long as it is sufficiently detailed, as this would quell rumours that the company had been printing unbacked Tethers to artificially drive up the price of Bitcoin, "the market's bellweather".[13]

Tether, however, shows little sign of mending its ways, having revealed its reserves for the first time, as part of its attempt to remain in compliance with the settlement with the New York Attorney General. It offers a breakdown of its reserves in a pie chart, which shows that as of 31 March 2021, the reserves consisted of 75.85 per cent of cash and equivalents, 12.55 per cent secured loans, 9.96 per cent incorporate bonds and precious metals, and 1.64 per cent in other investments, including digital currencies. Cash and equivalents cover: 65.39 per cent commercial paper, 24.2 per cent fiduciary deposits, 3.87 per cent cash, 3.6 per cent reverse repo notes and 2.49 per cent Treasury bills. Tether has not provided any further information about the commercial loans or the corporate bonds, such as the identity of the borrowers of the loans, the collateral backing the loans, or which agencies rated them or the rating.[14] Tether published the breakdown on its website, but that together with the reference to the independent accountant's assurance, is all.[15] The information is limited but the significance of the lack of information goes beyond Tether itself. "Tether is a key piece of plumbing for the roughly $2 trillion global crypto market. Traders use it to quickly transfer dollar value between exchanges to capture arbitrage opportunities when a bank wire is unavailable or too slow."[16] But if Tether's reserves are either not reliable or not what they seem, then the global crypto market may turn out to be a house of cards.[17]

In addition, Tether is and remains expensive to operate, a feature which may not seem obvious when focusing on its one-to-one link to the dollar. This is because the issuer and its investors, must provide and retain large amounts of collateral in low-yielding liquid form. Tether may not be able to expand as widely as it might wish and still keep sufficient dollars in reserve, even though it has weakened that commitment. Assuming that all the costs are passed on to the end-user, there is little difference between holding dollars in one's commercial account and using that account to pay bills, and to receive wire transfers from one's customers. It appears that fewer than 400 addresses hold over 80 per cent of all Tether. These owners could easily manipulate the market and the price of Tether itself. An illustration of this is when the "whales" (those holding enough of the coins to be able to manipulate the valuations) sent over $300 million in Tether to Binance.[18] That is a risk in itself but, in addition, Tether's market capitalization is still a fraction of that of Bitcoin. The current market cap for Bitcoin is $619.6 billion and for Tether, it is $21.3 billion, well behind Ether at $108.3 billion.

Quite apart from Tether's potential troubles, it is clear that few stablecoins have achieved the ideal characteristics of a stablecoin. The issue of "value" is where the problems lie. The value of stablecoins against reference assets may fluctuate more than digital instruments like e-money. Stablecoin pegs are managed through the actions of private investors, who deposit (withdraw) dollars with the Tether Treasury when the stablecoin trades at a premium (discount), a change in the relative supply that drives the peg back towards one.[19] Tether will argue that is what keeps the peg stable, but in the case of Tether, it appears that most of the fluctuations are driven the arbitrageurs' inability to employ their balance sheets to profit from price differentials. Others see even greater problems with stablecoins: "Their market capitalization may rise and fall rapidly with purchases and redemptions by investors. Worse yet, without additional private or public backstops, stablecoins can be subject to severe price discounts or self-fulfilling runs, especially when backed by risky or opaque assets and in times of market turmoil." Furthermore, "if stablecoins were to gain significant usage, runs on stablecoins could provoke fire sales of assets used to back their value".[20]

CRYPTOCURRENCIES AND COSTS

The claim is often made that cryptocurrencies and stablecoins offer not just fast but *cheaper* methods of payments, especially international payments. But it is often difficult to find out just what level of fees a user will be charged for purchasing Bitcoin, any of the altcoins or stablecoins by the issuer or the exchanges. The exchanges charge fees for moving money from one currency to another, regardless of whether the source or destination is a fiat currency or another crypto. In part, these exchanges just pass on the fees they have been charged by the sending account and the receiving account for carrying out the transaction, which typically involves two transfers: from the source to the exchange, the second from the exchange to the destination. The other part of the fee charged covers the exchanges costs and provides profits. In addition, there are fees which the cryptocurrency charges for performing operations within it, such as a transfer from one account to another, which usually varies with time. With many cryptocurrencies, a higher fee is charged for a faster transfer. In addition, cryptocurrencies with smart contracts have separate fees for executing the contract. The fees vary widely and can be very difficult to predict: for example, they can vary by as much as a 1000 per cent for Ethereum. The fees ultimately are destined for the accounts of the miners, who execute the transactions and the smart contracts.

The situation is no better with the fees charged for international transactions. Here is the heartfelt plea from an Ether-user from an online forum: "Fees are too damn high to send 20 USDC to someone is about $10–$15 worth of gas fees. How can I minimize gas fees when using a meta mask (a crypto wallet and gateway to crypto apps)? And is it true that if I send my gas fee too low, I would lose my ETH on a failed transaction?"[21] The question led to about 500 questions mostly posted by programmers, all trying to calculate the fees for various kinds of crypto, underlining the problems in estimating the charges for any transaction one wishes to undertake.[22] Clearly, regulators should also require fees for all transactions from the purchase of cryptoassets with fiat currencies, transfers of cryptoassets of all kinds should be transparent to the investor or user of such assets. This should be part of the consumer protection regulations.

It is also important to bear in mind that the prices, including the price of gas for using Ethereum, applies very widely as Ethereum is now the primary means of making payments or transferring cryptocurrencies from one account to another for almost all cryptos and stablecoins. This is why Ehereum's pricing is so important. The lack of transparency in the fees charged and the fact that these can be so high, undermines the claims of faster and cheaper methods of payment made by the cryptocurrency community and by stablecoins. They also face stiff competition from an ever increasing number of companies, such as Venmo, Currency Cloud and Rapyde, making the same offering with or without the need for a bank account and which do not require transferring fiat currency into a stablecoin.

Issuers of stablecoins may believe that they will be able to move into the spheres of retail payments, remittances and markets in financial claims such as securities. This is less likely in economies with a stable currency and a vastly superior payment systems. The real concern on the part of regulators and central banks is that these systems, which are too small to have any effect on monetary policy now, may grow to be a matter of concern. The point is that electronic money schemes which are licensed by the authorities must provide the central bank with any information that is required, including statistical information necessary for the purposes of monetary policy. Transparency over the fee structure is also a requirement, as part of consumer protection. That is the situation in the European Union, which introduced its E-Money Directive in September 2000 and revised it in 2009.[23]

If stablecoin issuers are to become legitimate and gain public support, then they will have to become subject to the same kind of requirements as the providers of electronic money are obliged to accept. For the European Union, these would include being licensed and subject to prudential supervision. Protection against criminal abuse, such as money laundering, must also be part of the design and implementation of electronic money schemes. The latest EU Directive dealing with money laundering and countering terrorist financing notes that the anonymity of virtual currencies allows for their potential misuse for criminal purposes. "To combat the risks associated with anonymity, national Financial Intelligence Units (FIUs) should be able to obtain information allowing them to associate virtual currency addresses to the identity of the owner of the virtual currency".[24] Section 17 adds that for the FIUs, "their unfettered access to information is essential to ensure that flows of money can be properly traced and illicit flows and networks detected at an early stage." One of the problems with stablecoin issuers is that users can deal directly with the exchange and the custody of funds without the intervention of any accountable trading platform or custodian.

Some of the essential requirements of electronic money do not apply to stablecoins. Issuers of electronic money are legally obliged to redeem electronic money at par, at the request of the e-money holder and charges have to be proportionate and related to the actual costs incurred by the e-money issuer. These regulations in the EU are aimed at maintaining price stability by avoiding too much e-money being issued, safeguarding liquidity and the short-term interest rates set by the central bank. Issuers of e-money in the EU are obliged to hold customers' funds in a separate credit institution or invested in secure, liquid low-risk assets as defined by the competent authorities of the home member state. This is to ensure that customers' funds are ring-fenced from the issuers' assets and cannot be seized by its creditors in the event of insolvency. The funds of the custodian bank must also be protected. They are also subject to capital and liquidity requirements.

In their recent article, Bullman and others argue that, "if issuers of tokenized currencies (or stablecoins) were subject to similar provisions and licensing requirements, they would obtain legitimation and could possibly gain acceptance in the retail payment market where they would compete with similar businesses that use traditional technology". But that is not quite the point. If these initiatives were to do so, they would "lose the users who do not want to interact with the regulated financial sector and prefer to bear the risk of holding their funds with unregulated entities rather than disclose their identities".[25]

It is also a question of the governance of the blockchain. "Governance collapses in cryptocurrency blockchains have become common ... Governance is about who makes the rules and who enforces them. It is about not only who controls the blockchain but also resolution mechanisms in case of technological collapse, contract default and crime. Similar technology solutions as in scalability and privacy issues have all been proposed but all seem to imply 'some degree of centralization' ... Technological solutions alone cannot suffice. Standardization and regulation will be much needed."[26]

But these restrictions are precisely those which have been rejected by the cryptocurrency community and its commitment to decentralization, together with freedom from the control of the central bank. That is their ideological commitment. Others, of course, are happy to take the risks as anonymity suits their nefarious purposes very well. And others are simply unaware of the risks involved or refuse to recognize them. The power of the "fear of missing out" (FOMO)[27] is well illustrated in surveys of people responding to initial coin offerings by buying stablecoins without even knowing what they are. And it can even hit the more sophisticated, as Nasdaq reported when the Coinbase Pro exchange designed for institutional investors, registered an outflow of over 35,000 Bitcoin early on 2 January 2021. These outflows usually end up in Coinbase's cold wallets for custody but instead Bitcoin's rally from October lows of $10,000 went "ballistic over the past four weeks, with prices rising from $19,000 to over $30,000".[28] None of these considerations stopped those jumping on the bandwagon of providing cryptocurrencies, nor the public being taken for a ride.

DECENTRALIZED FINANCE: A NEW LIFE FOR STABLECOINS?

The idea of decentralized finance (DeFi) apparently originated in discussions in August 2018 between Ethereum developers and other entrepreneurs about building open financial applications on blockchain technology. These would be non-custodial, as users are the only ones with access to their wallets, open as funds can be transferred globally and transparent as the code for these transactions is open to anyone to inspect.[29] Most DeFi smart contracts incorporate stablecoins at the core of their functionality. DeFi loans are one example in which tokens or stablecoins are organized by platform operators to construct liquidity pools, so that other users can borrow these by providing their cryptoasset collateral. Those on the supply side can deposit Ether tokens in, for example, Compound, which describes itself as an algorithmic, autonomous interest rate protocol built for developers, enabling them to earn interest on transactions which generate pool fees. Users can be on the demand side as well and can borrow from the pool as long as they have adequate collateral in another cryptoasset in the pool. That could be as much as 150 per cent of the value of the loan to compensate for market volatility. It is also possible to take out a flash loan (uncollateralized DeFi), which seems to be a matter of taking out a loan to take tokens out of one pool for fast arbitraging purposes to get a better rate of return.[30] This has to be completed in one transaction block so that the liquidity pool does not lose liquidity.[31] The Commodity Futures Trading Commission (CFTC) describes the lending protocols in more detail. The decentralized lending protocols allow users to deposit digital assets into a vault (e.g. Ether) and borrow another token (e.g. DAI). Some of these aim to create a stable digital token through borrowing/lending and some generate a rate of return. Borrowers deposit one digital asset into a smart contract and receive another token, usually valued at an amount below what has been provided as initial capital. The loan is denominated in another asset at an amount which is usually 50–75 per cent of the deposited capital. To ensure the lending protocol has enough capital, the deposited capital is sold if the borrower's capital drops below a liquidation ratio. The lending protocols often rely on outside data feeds to assess the value of the collateral deposited by users.

At first sight, it might be assumed that this lending is to provide other sources of finance for those without access to bank lending and to finance the real economy. But this is not the case. The loans are designed for those who already possess cryptoassets to enable them to exchange tokens between users so that they can earn from interest rate differentials. The uninitiated should be advised that they should not expect any of the protections which exist with bank or credit institution lending.[32] Aon, for example, announced in March 2021 a pilot with Nyama allowing cryptocurrency holders to cover against losses due to hacks or buggy software. But users will need to be tech savvy to use these services safely and the software is more complex than the already complex blockchain applications. Runs on liquidity could also raise problems. The CFTC task force recommended a wait and see approach, but also recommended that the CFTC should consider whether or not to impose strict liability on smart contract developers and/or miners to prevent spillover effects, amongst other considerations.

DeFi is expected to continue high rates of growth in 2021, having reached $13 billion by the end of December 2020, and reportedly having hit $40 billion in early 2021, based on industry data and cryptocurrency exchanges.[33] Nasdaq provides similar estimates for February 2021.[34] But the point to note is this: where is this growth to be found? All the areas cited by CFTC are all confined to cryptoasset users and serve only their interests. Small business owners and retail customers are concerned with developing their businesses, or making purchases such as property. The product offerings do not meet their concerns.

CHAPTER 4

Initial coin offerings: the "Wild West"

By April 2018, just over 82 per cent of initial coin offerings (ICOs) created their tokens using the Ethereum platform. Other platforms followed suit, including Waves, a Russian-based project founded in 2016, the second most popular platform after Ethereum, NEO (or Antshares), a Chinese platform NEM, and Stellar, claiming to be the best choice for ICOs that do not require a smart contract, as most do not. The ICO is a method of raising capital, using blockchain technology as part of their business model to provide a particular product or service. Sometimes, tokens are granted for the purpose of gathering a group of individuals interested in blockchain technology, or for social media or marketing reasons. Buyers are led to believe that their tokens will increase in value, or that they will become developers of the project, blockchain providers or used in marketing purposes.

When a cryptocurrency start-up wants to raise money, it usually publishes a "White Paper" which sets out details of the project, how much funding is required, and the length of the funding campaign. During the campaign investors buy some of the new tokens with fiat or digital currency. If the funds raised do not reach the minimum level required by the firm, the monies raised may be returned to the backers and the ICO will be regarded as unsuccessful. The ICOs are advertised on the internet and social media as well as through the blockchain community and its publications. The popularity of ICOs grew steadily from 2013 onwards, reaching its peak in 2017 through to the first half of 2018.

Between 2016 and 2017, over 3,000 ICOs raised billions of dollars, with estimations ranging from $3 billion to $75 billion with more funds raised in the first six months of 2017 than in the previous three and a half years. The first expected mega ICO took place in 2018: Telegram raised over $1.7 billion in two separate private token sale rounds, followed by EOS unexpectedly attracting $4.1 billion.

Telegram Open Network (TON) was launched in 2018 but it was not until June 2019 that details of the project were published by a Russian research agency. The project was developed by the Durov brothers, who later fled from Russia to reside in Saint Kitts and Nevis. TON was to be a new blockchain platform and native cryptocurrency called "gram" that used Telecom's existing encrypted instant messaging service. The tokens were not offered to the public, and the names of its backers were not revealed, with the exception of Sergey Solonin and David Yakobashvili. All seemed promising back then, but in May 2020, after US courts found that the ICO violated federal securities laws and prevented the global distribution of grams,[1] Telegram abandoned the Telegram Open Network and Gram Tokens and agreed to return more than $1.2 billion paid by investors.

EOS

Based on its White Paper, published on 1 June 2017, the EOS.IO blockchain platform was developed by a private company, Block.one and released as an open-source software project. Two weeks later, the Mainnet had not yet gone live, because the crypto tokens, EOS, were locked until 21 "miners" had been elected for the new network. Those who had bought tokens had to wait until 15 per cent of all tokens, the equivalent of 150 million were "staked" in a vote on block producer candidates. Staking tokens allows EOS holders to vote for up to 30 block producers, who verify transactions. The votes were weighted by how many tokens are staked. There was considerable speculation about the reasons for the delays in voting.[2] Over a year later, the project was still delayed, partly due to fears that it was over-centralized with a large proportion of the tokens held in China, with some fearing state intervention. Block.one, the company which launched EOS, was the largest token holder giving it the right to change the protocols and also to select the block producers, but even after a year, it had not yet done so. EOS uses a consensus model, delegated proof-of-stake, where a higher throughput of transactions is achieved by reducing the number of nodes participating in the consensus. Many crypto investors regarded this approach as too centralized. As time went on, EOS moved away from the whole idea of a constitution for the governing the chain.

It was hoped that the block providers would fund new tools, code improvements and decentralized apps, including community functions, lobbying costs and security audit. In September 2019, the Securities and Exchange Commission settled charges against Block.one for its unregistered ICO, which raised the equivalent of several billion dollars between June 2017 and June 2018. Block.one had not registered as a securities offering, as required. The result is that Block.one did not provide ICO investors with the information they were entitled to receive as participants in a securities offering. Block.one settled with the SEC for $24 million.

The members of the EOS ecosystem were disappointed to find that, as there was no way of making a decision about how to distribute the funds, all 34 million EOS were burnt on 8 May 2019, with thousands of new applications going with it.[3] By June 2020, the situation had still not been resolved. Block.one announced its intention to start voting, although as it holds 9.5 per cent of the EOS coins, that would make it a major single voter for the 21 validators with the largest share of tokens supporting them. Meanwhile a cryptocurrency investment fund launched a class-action lawsuit against Block.one and EOS, claiming that a "fraudulent scheme" failed to deliver on its primary promise of decentralization, one which has not apparently been settled at the time of writing.

However, it is still possible to buy EOS using US dollars or euros on the Coinbase, Binance and Kraken exchanges, and to sell EOS on an altcoin exchange for Bitcoin or Ethereum. It provided early investors with a return on investment of 240 per cent. Its market cap in June 2020 was $2.3 billion and its value at the time of writing is $3.24 and its market capitalization is $3 billion. The coin is clearly viewed as an asset, which people buy with a view to selling when the price rises.

But troubles may still lay ahead. The EOS blockchain is being used quite widely but it has not yet attracted major companies who want a highly secure database with high throughput. Block.one launched its initial coin offering to provide the funds to develop EOS. But by December 2020, Block.one still had not made any moves, beyond issuing EOS. The EOS token is the cryptocurrency of the EOS network. A developer simply needs to hold EOS, instead of spending them, to be eligible to use network resources and to build and run DApps.

TEZOS

Tezos is an open-source blockchain network linked to the digital token, a tez (XTZ), based on a proof-of-stake consensus mechanism. Its ICO in the summer of 2017 was successful, but it immediately became embroiled in a series of disagreements and lawsuits. It eventually got off the ground in 2018, with its price reaching record highs in February 2020.[4] The price hit $3.12 on 12 February 2020, a 54 per cent increase on the previous week alone, but fell back to $2.58 in June 2020. The proposition was led by Arthur Breitman (as L. M. Goodman) in a White Paper published in August 2014, Tezos was planned as a self-amending blockchain governance system that would allow holders of its protocol token, XTZ, to more easily vote and implement changes to the software without hard forks. The ICO took place through the Breitmans and their company Dynamic Ledger Solutions and raised $232 million. The legal disputes between the Breitmans and the appointed head of the Tezos Foundation, Johann Gevers, delayed the release of XTZ tokens to investors and the launch of the network. As with other unlicensed ICOs Tezos was criticized by the SEC, which demanded penalties for securities violations, despite pushbacks from stakeholders to exempt a wider range of tokens from securities regulation. Class action lawsuits were brought against Tezos, but in September 2020, with the Tezos Foundation having agreed to pay a $25 million settlement, the longstanding case was finally settled. However the case still left it unclear as to whether Tezos is a security or not.

TON, EOS and Tezos are three of the biggest and most notable of the 3,000 ICOs launched during 2017–18. Originally intended as ways to attract financial support for new ideas in the blockchain community, they became ways to raise funds for broader purposes with an ever-growing number of investors. The governance of such structures was not only unclear, but seemed to change on the whim of either the owners of the company or those owning the largest number of coins. The billions of dollars raised were not invested according to the original White Papers or they were not invested at all. Of course, the investors can cash in their volatile investments when they wish, but the owners retain substantial funds in many cases. Some of the coins remain in existence, but many did not survive long after their ICOs reached either a target price or the maximum price they were likely to meet during the period of the offering.

The distribution of ICOs by market capitalization shows that most ICOs (41 per cent) aim to collect between $10 million and $100 million, with 18 per cent seeking between $1 million and $10 million.[5] The actual amount raised was often much less than the goals set out in the White Paper. Very often these provided very little information about the issuing entities, or the details of the backers of the project, including no location or contact details. Usually the White Paper focused on long and detailed technical descriptions of the project with possibly some indication of the use and benefits of the technology. Most investors would not be able to assess whether the proposed technical advances are feasible or when they would be likely to be completed. But many investors, acting partly through the "fear of missing out" and certainly with the hope of short-term gains, piled funds into the ICOs. A joint report from PWC and the Swiss Crypto Valley Association estimated that the volume of ICOs reached $13.7 billion in the first five months of 2018.

Companies have been able to raise funds with surprising speed; for example, TenX raised $80 million, the equivalent of 245,832 Ether (ETH), which were then exchanged for the company's own PAY tokens at a rate of 350 Pay to 1ETH. About 4,000 people took part in the sale which lasted for under seven minutes. By 2019, the company later had to restructure to comply with regulations in Singapore, where the company is located. A company, possibly created by a single person, offering the Useless Ethereum Token managed to raise $200,000 in contributions. One would think the name of the offering alone would dissuade people from investing in it. The speed with which people were prepared to invest in companies offering new cryptoassets without knowing anything about the company or the nature of the offering shows how easy it was to defraud them. Those who invested in the Useless Ethereum Token lost their money entirely. Whoever was responsible for that offering simply disappeared. It is unclear whether or not TenX was a scam. The company announced that it proposed to discontinue its services in January 2021 with the TenX team telling its users to withdraw their funds from their TenX wallets as soon as possible. TenX failed to deliver its own debit card, partnered with Wirecard, which then collapsed in June 2020, owing $4 billion.[6] That ultimately led to the closure of TenX.[7]

Examples of fraud, scams and Ponzi schemes amongst the ICOs abound. For example, Centra Tech launched a crypto project in 2017, claiming that they would provide a crypto debit card, supposedly issued by Visa or Mastercard. They claimed to have 38 state money transmission licences and even invented a Harvard graduate to bolster their credibility. They provided celebrity endorsements from the boxer Floyd Mayweather and the music producer, DJ Khaled to boost the sale of Centra tokens. In December 2017 the scheme unravelled when a project investor filed suit, and in 2018, the SEC charged two of the founders, Sam Sharma and Robert Farkas with conducting an illegal ICO that defrauded investors to the tune of $25 million.

A quick and superficial reading of PlexCoin's White Paper would suggest that it was a large company, with considerable expertise. It claimed to have a team of 53 people from all over the world, and that its card would be accepted everywhere, because it was linked to Visa. A pre-sale for registered members took place on 5 August 2017 at which it was hoped to sell 400,000 PlexCoin, with a return on investments of a mouthwatering 629 per cent at sale level 2, after 29 days or less. Small wonder that many invested, only to find that not only did they not receive the profits, but that by 4 December, the SEC had announced it had obtained an emergency asset freeze to halt a fraud that had raised up to $15 million from thousands of investors (by falsely promising a 13-fold profit in less than a month). The company's owners were fined nearly $7 million and faced further fraud charges in Cleveland, Ohio in July 2020. The company claimed to be based in Singapore, but was actually based in the United States, which is why the SEC acted. On 17 March 2021, the SEC issued a notice advising investors to continue to check the SEC's website concerning the distribution of frozen assets to investors.[8]

A study published on 11 July 2018 by the ICO advisory firm, Statis Group found that over 70 per cent of ICO funding by dollar volume went to higher-quality projects, but over 80 per cent of the projects by the number of shares were identified as scams. It found that 4 per cent of the ICOs had failed and that 3 per cent had "gone dead", that is, they were not listed on exchanges for trading nor had they arranged a code contribution in Github (the open-source software development platform) for three months. The Statis report reckoned that the total funding of coins and tokens in 2017 was $11.9 billion of which $1.34 billion was invested in scams. Most of the money which was lost went to Pincoin ($600 million), Arisebank ($600 million) and Savedroid ($50 million). Techcrunch published a report, based on data from Coinopsy and Deadcoins, which found that over a thousand crypto projects had already died by 30 June 2018.

The cybersecurity company, Carbon Black, calculated that $1.1 billion in terms of digital currency was stolen in the first six months of 2018. There were also widespread reports of fraudulent ICOs, where either the cryptoassets did not exist, or the issuer/developers disappeared after the ICO. Ernst & Young produced a study of the top ICOs in 2017, representing 87 per cent of all ICO funding. They then followed up with a study of the same group of companies in 2018. Of these ICOs, 87 per cent were below their listing price and 30 per cent had lost all value. Only 29 per cent had working products or prototypes, up by 13 per cent from 2017. Of these, seven companies accepted payment in fiat currencies as well as ICO tokens, which reduces the value for token holders. And none had succeeded in reducing the dominance of Ethereum.[9] Other sources estimate that the total raised in 2018 was $8.27 billion, of which the blockchain protocol EOS, gained $4.2 billion and the messaging app Telegram, $1.7 billion.

These figures do not, however, accord with those produced by Cointelegraph, based on data provided by ICObench. According to Cointelegraph, in 2018, 2,284 ICOs were launched and concluded. Investors could choose, on average, between 482 token sales opening every day of the year. The total amount raised was $11.4 billion. The closing months of the year saw a downturn with November 2018, bringing in $0.36 billion. In 2019, the fall in funding continued but was even more dramatic. Cointelegraph, relying on a report from another research firm, CB Insights, stated that ICO funding fell by 95 per cent to $371 million in 2019. Tokendata, on the other hand, reported that ICOs raised $1.97 billion from 93 companies by June 2019. The variation in results is partly due to the number of databases in use, the lack of a single global database and the fact that ICOs are issued in many different jurisdictions and are limited in duration and scope.

Other reports, such as the ICO Market Report 2018/19, concluded that a clear majority of the tokens of the ICOs of 2018 have never been traded on secondary markets or have already been delisted. Investors who bought tokens in 2018 had a 23 per cent chance that their investment was in the profit zone after 30 days, but if the token was traded on a crypto exchange, their chance of making a profit fell to 8 per cent.[10] The report concluded that the United States, Singapore and the British Virgin Islands, were central hubs for ICOs in 2018. During that year, the ICOs raised $14 billion, most of which, 90 per cent, were based on the Ethereum blockchain. By July 2019, 46 per cent of tokens were in the red compared with their ICO price and over 70 per cent of tokens had lost all, or substantially all of their value. Only 7.57 per cent were in a position to be profitable.

INITIAL COIN OFFERINGS AND WHITE PAPERS

The descriptions of these ICOs illustrate the fact that most ICOs are not really creating a new business, but are simply exploiting an existing business model. Of course, the so-called "White Papers", the accompanying documents for an ICO do not say that. They claim that the funds will be used to develop a new approach to blockchains and exciting developments, which will take place once the funding is received. The ICO often refers only to the first offer to the public, which may take place after one or two offerings have been made to a presale or private investor group without mentioning the proposals for lock-up periods. This has given rise to so-called "pump and dump" schemes, where an individual or more often, a group, plan to make a profit by intensive marketing of the new coins, creating an artificial supply. Investors and traders rush to buy the tokens. Once the scammers sell all their coins, demand falls and the price suddenly crashes.

With the demise of so many ICOs and fraudulent or opaque White Papers during 2018, Cointelegraph offered some reputable advice on the require-ments for White Papers. This was after the various ICOs had raised about $5 billion in total funds, so the guidance was rather late in the day. For all that, it was good advice. The main points were that the contents of the ICO White Paper should cover the entire project, including market analysis, the vision of the project, its development strategy, architecture, goals, information about the token and its distribution, legal issues, available resources, a description of the team, early investors and advisors.[11] The Guide also advised those considering the launch of an ICO to check the regulations in the relevant jurisdiction before the launch.

What the Guide does not specifically mention is that the ICO White Paper should publish the name, address, contact details for the company as well as its ownership and any information confirming that the company is in fact a legal entity in the jurisdiction in which the company is located. Presumably that comes under "Everything" with reference to what the White Paper should contain. Perhaps that also includes information about precisely how their funds are going to be used and exactly what rights are being given in return for these funds, but these references are not given in the advice. This information was not part of many White Papers issued for ICOs. But by the time, Cointelegraph published its Guide, ICOs were either legal, regulated, or subject to future regulations. The omissions in the Guidance were addressed in the IPO (initial public offerings) regulations, which applied to the ICOs.

As noted above White Papers often covered only the technical details of the project. Blockchain enthusiasts will be able to examine all the details of the project and will be able to expose any obvious flaws. But other investors will be unlikely to be able to assess the feasibility of the project. Explanations in laymen's terms would help. Similarly information about how the technology is to be developed should have been included. Nor was it clear whether the funds the investors provide would be pooled or segregated, although many of the proposals lacked the governance arrangements to make segregation possible.

The ICOs frequently failed to set out detailed information about the tokens, such as what the tokens could buy, how they could be bought and sold, and how many would be created and when. Investors were not told what portion of the project's currency would be distributed among the development team and how many would be available for investors to buy. It was often not made clear how many tokens would be sold during each stage of the token sale. So even Cointelegraph's Guide omitted some of the crucial detail missing from so many White Papers in the past.

Nevertheless, it was a significant step forward. In the Guide's last section headed, "Compliance becomes cool", Cointelegraph wrote "the market started its steady shift from the unregulated Wild West like era to a regulated eco system recognized by large financial institutions … while most countries are still struggling to roll out definite regulatory frameworks … the SEC and

CFTC came in with an iron fist and started to prosecute bad actors".[12] In other words, many in the crypto community now recognized that the many headlines describing ICOs as scams, as indeed many found to their cost, were damaging to the industry and things had to change. There were some who had seen the risks, such as Jay Clayton and Chris Giancarlo who both expressed concern about the uncontrolled nature of the ICOs. By March 2018 Facebook, Twitter and Google had all banned ICO advertisements. The Reserve Bank of India announced that it would no longer provide services to any person or business that deals in cryptocurrencies. Perhaps because they saw insurmountable regulatory obstacles ahead, many ICOs started cashing out at the end of 2018. According to the software development firm, Santiment, ICOs were transacting ETH at breakneck speed, with over 400,000 ETH moving out of wallets during late November and early December 2018.[13] With the total lack of clarity about the rights of investors and issues of governance, auditing and accounting, as well as custody of assets, and reliability of the wallets, the ICOs were a far riskier undertaking than investors had realized.

TRADING PLATFORMS AND EXCHANGES

Cryptoassets can be traded or exchanged for fiat currencies or other cryptoassets after issuance on specialized trading platforms or exchanges. It is very difficult to estimate how many of these there are. A number of websites list these platforms or exchanges. Cryptowisser lists over 500 with another four established in 2020. Many sites select the best sites out of the wide range on offer: Finder.com lists the best for beginners, for USD, for low fees, for altcoins and for trading. Others such as Coinswitch-top10, blokt.com-top12 and CoinMarketCap rank 306 exchanges in terms of traffic, liquidity, and trading volumes of spot markets. In June 2018, Forbes selected the top 15 exchanges,. Of those 15, two were hacked: Bithumb lost $18 million and UPbit lost $48.5 million, and, although South Korean investors have been reimbursed (both exchanges are based in South Korea), foreign investors have not.

In June 2020, the Ontario Securities Commission published its investigation into the collapse of the cryptocurrency exchange, QuadrigaCX owing over 76,000 clients $215 million in assets. Its founder, Gerald Cotten, who apparently died while on honeymoon in India, was found to have run a Ponzi scheme and was able to misuse client assets for years, unchecked and undetected Although it would be wrong to suggest that this happens with the majority of exchanges, nevertheless there are serious risks associated with these platforms and exchanges. Most are unregulated, with inadequate cyber security or separation of traders' or investors' assets. Neither are they required to have circuit breakers to halt trading during wild price swings or "flash crashes".

It is difficult to know what fees are charged to issuers and the level of transaction fees, especially when firms provide discounts to their most active traders. It is, however, clear that billions of dollars have been earned in fees and charges by the exchanges with the lion's share going to the top exchanges. Listing fees range from $50,000 to $1 million with some of the largest trading platforms charging 0.3 per cent on average. The fact that such exchanges are largely unregulated, comparatively easy to establish, must make setting up a platform or exchange an attractive proposition, a way of making easy money.

The next chapter will examine the developing regulatory response. This will vary depending on the jurisdiction, partly because the nature of the coins or tokens was difficult to determine: are they assets, securities, digital currencies? Where would they fit in existing regulatory frameworks? There was a growing recognition on the part of the cryptocurrency world that the Wild West days could not continue. The trend towards compliance would continue through 2019 and 2020 and looks set to continue in 2021. This chapter and earlier chapters have illustrated the extent to which this hitherto unregulated market has led to fraud and criminality, a lack of regard of the rights and interests of consumers

CHAPTER 5

The regulatory response to ICOs

The regulatory response to the initial coin offerings of 2017–18 proceeded slowly and varied considerably between one jurisdiction and another. This was in part because there was no agreed classification of cryptoassets. Depending on how they were used by the issuer they could be construed as a means of exchange, a store of value, or investment tokens, supposedly providing ownership rights, or dividends. And utility tokens provide access to a specific product or service. The situation is even more confusing because some cryptoassets fall into more than one category.

Similarly developments in the cryptocurrency world also led to further changes in the approach to regulation. The differences in approach meant that companies in the virtual asset or currency business could select the jurisdiction which best suited their purposes. The fact that cryptocurrencies have become multibillion-dollar industries has, of course, attracted investors in every part of the world.

THE UNITED STATES

The United States regulatory structure enabled the regulatory authorities to accommodate cryptoassets with ease. On 1 December 2017, the CFTC first approved trading in Bitcoin futures and then later virtual currencies. This might seem odd at first, but the Commodity Exchange Act gives such a broad definition of "commodity" that it can cover "all services, rights and interests ... in which contracts for future delivery are presently or in the future dealt with".[1] The CFTC's focus is on the risk transfer markets and derivatives, which are largely traded by big institutions, not on the retail market, which is the SEC's concern. The then chairman of the CFTC, Chris Giancarlo was a well-known advocate of virtual currencies. The CFTC has jurisdiction when a virtual currency is used in a derivatives contract or if there is fraud or manipulation involving a virtual currency traded in interstate commerce. The CFTC issued a statement supporting interpretive guidance on actual delivery of virtual assets in March 2020. The CFTC concluded that an actual delivery has occurred when the customer has the ability to take possession and control of the "entire quantity of the commodity" however it was purchased (e.g. using leverage) and is able to use "freely in commerce" no later than 28 days from the date of the transaction. Furthermore, the offeror and counterparty "cannot retain any interest in, legal right or control over any of the commodity" however it was purchased. The CFTC did allow a little more flexibility with regard to custodial arrangements "to hold virtual currency in a manner consistent with actual delivery requirements".[2] It is not clear that this exception is sufficiently strong enough to protect consumers, since so much depends on the choice of custodial arrangements. The custodians would have to be approved. The CFTC gives some useful examples of actual deliveries and actual delivery failures. It is sufficient to cite two here:

1. Actual delivery will have occurred within 28 days if ... there is a record on the public distributed ledger or blockchain address of the transfer in full of the purchased virtual currency to the purchaser's blockchain address over which the purchaser maintains full possession and control.

2. Actual delivery will not have occurred if within 28 days of the transaction, a book entry is made by the offeror purporting to show that the delivery of the virtual currency has been made to the customer, but the counterparty seller or offeror has not actually delivered the entire quantity of the virtual currency purchased.[3]

These rules are obviously important, but it is not clear that they confirm legal rights to the virtual assets once purchased or what actions are open to the buyer in the event of non-delivery, especially when the assets can be kept by a custodian. The experiences of the last few years suggests that stronger safeguards are required.

The CFTC, however, has powers of enforcement, such as the significant action taken against Coinbase on 19 March 2021, for "reckless, false, misleading or inaccurate" reporting as well as "wash trading" by a former employee on Coinbase's GDAX's platform. Between January 2015 and September 2018, Coinbase operated two automated trading programmes, Hedger and Replicator, which generated orders that at times matched each other. In practice, the programs matched orders with one another in trading pairs, resulting in trades between accounts owned by Coinbase. The company then provided that information to a wide range of reporting services. This transactional information is used by market participants for price discovery related to trading or owning digital assets, "and potentially resulted in a perceived volume and level of liquidity in digital assets, including Bitcoin, that was false, misleading or inaccurate".[4] This is extremely important, partly because of the reliance on Coinbase for price discovery, but also because it gives a false impression of the growth in the market for cryptoassets and distorts the value of Bitcoin. Buyers looking at Coinbase were led astray when they relied on Coinbase for their decision as to when and whether to purchase Bitcoins.

The Securities Exchange Commission

In 2017, the SEC stepped in to warn market participants that offers and sales of digital assets by "virtual" organizations are subject to securities laws. The SEC's investigation centred on the Decentralized Autonomous Organization (DAO), established by Slock.it UG, a German corporation with a view to assessing whether or not they had violated federal securities laws.[5] The DAO was designed to create and hold assets, through the sale of DAO tokens to investors and these assets would be used to fund projects, which would "produce profits that the DAO token holders would share in. The DAO token holders could sell their tokens on a number of web-based platforms, which allowed for secondary trading in the DAO tokens.[6] But, as we detailed in Chapter 2, before any projects were funded, a hacker used a flaw in the DAO's code to steal about one-third of the assets. In this case, the investors were more fortunate than others investing in ICOs in that Slock.it's founders and others found a way in which DAO token holders could choose to have their investments returned to them.

The ICO for DAO raised 1.15 billion tokens in exchange for 12 million Ether, valued at about $150 million, in May 2016. T Token holders were given the impression that they would be able to vote on the funding of a particular proposal, but holders needed some technical knowledge in order to enable them to vote. The snag was that it involved token holders tying up their tokens until the voting cycle was completed. A vote could only be held after the "Curators", selected by Slock.it, had determined which projects would be submitted to a vote and funded by the DAO. The Curators' role was to ensure that any proposal for funding came from an identifiable person or organization, and confirm that the smart contracts involved reflected the code the contractor claimed to have deployed on the Ethereum blockchain. The Curators had the power to determine which proposals reached the White List and the way in which the White List operated often according to their own subjective criteria. The quorum requirement for votes could be reduced by 50 per cent every other week. Token holders had less power over the use of their funds than many may have assumed. But they could still buy and sell their tokens on a number of platforms as long as they were customers of the platform with one platform executing over 500,000 transactions between May and September 2016. Meanwhile about one third of the funds raised was diverted from the DAO by an "attacker" and was only resolved by a "hard fork." The majority of the Ethereum network carried out the software updates, transferring the funds to a new address where the DAO token holders could exchange their tokens for Ether.

The SEC's report uses the example of the DAO and its operations to show that federal securities regulations apply to various activities, including distributed ledger technology, regardless of the type of organization or technology used.[7] The Securities Act (1933, section 5) requires that the offer or sale of securities to the public should be accompanied by "full and fair disclosure" in the form of a statutory prospectus which provides enough information for prospective investors to make an informed decision. This includes information about the identity and background of the management, and the price and the number of securities to be offered. As we have seen the "White Papers" accompanying the ICOs frequently did not have such basic information.

The SEC clearly identified digital currencies as "securities", which includes an "investment contract", in a "common venture" "premised on a reasonable expectation of profits to be derived from the entrepreneurial or managerial efforts of others". The SEC follows the famous "Howey case", in which the decision about whether or not something is a security should be based on the "economic realities underlying a transaction".[8]

Nor does it depend solely on an investment of money, since the investment can take the form of "goods and services" or as investors did in the case of the DAO, the tokens were received in exchange for ETH. They were also investing in a common enterprise and reasonably expected to earn profits through that enterprise when they sent ETH to the DAO's Ethereum Blockchain in exchange for DAO tokens. The investors' profits were to be derived from the managerial efforts of others, as described above. Through their conduct and marketing materials, claiming to be experts in Ethereum, they led investors to believe they would be able to make sufficient managerial efforts to make the DAO a success.

The voting rights given to the token holders were indeed limited and did not provide them with any meaningful control over the enterprise, especially when they could only vote on proposals, which had been cleared by the Curators. Draft proposals were discussed in online forums, but the terms of any subsequent contracts were intentionally vague, and were not subject to negotiation or feedback. Of course, even if they had understood, it would have been difficult for DAO token holders to act together, given the widespread of token holders and the fact that their real-world identities were not known. The structure of the DAO meant that, although it appeared to resemble a partnership, it could not operate as such. A partnership vote is in fact just a single shareholder vote in a corporation.[9] But this still does not negate the existence of an investment contract. The emphasis must be placed on the economic reality.[10]

All of this leads to the application of securities laws to such offerings in the United States. Offers and sales of securities have to be registered with the SEC. During the offering period, the DAO offered and sold DAO tokens in exchange for ETH on the DAO website which was publicly accessible, including to individuals in the United States. According to SEC rules, the website should have been registered as a national securities exchange. By providing a "marketplace for bringing together purchasers and sellers of securities", the DAO was operating like a stock exchange by bringing together orders for securities of multiple buyers and sellers and using established non-discretionary measures for the interaction of such orders and the buyer and sellers agree to the terms of the trade.

The SEC concluded that those who offer and sell securities in the United States must comply with these laws, including the requirement to register with the Commission. Registration is designed to provide investors with the information and the protection they need to make informed investment decisions, whether or not the issuer is a traditional company or a decentralized autonomous organization, or whether the securities are purchased using US dollars or virtual currencies or whether they are distributed in certificated form or through distributed ledger technology. At least part of this is what the cryptocurrency community had come to realize during 2017 and 2018, and that unregulated ICOs led to fraud. What may not have been recognized to the same extent was that the decentralized organization was not quite as decentralized as it appeared. Just like the DAO, crucial decision making may not be widely shared. Indeed, a DAO might be controlled by only a handful with the most computing power or tokens, retained by the issuers.

By defining digital or virtual currencies as assets or securities, the US was able to include virtual currencies in its existing legislation. By May 2020, the SEC had successfully pursued a large number of ICOs for their failure to register with the SEC.

Reference has already been made to the so-called "Howey test". This arose from a Supreme Court ruling in 1946, in the case of *SEC v W. J. Howey Co.* which involved a Florida citrus grove development. The Supreme Court in establishing its verdict defined the nature of an "investment contract" and what would therefore fall under the Securities Act 1933 (and the Securities and Exchange Act 1934). An "investment contract" was defined as "a contract, transaction or scheme whereby a person invests his money in a common enterprise and is led to expect profits solely from the efforts of a promoter of a third party, it being immaterial whether the shares of the enterprise are evidenced in formal certificates or by nominal interests in the physical acts as employed in the enterprise".[11] In other words for an investment contract to exist it needed to meet four criteria: an investment of money; in a common enterprise; with an expectation of profits; solely from the efforts of others.[12]

The Act also provides for a very wide definition as to what constitutes a security:

> A 'security' means any note, stock, treasury stock, bond, debenture, evidence of indebtedness, certificate of interest or participation in any-profit-sharing agreement, collateral-trust certificate, preorganization certificate or subscription, transferable share, investment contract, voting-trust certificate, certificate of deposit for security, fractional undivided interest in oil, gas, or other mineral rights, or in general, any interest, or instrument commonly known as a 'security' or any certificate of interest or participation in, temporary or interim certificate for, receipt for, guarantee of, or warrant or right to subscribe to or purchase, any of the foregoing.

The SEC's framework for analyzing whether a digital asset is an investment contract and whether offers and sales of a digital asset are securities transactions are evaluated against these four criteria. If it is judged to be so, then the digital asset falls under the existing securities laws, which would turn an ICO into an initial public offering, an IPO, and so subject to a series of regulations, including the information that must be provided to potential investors to enable them to make informed investment decisions.

The SEC set out its "Framework for 'Investment Contract' Analysis of Digital Assets" in April 2019. One of the key issues it highlighted was that although the structure of a digital asset may ostensibly by decentralized, the fact is that almost every aspect of its development is in the hands of its developers or "active participants" (AP), even if it has to be confirmed by a majority of stakeholders or miners, and so meets the third criteria of the Howey test regarding "the reliance on the efforts of others".[13] Related to that is the issue of whether or not the digital asset increases in value, and if so, does that come about because of the efforts of the AP; the way in which the asset is marketed and whether or not it is primarily used as a means of exchange. This might suggest that there may not be a one size fits all in the case of digital assets and each case will need to be decided on its merits, unless the courts can give clear guidance. That may happen in the case of Plexcoin, but at the time of writing, that remains to be seen.

However, the same point applies to the SEC as to the CFTC. In each case, the agency's approach has largely involved enforcement actions. The SEC, as we have seen, has largely protected investors by requiring offerings of digital assets to be registered as securities, when the SEC was able to show that the offering fulfilled the criteria set out in the Howey test. The SEC issued the "Framework for 'Investment Contract' Analysis of Digital Assets" in April 2019, setting out the criteria for determining whether or not an asset is a "security" and if the offering is an "investment contract". This was issued as guidance to those considering an ICO. As well as enforcement actions, the SEC has refused to approve various vehicles designed to allow investment in digital assets, such as a Bitcoin exchange-traded fund (ETF), citing the absence of regulation of a spot market in cryptocurrencies on the grounds that applicants had failed to demonstrate that the spot market was resistant to market manipulation and that they were sufficiently supervised.

The point here is that both the SEC and the CFTC are using existing legislation primarily through enforcement actions. What has not yet emerged is a comprehensive approach to the regulation of cryptocurrencies. The current actions of the SEC and the CFTC do provide clear guidance over key aspects of cryptoassets, often regarded as a form of investment, and the ICOs clearly seek to attract funds without providing adequate information to potential investors. The enforcement actions taken, limited in range though they may be, have been upheld in the courts. Having said that, it may well be time for a more comprehensive framework to be provided so that investors in the cryptoasset market and the digital asset providers are clear about the nature of the federal oversight.

The newly appointed Chairman of the SEC, Gary Gensler, stated that

> There are many challenges and gaps for investor protection in these markets. Tokens currently on the market that are securities may be offered, sold, and traded in non-compliance with the federal securities laws. Furthermore, none of the exchanges trading crypto tokens has registered yet as an exchange with the SEC. Altogether, this has led to substantially less investor protection than in our traditional securities markets, and to correspondingly greater opportunities for fraud and manipulation ... I look forward to working with fellow regulators and with Congress to fill the gaps of investor protection in the crypto markets."[14]

Clearly any more detailed legislation framework for cryptoassets will take some time to be developed.

THE EUROPEAN UNION

As a result of the SEC's actions, a number of issuers structured their ICOs to prevent US citizens or residents from obtaining tokens and thereby avoiding US securities regulation. EU citizens and residents were still able to invest in tokens, but ICOs did not have to publish and register a prospectus at that time. The debate over the definition of tokens also took place in the EU and whether or not they counted as securities. If they are investment tokens, then they may count as securities, while pure currency and utility tokens are exempted from securities legislation. To complicate matters further, hybrid tokens are often issued, which often comprise elements of one or more of the kinds identified here. There is no regulation specifically and expressly tailored for ICOs. But, on the other hand, if the tokens are to count as securities, then offering tokens for sale without a prospectus, can give rise to serious civil and criminal liabilities. In the context of EU law, the issue is whether or not tokens are securities. But answering that question is not as straightforward as it is in US securities law.

In some respects, however, they are similar. For example, like securities, tokens can be sold on secondary markets and thus are transferable. Tokens would have to be negotiable as well, that is, easily traded on capital markets. The fact that they are actively traded on cryptocurrency platforms is taken to indicate that they would be easily traded on capital markets, a concept in EU law which is "broad and meant to include all contexts where buying and selling interests in securities meet".[15] It is also argued that for tokens to be regarded as securities they must be standardized as "classes of securities" with certain qualities and the claims they represent must not be individually negotiated with investors. Tokens can be utility tokens, currency or investment tokens, but all that matters is that the issuer offers tokens which share the same characteristics.

Utility tokens, however, cannot be compared with shares because they do not involve any property rights in the underlying company, but grant "membership rights" in the sense that they can make use of the blockchain vehicle. If the investors have voting rights, then these are designed to help investors improve the working of the product; for example, EOS tokens which give investors the right to vote on the development of meta-level, scalable blockchains. Currency tokens are not regarded as securities under EU law. Although denominated in a unit of account they do not have the status of legal tender, although they can be converted into fiat currencies on crypto exchanges or even for commodities on an e-commerce platform like Open Bazaar. Nor do they count as E-Money under the EU Directive, which describes it as "electronically ... stored monetary value as represented by a claim on the issuer which is issued on receipt of funds for the purpose of making payment transactions ... and which is accepted by a natural or legal person other than the electronic money issuer".[16] The point here is that crypto coins do not confer a claim against the issuing entity. Nor are they securities.

It is against this background that the EU regulatory authorities have to consider how cryptocurrencies and crypto tokens should be classified and regulated. Although cryptoassets are not regarded as fiat money in any EU member state, the European Banking Authority (EBA) has considered whether or not they are "electronic money" or can be regarded as "funds" under the second Payment Services Directive (PSD2). Only rarely can such assets count as electronic money and then only if they meet certain criteria.[17] Cryptoassets are not banknotes, coins or scriptural money.[18] To a large extent, cryptoassets do not fall within the scope of current EU financial services regulation. But that still leaves consumer protection issues and concerns about a level playing field.

The EBA has stressed the risks to consumers, including the lack of conduct of business rules, including specific disclosures about the risks involved in cryptocurrency activities, or information about the companies concerned, including, especially in the case of ICOs, misleading marketing and promotions, no arrangements for segregating consumers' assets and those of the firm, no compensation scheme or any legal framework determining the rights and obligations of each party. The problem the EBA identifies is that the existing EU legal framework does not apply to many forms of cryptoasset activity. This is especially true of cryptoasset custodian wallet provision and cryptoasset trading platforms. The EBA has not, however, proposed any specific extension of the legal framework so that cryptoassets are included. Their only recommendation has been for national regulatory authorities to monitor the business practices of financial institutions over their involvement with cryptoassets, taking note of cryptoasset advertising and ensuring high levels of consumer protection for consumers.

The European Securities and Markets Authority (ESMA) identified similar problems as the EBA in that not all of the cryptoassets qualify as transferable securities. If they can be classified as securities, then a full set of EU rules apply to their issuer and/or firms providing investment services for these assets. Where they cannot be classified as securities, then ESMA believes that the absence of applicable regulations leaves consumers exposed to financial risks.

If cryptoassets qualify as financial instruments, then a whole range of legal provisions will potentially apply to them. These include the Prospectus Directive, the Transparency Directive, which requires accurate, comprehensive and timely information about the issuers whose securities are admitted to trading on a regulated market. They would then have to face the complexities of the Markets in Financial Instruments Directive (MiFID II). How this would apply depends on the type of platform. Most likely those platforms trading with a central order book and/or matching orders will come under the regulations for regulated markets or multilateral trading facilities. Trade reporting requirements as set out in Markets in Financial Instruments and amending regulations (MiFIR) covering pre- and post-trade data would also apply.

ESMA also drew attention to the fact that the EU does not have an agreed definition of record-keeping and safe-keeping. This role is carried out by a wide range of entities, such as custodian banks, registrars, notaries, depositaries or central securities depositories. The rules also depend on whether the record-keeping is at the issuer level or the investor-level, but even then the rules vary from one member state to another. Even if these rules were harmonized at EU level, it is not clear how these would apply to cryptoassets. Control of the private keys on behalf of clients might be regarded as safe-keeping services and along with rules ensuring the safe-keeping and segregation of client assets, should apply to the providers of these services. The problem is that the legal implications of holding private keys on behalf of clients will have to be clarified. Multi signature wallets, where several private keys may be held by different individuals, instead of one will also have to be taken into account. Rules for cryptoassets will inevitably be more complicated. ESMA takes the view that it is impossible to fit all versions of cryptoassets into the existing regulatory frameworks and therefore recommended a "bespoke regime" for cryptoassets.

European Commission Consultation Paper, December 2019

The publication in December 2019, of the European Commission's Consultation Paper made it plain that the Commission is committed to developing and promoting blockchain technology across the EU and by defining cryptoassets as a "digital asset that may depend on cryptography and exists on a distributed ledger"[19] put cryptoassets as one of the major applications of blockchain for finance. This consultation relied heavily on the advice offered by the EBA and ESMA.

Where cryptoassets are already covered by existing regulations, such as MiFID II or the Electronic Money Directive, the Commission is in the process of assessing whether such legislation can be effectively applied. For cryptoassets, which are not currently covered by the EU legislation, the Commission is considering a "possible proportionate common regulatory approach at EU level to address potential consumer/investor protection and market integrity concerns".[20] This applies to cryptoassets which do not constitute financial instruments, such as stablecoins, e-money tokens and utility tokens and is designed to regulate the public offering of cryptoassets; admission of cryptoassets to trading on a trading platform; the licensing of cryptoasset service providers; and the implementation of market abuse rules for cryptoasset businesses. It covers all asset-referenced tokens, which maintain a stable value by reference to the value of several fiat currencies, several commodities or several cryptoassets, and includes Libra, USDC, a stablecoin issued by Circle, and any cryptoassets that are digital representations of value or rights which might be transferred and stored electronically using DLT, such as Bitcoins as well as other similar tokens.

The Consultation Paper proposed that issuers of asset-referenced tokens must be a legal entity established in the EU and must be able to demonstrate own funds of more than €350,000 or 2 per cent of the average of reserve assets and maintain the reserves in custody at all times – with a credit institution for non-cryptoassets. Each creation/destruction of tokens must be reflected by a corresponding increase/decrease in reserves. E-money tokens have to comply with the e-money Directive and can only be issued by an EU legal identity licensed as a credit institution in the EU.

The paper recommended that the content of the White Papers must include a description of the issuer, the offered tokens and rights and risks associated with them. In addition, for asset-based tokens, the White Paper must contain a detailed description of the reserve assets and the custody arrangements. This White Paper must be approved by the relevant national competent authority in the EU member state before publication. This is also part of the licensing process for the issuer of such a token. For e-money tokens, the White Paper must describe the redemption rights of token holders and the conditions for exercising such rights. It does not require pre-approval but must be submitted to the National Competent Authority at least 20 days before it is published.

European Commission proposal for a regulation on Markets in Crypto Assets, September 2020

In September 2020, as part of its Digital Finance package, the European Commission drafted comprehensive regulation for Markets in Crypto Assets (MiCA), the most extensive regulation of cryptoassets to date, covering Bitcoin and Ethereum, utility tokens, stablecoins and Libra. It sets out a regime to regulate issuers of cryptoassets and providers of cryptoasset services, including exchanges, custodians, trading platforms for cryptoassets, execution of orders for cryptoassets on behalf of third parties, placing of cryptoassets and providing advice of cryptoassets. The proposed regulation distinguishes between the following types of cryptoassets:

- e-money tokens, defined as cryptoassets, the main purpose of which is to be used as a means of exchange, purporting to maintain a stable value by referring to the fiat currency that is legal tender.
- asset-referenced tokens. These are cryptoassets, purporting to maintain a stable value by referencing the value of several fiat currencies which are legal tender, one or several commodities, one or several cryptoassets or a combination of such assets.
- cryptoassets are defined as a digital representation of value or rights that may be transferred or stored electronically, using DLT or similar technology.
- utility tokens: a type of cryptoasset intended to provide digital access to a good or service, available on DLT and is only accepted by the issuer of that token.

Its aim is to establish a regulatory framework for cryptoassets and their service providers not currently subject to provisions on consumer and investor protection and market integrity, through a single, uniform licensing regime across all member states by 2024. The intention is to "enable and support the potential of digital finance in terms of innovation and competition while mitigating the risks ... the first objective is one of legal certainty. For the cryptoasset markets to develop within the EU, there is a need for a sound legal framework, clearly defining the regulatory treatment of all cryptoassets that are not covered by existing financial services regulation. The second objective is to support innovation", hence "the proposal on a DLT pilot regime".[21]

The pilot regime on DLT market infrastructure and digital operational resistance has been in the process of development since 2018 and relies heavily on all the above consultations. However, the proposal takes the form of a Regulation so that, once adopted, it will lay down a single set of rules that will apply immediately throughout the Single Market. It will therefore override any specific regulations in one or other of the member states, except where these are in line with MiCA. It draws heavily on the reports issued by EBA and ESMA, setting out detailed requirements for transparency and disclosure requirements for issuance and admission of trading in cryptoassets; the authorization and supervision of cryptoasset service providers and issuers of asset-referenced tokens, issuers of electronic money tokens and cryptoasset service providers; consumer protection rules for the issuance, trading, exchange and custody of cryptoassets and measures to prevent market abuse to ensure the integrity of cryptoasset markets. The detailed rules applicable to cryptoasset services providers include capital requirements for custodians, who must keep its customers' cryptoassets on DLT addresses that are different from its own and file quarterly reports on the cryptoasset positions they hold for each client. Customers can hold their cryptoasset custodian liable for any losses due to hacks or malfunctions.

One of the key points, already mentioned in connection with the Consultation Paper, is the requirement that an issuer of cryptoassets must be a legal entity and has provided a White Paper with detailed points such as a warning that the assets may lose their value, may not always be transferable and may not be liquid. As we have noted, too many ICOs lacked any of this information. Failure to comply with these and other detailed requirements, and a holder of these assets may sue the issuer. Issuers of asset-referenced tokens must be authorized by the regulatory authority in their home country, the identity of the members of the applicant issuer and details of the governance arrangements must be presented. A White Paper must be issued, which must include, amongst other items, detailed information on the nature and enforceability of rights, including any direct redemption right, and how such rights will be handled in the case of insolvency. These issuers must also have "robust governance arrangements", including sound administrative and accounting procedures, and the custody of reserve assets. Other issues highlighted include the quality and quantity of reserve assets, where and how they are invested and who has custody of them. Similar requirements apply to issuers of electronic money tokens, especially significant e-money tokens and cryptoasset service providers, such as custodial providers. The latter must offer prudential safeguards and the minimum capital requirements at all times.

I have focused on some of these detailed rules because most jurisdictions did not have them fully in place before 2017. If they had been in place and enforced throughout the cryptoassets market, then more may have survived and many retail investors in particular would not have lost so much money. The regulation is not new in so far as such regulations are part of the framework surrounding financial markets generally. The only difference is the efforts to make the details relevant to each type of cryptoassets. What is noteworthy is that this comprehensive Regulation directs all the providers towards centralization, but perhaps the decentralization experiment cannot provide the necessary conditions for trust.

The proposal also allows for a quite different approach to pilot schemes for DLT. Other regulatory authorities have, as we shall see, set up specific, mostly proof-of-concept schemes under the auspices of the central bank. The proposal is for a regulatory "sandbox" for certain providers of DLT and blockchain services, such as those providing multilateral trading facilities, securities settlement systems for authorized investment, or market operator firms, or a Central Securities Depository. Once given special permission, these firms are exempted from certain regulations, but must fulfil different special requirements under the Pilot Regime, such as limitations on securities and general requirements to avoid risks for a period of six years. It is a very cautious approach, allowing for little flexibility and experimentation. But it is an attempt to understand which rules are feasible in a changing world. Neither the results of the "sandbox" nor the content of the Commission's Proposal will be known for some time. The proposed regulation had its first reading in the Committee on Economic and Monetary Affairs in June 2021, at which point over a thousand amendments were proposed. All of these have to be translated and distributed to the Econ Committee, which votes on the amendments and agrees the text. If there are differences between the original proposal and that of the Parliament, then the Council, the Commission and the Parliament have to agree on a final version, after the usual "horse trading" between them. Once that is agreed, it is that version which is voted upon by the whole House. That is unlikely to happen before October 2021. The text of the Regulation, due to come into force in 2024, may differ from the original proposal. At the time of writing the final text of the Regulation on Markets in Crypto Assets is unclear.

It is not possible to survey all the countries in which cryptoassets found a home, but three others are significant for a variety of reasons. They are Singapore, Malta and Switzerland, each of which began to change the legislative framework to accommodate digital assets before the United States and the European Union.

SINGAPORE

In 2017, the Monetary Authority of Singapore (MAS) stated in its Guidance that it would regulate digital tokens if these fell within the definition of securities regulated by the Securities and Futures Act. The list of such products included shares, conferring or representing in a corporation, a debenture, a unit in a business trust, a securities-based derivatives contract, or a unit in a collective investment scheme. Any offering of digital tokens deemed to be securities must comply with the securities regulations. Responding to parliamentary questions about the regulation of cryptocurrencies and ICOs on 2 October 2017, the minister responsible stressed that the MAS would only regulate with regard to money laundering and terrorist financing, but that no specific regulation had been issued regarding ICOs.

However, "Digital tokens", defined as "transferable units generated within a distributed network that tracks ownership of the units through the application of blockchain technology" do not constitute securities.[22] The digital token is a "cryptographically-secured representation of a token-holders rights' to perform certain functions within or receive benefits from a token network". So open digital offerings, in which the initial sale of tokens is not restricted to a small number of participants, open access to platform services, project governance decisions and enabling payments were not regulated as securities in Singapore. The clarity of MAS's guidance made Singapore a leading home of open digital offerings in 2017 and 2018. By the second half of 2018, about 21 per cent of the world's ICOs took place in Singapore, although some were Asia-based projects given the unfavourable regulatory environment in other Asian countries. The value of the 2018 ICOs was $730 million but they raised over $1.6 billion.[23] Singapore became the third most favourable country for ICOs in 2018, with eleven of the largest hundred ICOs ranked by funds raised held by firms in Singapore. As the tokens being offered were not classed as securities, the ICOs were largely unregulated. MAS expected ICO issuers "to conduct their own independent legal due diligence that the tokens are not securities, but also to address the anti-money laundering and counter financing of terrorism risks when issuing tokens".[24] Indeed, the ICO excitement reached a peak when one Singaporean ICO, TenX raised $80 million in seven minutes in June 2017.

By April 2019, however, the tone of MAS's Guidance began to change as it began to examine the structure and characteristics of, including the rights attached to, a digital token in determining if the digital token is a type of capital markets product under the Securities and Futures Act. If any of these tokens constitutes a capital markets product, then anyone operating a platform on which digital tokens are being offered, issued, or traded, may find that they should be licensed under the SFA, the Financial Advisers Act, or as a recognized market operator under the SFA, or that the exchange itself must be approved. All of these regulations also have an extra-territorial application if any of these take place partly in and partly outside Singapore.

The final part of the Guidance referred to the Payment Services Act, January 2019, which will apply to anyone providing any service of dealing in digital payment tokens or any service of facilitating the exchange of digital payment tokens must be licensed. They would be required to comply with the anti-money laundering and anti-terrorism financing regulations and to put in place policies, procedures and controls to handle these risks. This new licensing regime allows MAS to regulate a wide range of payment services to match the scope and scale of services provided, such as account issuance, domestic money transfers, cross-border transfers, merchant acquisition, e-money issuance, digital payment token dealing and exchanges and money changing. The license will apply only to the services provided. The regulation proposed is light and aims to facilitate a "permanent sandbox" to encourage innovation and investment. Singapore has acted to remain as a centre for cryptoasset technology, whilst ensuring that the wild days of 2017 were over. The regulator described the Payment Service Act (PSA) as a "forward-looking and flexible regulatory framework for the payments industry ... allowing rules to be applied proportionately and to be robust to changing business models. The PSA will facilitate growth and innovation while mitigating risk and fostering confidence in our payments landscape".[25]

In a response to a written parliamentary question about the regulation of cryptoassets in Singapore, the minister set out the current regulatory situation on 5 April 2021. Despite all the hype about Singapore as a crypto centre, the size of the market is very small: the combined peak daily trading volumes of the three major SGD-quoted cryptocurrencies, Bitcoin, Ethereum and XRP, was 2 per cent of the average daily trading volume of securities on SGX in 2020. Cryptocurrency derivatives traded through financial institutions amounted to less than 1 per cent of the derivatives trading activity on SGX. Cryptocurrencies are less than 0.01 per cent of the assets in funds managed by MAS-regulated fund managers. Retail investors are not allowed to purchase cryptoassets. Exchanges offering trading of cryptocurrencies are regulated as digital payment token service providers under the PSA, must be licensed by MAS and conform to AML/CFT regulations. Securities tokens are regulated in the same way as securities, but only three of over 60 Recognised Market Operators offer trading in securities tokens, which cannot be offered to retail investors. Finally, "MAS has stepped up its surveillance of the cryptocurrency sector, to identify suspicious networks and higher risk activities for further supervisory scrutiny".[26]

MALTA

In 2017 Malta's government dreamed of becoming the "Blockchain Island". Its Digital Economy Parliamentary Secretary announced in February 2018 that it would "provide the necessary legal certainty to allow the industry to flourish"[27] resulting in the enactment of three bills, all of which became law in November 2018, following the launch of the Malta Digital Innovation Authority in September. The Virtual Financial Assets Act established VFA Agents as gatekeepers. These agents are required to have robust "know your client" systems and controls in place, including verifying the source of funds of clients, whose primary wealth comes from DLT assets such as Bitcoins. The Maltese Financial Services Authority (MFSA) registered its first VFA agents in May 2019, six months after the Act came into force. Currently about 20 agents are registered, but no businesses have yet been licensed under the VFA framework, although many are considering it on promises of a friendly, understanding regulatory environment.

The Initial Virtual Financial Asset Offering Act covers the ICOs. Although the issuer does not have to be registered with the MFSA, they do have to appoint a registered VHA agent. The Act sets out the requirements for the contents of the White Paper, including the reasons for the offering, characteristics of the financial assets offered and how the funds raised through the offering will be allocated. The White Paper can only be issued with the MFSA's approval.

The Act that established the Maltese Digital Innovation Authority (MDIA) sets out seven roles for the Authority, including "protecting users of innovative technology arrangements" and "promoting legal certainty in the law applying to innovative technology arrangements".[28] The MDIA was established to maintain Malta's reputation as a centre of innovation in technology by promoting education about ethical standards and legal certainty as it applies to innovation. Its aim "to secure the integrity of the Maltese DLT market and that any policies adopted in Malta will not be disconnected from DLT international policies and rules".[29]

As we saw in Chapter 2, hopes were raised that Malta would fulfil its dream when it appeared that Binance, the world's top exchange, was considering moving to Malta after facing regulatory difficulties in Japan. Binance was indeed close to the Maltese government at the time and to Prime Minister Muscat, in particular. Binace's founder, Zhao Changpeng, personally thanked the Prime Minister for his welcome and Malta's aim of becoming global trailblazers in the regulation of blockchain business. Muscat talked about cryptocurrencies as the future of money and was putting in place plans for it.

The investigative journalist, Caruana Galizia, commented that "Malta is set to become the Bitcoin money laundering capital of this part of the world – and that the preparations are already being made for it. And that whoever has a vested interest in the heightened use of cryptocurrencies is already (funneling) money into the Labour Party and a couple of Panama companies, and calling the shots."[30] She was murdered by a car bomb on 16 October 2017, but her influence lingered after her death, leading ultimately to the resignation of three members of Muscat's cabinet, followed by the prime minister himself. He was replaced by Robert Abela, elected leader of the Labour Party on 11 January, and who then became prime minister on 13 January 2020.

It is difficult to determine whether or not the political scandals played a part in the failure of so many companies to register. After the legislation was passed in 2018, companies were invited to operate on the island during a transition phase. On 24 April 2020, the MFSA stated that it was "aware of a number of entities which have availed themselves of the transitory provisions, thus were providing VFA services but have failed to submit either a Letter of Intent to initiate the application process for a VFA Services License or a cessation of activities notification".[31] By December 2020, 27 companies had actually submitted an application, one VFASP license had been issued with a further 12 having received in-principle approvals.[32] At the time of writing neither Binance nor Palladium have applied for a license.

However, by May 2021, Crypto.com became the first cryptocurrency company to receive Malta's Class 3 Virtual Financial Assets Licence. It has become one of the largest platforms for digital asset trading, with active users having reached 5 million by October 2020, before reaching 10 million in February 2021. Crypto.com is a principal member of the Visa network and is hoping to extend its fiat lending programme during 2021, allowing Crypto.com Visa cardholders to use their cryptocurrency balance as loan collateral. Cointelegraph notes that $71 billion in crypto has passed through Malta since 2017. The Financial Action Task Force (FATF) in its discussions in Paris in June 2021 reportedly expressed concerns about Malta's push to become "Blockchain Island" in 2017 and 2018 when the sector was less regulated. The question was whether or not Malta should be on a list of countries that have fallen short of their obligations to prevent financial crime. Concerns were also expressed about its law enforcement regime.[33] The outcome of such discussions is not yet clear. The MFSA took part in the consultation process launched by the EU Commission, based on its experience gained through the implementation of the Virtual Financial Assets legislation. Malta will be obliged to apply MiCA when all the details have been finalized and approved by the European Parliament and the Commission.

CANADA

Canada allows the use of digital currencies, including cryptocurrencies, although they are not regarded as legal tender. Canada's tax laws apply to cryptocurrency transactions although Canada's Revenue Agency classifies cryptocurrencies as commodities and any payment made using cryptocurrencies should be regarded as a barter transaction, that is the exchange of one commodity for another. Despite that novel classification, goods purchased using digital currency must be "included in the seller's income for tax purposes".[34] The amount included would be valued in Canadian dollars. If considered income, then the whole amount is taxable, but if it can be argued that the transaction can be treated as a capital loss or gain then only one half of the capital gain is taxable, which, of course, opens up the issue of when the transaction counts as income and when it counts as capital. There is no escape from the taxman with digital currencies!

In 2014, the Governor General of Canada gave his royal assent to Bill-C31,[35] which included amendments bringing the virtual currencies, including Bitcoin, under the money-laundering and terrorist financing rules. The law treats virtual currencies, including Bitcoin as "money service businesses" for the purposes of anti-money-laundering laws. Companies dealing in virtual currencies are required to register with the Financial Transactions and Reports Analysis Centre of Canada (Fintrac) and they must keep and retain prescribed records, report suspicious transactions and determine if any of their customers are "politically exposed persons". The law also applies to virtual currency exchanges operating outside Canada, "who direct services at persons or entities in Canada". It also bars banks from opening or maintaining accounts or having a "correspondent banking relationship" with companies dealing in virtual currencies, "unless that person or entity is registered with the centre".[36]

However, the amending regulations were not issued in draft form until July 2019 and finally took effect on 1 June 2021. The aim of these regulations was always to improve the effectiveness of Canada's anti-money laundering and counter-terrorism financing regime and to bring this up to international standards, especially in the light of FATF's recent review of Canada's laws and regulations. The regulations needed overhauling in order to take account of FinTech and new business models leveraging prepaid cards and virtual currencies. The definition of virtual currencies has been changed from a "digital representation of value that can be used for payment or investment purposes that is not a fiat currency and that can be readily exchanged for funds or for another virtual currency that can be readily exchanged for funds" or "information that enables a person or entity to have access to such digital currency" to "a digital representation of value that can be used for payment or investment purposes that is not a fiat currency and that can be readily exchanged for funds or for another virtual currency that can be readily exchanged for funds, or a private key of a cryptographic system that enables a person or entity to have access to a digital representation of value".[37] The aim was to offer a more precise definition for virtual currencies, and to create a level regulatory playing field that applies to digital representations of value to other use cases, such as tokens that can be used either for payment purposes (such as Bitcoins or stablecoins) or investment purposes (such as security tokens). They then fall under the Proceeds of Crime (Money Laundering) and Terrorist Financing Act, through a framework of requiring the registration of entities dealing in virtual currencies as money service businesses. As such, they are subject to the same record-keeping, verification procedures, suspicious transaction reporting and registration requirements as MSBs dealing in fiat currencies. In February 2020, the Virtual Currency Travel Rule, which requires financial entities and MSBs to keep a record of electronic fund international transfers, including virtual currency transactions, took effect. Most of the legislation is now in effect, but the requirement that MSBs register with Fintrac and implement complete AML plans will take effect in June 2021.[38]

The legislation goes further by identifying certain transactions in cryptoassets as "securities" if transactions in such assets fulfil the criteria for an investment contract, defined in the same terms as the "Howey" test we discussed earlier. The securities laws, which are enacted on a provincial and territorial bases, not federally, have been largely harmonized throughout Canada.

The securities administrators are all represented by the Canadian Securities Administrators (CSA), which issued two staff notices in 2018 and a third in January 2020, that together make clear that cryptoassets will be defined as securities, even when the offerings of tokens are purported to be utility tokens. The platforms on which cryptoassets are traded would also be subject to securities and/or derivatives regulations and requirements.[39] Despite being the "world's first" and leading the way in developing appropriate legislation for cryptoassets, it took five years for Canada to set out the regulations and another two years to see full implementation.

SWITZERLAND

Switzerland has both sought to encourage innovative FinTech companies, especially in Zug, whilst also keeping an eye on the risks associated with ICOs. This has led to a gradual development in the regulatory framework. At first there were no ICO specific regulations, but depending on the design of the ICOs, financial market laws were applicable instead.

In 2014, the Swiss Federal Council published a report on virtual currencies, setting out their legal status, and its economic importance as a means of payment, which it regarded as insignificant at the time and which was not expected to change in the foreseeable future. It recognized that the users of virtual currencies faced substantial risks and abuses, but it was thought that there were sufficient safeguards in place, since contracts with virtual currencies are enforceable in principle and penalties can be imposed for criminal offences. Certain business models would fall under the regulation and supervision of the Swiss Financial Market Supervisory Authority (FINMA). The report noted that it was difficult to investigate criminal offences and seize assets, since "virtual currencies are for the most part managed on a decentralized and cross-border basis and therefore contact people are lacking for the prosecution authorities".[40] And much of the responsibility thereby lies with the users themselves. This somewhat complacent attitude began to change as the decade wore on.

The Federal Department of Finance, FINMA and the Federal Office of Justice set up a blockchain/ICO working group in January 2018. Its purpose was to examine the legal framework and identify any necessary action in conjunction with the sector. The aim was to increase legal certainty and ensure technology-neutral regulation. Before the final report was published, FINMA issued new guidelines in 2017 and updated them in February 2018. These made it clear that there are no specific regulatory requirements for ICOs.

The now familiar classification of tokens into three categories: payment, utility and asset tokens (with the possibility of hybrid tokens, as the latter two categories can also be payment tokens), determines the applicable regulatory regime. Some may be classified as securities, publicly offered for sale, and under the code of obligations, the only formal requirement is for a register of the number and denomination of the uncertificated securities issued and the creditors recorded, which can be digitally recorded on a blockchain. Payment and utility tokens are not regarded as securities. Asset tokens are regarded as securities if they meet either the general requirements for securities or if it is a derivative, i.e. the value of the conferred claim depends on an underlying asset. The legal implications of treatment as a security depend on whether they are "certificated" or "uncertificated", where the latter are fully dematerialized securities, i.e. have no documents of any kind.

Since the introduction in February 2019 of the blockchain based solution provided by Daura AG, companies limited by shares have been able to issue securities not only in digital form but also "tokenized". By transferring these tokens on the blockchain, uncertified securities can easily be transferred worldwide between registered platform users.

The Swiss draft DLT law was approved by the Swiss Federal Council, the Swiss Federal National Council, as well as the Economic Affairs and Taxation Committee and was then passed by the Swiss Federal Council of States in February 2021. The law was passed in response to a further report by the Swiss Federal Council, "Legal Framework for Distributed Ledger Technology and Blockchain in Switzerland". The Act to Adapt Federal Law to Distributed Ledger Technology consists of amendments to various civil and financial market laws, such as the Swiss Code of Obligations, the Federal Act on Debt Enforcement and Bankruptcy, the Federal Act on International Private Law; and anti-money laundering requirements, to enable the introduction of ledger-based securities stored on a blockchain. The Act provides greater legal certainty for tokens in the form of cryptocurrencies, legally classified as "intangible assets", to be transferred from one person or company to another by means of digital registers. It introduces a new category of "ledger-based securities", a right, which must have the agreement of both parties, is registered in a ledger-based security register and can only be claimed and transferred through this register – an interesting way of securing rights of ownership of a digital or virtual asset. The register must meet a number of requirements, including giving creditors but not debtors, power of disposal of their assets. Maintenance of the register must meet certain requirements. Debtors of ledger based securities are obliged to provide information on the content of ledger based rights, the functioning and integrity of the ledger-based security register to potential purchasers, and are responsible for any damages from false or misleading statements. If there are any bankruptcy proceedings, the cryptoassets must be segregated and held by a custodian.

The Financial Markets and Infrastructure Act adds DTL trading systems to the list of financial market infrastructures and DLT securities are included in the list of securities, but added as a new category. A DLT trading system is defined as an "institution for multi-lateral trading of DLT securities whose purpose is the simultaneous exchange of bids between several participants and the conclusion of contracts based on non-discriminatory rules". The exchange will, provided it fulfils certain conditions, require a license from FINMA.[41]

JAPAN

Japan first introduced regulations to protect retail consumers in 2012. Changes in regulation followed the hack of the cryptocurrency exchange, Mt Gox in 2014 with losses of $473 million. As we discussed in Chapter 2, Mt Gox was the largest Bitcoin exchange in the world at the time, handling as much as 80 per cent of all transactions, but by February 2014, Mt Gox had filed for bankruptcy in Tokyo and in the United States. Japan's Financial Services Agency established a working group on "sophistication of payment and settle-ment operations" in 2014/15. The working group's report recommended the introduction of a registration system for cryptocurrency exchange business; making cryptocurrency transactions subject to money laundering require-ments; and the introduction of a system to protect cryptocurrency users.

These proposals were incorporated into the Payment Services Act in 2016 and took effect on 1 April 2017. The Act itself is quite detailed. It defines a cryptocurrency as a "property value which can be used as payment for the purchase or rental of goods or provisions of services by 'unspecified persons' and is transferable via an electronic data processing system". It is limited to "property values that are stored electronically on electronic devices".[42] The Payment Services Act, states that the operators of a cryptocurrency exchange must be a stock company and must be registered with the local Finance Bureau or a "foreign cryptocurrency exchange business" subject to the equivalent registration requirements as in Japan. A foreign company can only operate in Japan if they have a representative, resident in Japan. Applicants must provide documents showing that they have a system for properly running a cryptocurrency exchange.

The Act also requires cryptocurrency exchanges to protect the data they hold, to provide information regarding fees and other contract terms to their customers and to separate client funds or currencies from their own funds, presumably holding the former in separate accounts. The management of funds must be reviewed by certified public accountants or accountancy firms. Complaints about the exchanges must be handled by a designated dispute resolution centre with expertise in cryptocurrencies or the exchange must establish its own system.[43]

The Prevention of Transfer of Criminal Proceeds was also amended at the same time to add cryptocurrency exchanges to the list of entities subject to money-laundering regulations. The exchanges must check the identities of customers who open accounts, keep transaction records, and notify the authorities about suspicious transactions.

Following the hacking of another large virtual currency exchange, Coincheck with losses to date of $530 million, the Japan Financial Services Authority (JFSA) undertook a series of on-site investigations, which, not surprisingly meant that many exchanges' internal management and operational systems were shown to be inadequate. Despite virtual currencies not being regulated, the volatility in their value had attracted speculators and investors rather than being used as a means of payment. The JFSA had already issued alerts to the public in 2017, warning them that investments in ICOs could be very volatile and that some of the ICOs were engaged in fraudulent activities. The Coincheck affair finally led to further amendments to the Payment Services Act and the Financial Instruments and Exchange Act.

The 2019 Amendment to the two Acts was promulgated in June 2019 and took effect in June 2020. It added cryptoassets to the list of financial instruments, so that the existing regulations for derivatives trading applied to cryptoassets derivative transactions. About half of the registered cryptoasset exchanges allow customers to engage in margin trading of cryptoassets, a risky investment for the retail investor. The application of these rules to cryptoasset derivative trading provides some protection for consumers. The 2019 Amendment also prohibits various unfair trading practices involving cryptoasset-related transactions and cryptoasset derivative transactions, such as various manipulative trading activities applicable to trading in securities. Interestingly enough, insider dealing was not added to the list because of the difficulties of identifying the issuer of a cryptoasset. This, however, is a crucial item of information that should be accessible to investors and regulators. It is a significant gap.

In addition, ICOs are now expressly regulated by the JFSA. The 2019 Amendment introduced a new category of securities, "electronic recording transfer rights". Unless they fall into the category of private placements, the public offering of cryptoassets is now subject to the registration requirements and rules governing issuing a prospectus. To engage in brokerage activities for electronic recording transfer rights a broker-dealer must be registered as a financial instruments broker-dealer, although there are certain very limited exceptions. The legislation also expands the scope of collective investment schemes by including interests in such schemes being acquired through the contribution of cryptoassets. Custody of cryptoassets is more carefully regulated than ever before, as virtual asset service providers must have the same level of accountability as virtual asset service providers (VASPs) offering exchange services. Only broker-dealers registered under the Financial Instruments and Exchange Act (FIEA) can hold electronic recording transfer rights on behalf of clients for trading purposes. Cryptoasset custodians must register as a cryptocurrency exchange. Since April 2020, they are required to segregate customers' funds from their own, which requires them to deposit customers' cash in a third-party entity. If not in the form of segregated "cold wallets", cryptoasset exchanges must hold "the same kind and same quantities of cryptoassets" as the customers' cryptoassets if they are held in "hot wallets" according to the Payment Services Act, as amended, 2019.

FURTHER INNOVATIONS AND REGULATORY DEVELOPMENTS

At this stage in the development of cryptoassets, various jurisdictions developed their own approaches to regulating them. The variation in the approaches adopted was partly due to differences in the structure of financial services regulation in each country and the uncertainty as to how these assets should be defined and classified. It is their classification which determined the exact nature of regulation. In addition, some jurisdictions were anxious not to be seen to stifle innovation and therefore were slower to incorporate cryptoassets into their regulatory framework. However, these problems had to be overcome to ensure that consumers were protected and that people did not buy cryptoassets on false or misleading prospectuses.

However, Facebook's proposal in 2019 for a global stablecoin, Libra, prompted the actions of the international standard-setting bodies. The risks involved in global stablecoins are far greater than those that came into being through the proliferation of ICOs. Although those presented risks to consumers, allowed for fraud and money laundering, they did not present threats to the global financial system. In the next chapter will shall examine the international regulatory response to stablecoins and global stablecoins in particular.

CHAPTER 6

Global stablecoins: Libra

In this chapter, we shall examine in detail the initial launch of Facebook's Libra on the world. It illustrates all the issues involved in attempting to provide an alternative to a fiat currency and the need for safeguards.

In June 2019, Mark Zuckerberg's White Paper introduced Libra to the world. The original proposals have subsequently been watered down considerably and this chapter will explore the reasons for that.[1] Libra was intended to be a global stablecoin, tied to a basket of currencies, instead of being tied to just one fiat currency or asset. The plan was to back Libra with a collection of low volatility assets, such as bank deposits and short-term government securities in currencies from stable and reputable central banks. For each Libra issued an equal value of such currency, or highly liquid government bonds would be placed on deposit with a reliable repository. But given the basket of currencies approach, it is inevitable that the value of the basket would fluctuate over time in response to developments in trade and their economies. Although Libra acknowledges that the value of the stablecoin fluctuates with the value of domestic or international trade currencies, it did not explain how the exchange rate would be calculated and made transparent to Libra holders. This is especially important for local currencies, where an increasing use of Libra could lead to another kind of "dollarization" of the currency, which in turn could lead to a depreciation of the local currency.

The governance of the Libra blockchain and Libra reserve is in the hands of the Libra Association, an independent, not-for-profit membership organization based in Geneva. The Association itself would include any entity that operates a validator node and holds a sufficient stake in Libra, the minimum being $10 million, which provides the investment entity with one vote but the same entity cannot present itself twice. Some of the founder members included Visa, Mastercard, Spotify, Paypal, Uber, Lyft and Vodafone, but Visa, Mastercard, Strip, eBay and Paypal since pulled out. It is interesting to note that the tech giants, Apple, Amazon and Google did not join the enterprise in the first place and neither did any of the major banks.[2]

The Libra Association will "strive to be a neutral international association". It is the only party that is able to create (mint) and destroy (burn) Libra coins. They are only created when authorized resellers have purchased these coins from the Association with fiat assets to fully back the new ones and are burned only when the authorized resellers sell Libra coins to the Association in exchange for the underlying assets. The resellers will always be able to sell Libras to the Reserve at a price which is equal to the value of the basket. The Libra Reserve acts as a "buyer of last resort" in accordance with the Reserve Management Policy set out by the Libra Association, which is responsible for managing the reserves.

Unlike many other stablecoins, the intention is to have sufficient reserves to back all the Libra in existence. Libra expected to work with a competitive group of exchanges and other liquidity providers, so that users can be confident that the value of their Libra will be relatively stable over time. The money was expected to come from two sources: investors in the separate Investment Tokens and users of Libra. For new Libra coins to be created, there must be an equivalent purchase of Libra for fiat currency and the transfer of that to the reserve. The Association will pay out incentives in Libra coin to the Founding Members to encourage adoption by users, merchants and developers. But customers who transfer the value into the system will in effect give up their right to collect interest on their capital. Instead, the interest earned on their deposits and securities will be used to pay the system's operating costs – to fund investments in the growth and development of the ecosystem, grants to non-profits, engineering research, etc. Having covered those costs, part of the remaining returns will go to pay dividends to early investors in the Libra Investment Tokens for their initial contributions.

The assets in the reserve, the authors of the White Paper pointed out, are low risk and low yield, and the early investors will only obtain any profit on their investments if the network is successful and if the reserve grows quickly and substantially. In other words, the resellers are the conduits through which funds are collected from the users and then recycled to generate liquidity. These interest-free funds, obtained by the resellers, will be used for investments in financial assets, earning market rates of return, enabling the private, corporate members of the Association and the authorized resellers to profit from earning market rates of return from the fiat currencies they have garnered throughout the world at zero interest. Not only do those who purchase Libra coins receive no interest on the capital, but they pay fees to the authorized resellers for the privilege of doing so. A neat plan: a way of using the funds from unsuspecting purchasers to fund the growth of the project.

THE RESERVE AND TRANSACTIONS

The Libra Reserve is a collection of low-volatility assets, including bank deposits and government securities in currencies from stable and reputable central banks. It is designed to counteract any fluctuations in the value of Libra due to any movements in the value of any of the currencies making up the basket of currencies. The Association will only invest in sovereign debt from stable governments with a low default probability, with a low risk of high inflation, and debt issued by "multiple governments". For the purposes of liquidity, the Association will rely on short-term securities issued by these governments, that were all traded in liquid markets, whose daily trading volume runs into "tens or even hundreds of billions. This allows the size of the reserve to be easily adjusted as the number of Libra in circulation expands or contracts".[3]

Who holds the reserves? "The reserve will be held by a geographically distributed network of custodians with investment-grade credit-rating to limit counterparty risk. Safeguarding the reserve's assets, providing high auditability and transparency, avoiding the risks of a centralized reserve, and achieving operational efficiency are the key parameters in custody selection and design."[4]

As far as users of the currency are concerned, their contact is not with the reserve, but instead with the authorized resellers which will be the only entities authorized by the Association to transact large amounts of fiat currency and Libra in and out of the reserve. The authorized sellers will integrate with the exchanges and other institutions that buy and sell cryptocurrencies to users who wish to convert from cash to Libra and back again. The Association will encourage the listing of Libra on multiple regulated electronic exchanges throughout the world. They offer web portals and apps for users to buy and sell Libra.

Libra would be a permissioned blockchain initially, which means that access is granted to run a validator node. In a "permissionless blockchain" anyone who meets the technical requirements can run a validator node. However, the aim is for the Libra network to become a permissionless network in due course: "we do not believe there is a proven solution that can deliver the scale, stability and security needed to support billions of people and transactions across the globe through a 'permissionless network,' this will be five years after the launch as a result of working with the 'community' to research and implement the transition".[5] The White Paper also refers to the requirements to build its blockchain, which needs to scale to billions of accounts and be secure and flexible enough so that it can support Libra's ecosystem governance as well as future innovation. The proposal is to use a specific consensus protocol (Byzantine fault tolerant), which has a much higher throughput than the Bitcoin "proof-of-work" as well as a new computer language, "Move" which makes it easier to write a smart contract and better reflect the author's intent. It appears from the original White Paper that both the new blockchain, and the "new" computer language were still in the process of being designed and developed.

CALIBRA

Central to Facebook's Libra project is Calibra. As a newly founded subsidiary of Facebook it is tasked with developing Facebook's digital wallet and to integrate that wallet into Facebook's messenger platforms (Instagram, Messenger and What'sApp).[6] By doing so, Calibra would gain access to the 2.2 billion plus users of Facebook: an enviable market. Bundled into Facebook's digital ecosystem it would have the potential to become one of the first widely used digital wallets with the aim of making payments with Libra as easy as sending a text message, a photo or a video from a mobile phone. Kevin Weil, a senior executive of Calibra, stated that the company hoped to partner with "local businesses such as convenience stores where people could hand over cash and load libra directly on a mobile phone and vice versa" and "they (would) have a scanner and you have a QR code on your phone. That's the way you would physically do it in a store".[7] Calibra would partner with the "authorised resellers" of Libra, cryptocurrency exchanges and liquidity providers to help people change fiat currency from their bank account into libra online.

The White Paper claimed that Libra user payment information will be kept separate from Facebook social media data. Users will have to provide a government issued photo ID and other verification information when they first sign up, and their identity will not be tied to their publicly visible transactions. Data will only be shared on specific occasions for anonymized research or adoption measurement, to address fraud or in response to a request from law enforcement. The Association will not be involved in processing transactions and will not store any personal data of Libra's users. Transactions will be processed and stored by the validator nodes without being linked to a user's real-world identity. When stored on the Libra blockchain, a transaction will be associated with metadata concerning the time at which the transaction was committed to the blockchain and the validator node that added the transaction to the blockchain. The Association will oversee the evolution of the blockchain protocol and the validator node that will be added to the blockchain.

The links of Calibra with Facebook, however, have led many to conclude that Facebook would have access to extensive data for its own use and that it could create a vast database, well beyond that of any other private institution, as well as extend further its control over other areas of their users' lives. It is likely that many Facebook users will not know about or even consider what power they place in the hands of one company. The company has already shown that it does not respect its clients' privacy, most notably as seen in the Cambridge Analytica scandal, which saw the British datascience consultancy firm obtain the personal data of millions of Facebook users without their consent for voter profiling, micromarketing and other services it offered to US political campaigns and marketing clients.

Although transferring client data to Calibra would require client consent, at least under EU and Australian data protection laws, since Facebook clients have given their consent to use their data for social media, not financial services. There are other issues with digital wallets, not least with insurance. The

Libra proposals could lead to the wallets "storing potentially trillions of dollars without depository insurance. They would be unique target for hackers, who stole over $1 bn from cryptocurrency exchanges in the first nine months of 2018".[8]

The problem remains that there is huge scepticism that Libra would respect privacy. The financial incentives for Facebook – of acquiring such extensive "Big Data" are obvious, but the lack of trust in Facebook has undermined Libra from the start. More recently, other concerns have arisen over Facebook, concerning censorship and the closure of people's accounts who have views with which it disagrees. The possibility that one's Libra account could be closed or one could be refused cannot be ruled out.

A DIGITAL IDENTITY

The original Libra White Paper states that "an additional goal of the Association is to develop and promote an open identity standard. We believe that decentralized and portable digital identity is a prerequisite to financial inclusion and competition".[9] This would be a dramatic step forward, given the ease with which one can assume any identity on the internet, or as a *New Yorker* cartoon put it , "on the internet no one knows you are a dog". However, it is thought that having a digital identity would revolutionize many transactions on the internet, such as internet shopping and payments, since one would no longer have to reveal detailed information about oneself, such as date of birth, bank account details, etc every time. But the White Paper has not offered an explanation or further work as to how this could be achieved. Before the publication of the first White Paper, Mark Zuckerberg said he was investigating the blockchain's potential to allow internet users to log into various services via one set of credentials without relying on third parties.[10]

Work has already been done by others on a set of open standards for verifiable credentials.[11] The first step is the requirement for an independent institution to establish the identity in the first place, the second to provide a private key (to be used in all internet transactions and recorded on the blockchain). The problem is that, since people lose keys or forget them entirely, custodians are required, possibly for different aspects of the key, such as biometric identity. New technology that ultimately relies on individuals to keep digital identities safe is not enough. Almost one third of Bitcoins have been lost, thanks to lost passwords and hard wallets residing in landfill sites. The interesting questions in relation to Facebook are who would provide the externally verified digital identity? And who would be its custodian? Even more interesting is whether Facebook is really interested in establishing a digital identity. Libra's blockchain will be pseudonymous, that is, like many crypto networks, it will allow users to hold one or more addresses not linked to their real-life identities.

GOVERNANCE

The Libra Association serves to distance Facebook from Libra: the final decision-making authority rests with the Association, not with Facebook. The aim is for there to be up to 100 members of the Libra Association at the time of the launch. Each will pay up to $10 million into Libra's capital at launch, in return for certain decision-making rights. The Association is made up of the validator nodes of the Libra network, such as the global companies who provided $10 million of capital, but eventually, the Association will include any entity operating a validator node and that holds a sufficient stake in Libra. In the early years of the Libra network, there are planned additional roles besides developing and securing the network, such as raising funds from the members as well as other investors through the sale of Libra Investment Tokens; the design and implementation of incentive programs, including the distribution of dividends to Libra Investment Token Investors. As the Libra network matures into a fully permission-based blockchain in which anyone can serve as a node, these roles may no longer be required.

The Council consists of individual representatives of the Association, each $10 million investment entitles one vote in the Council, subject to a cap on voting rights of 1 per cent for each member. The Council is vested with powers to elect and remove the members of the Libra Association Board, approve and remove the managing director, approve the annual budget and publish recommendations on behalf of the Association including rules that govern the Libra Blockchain Ledger, which could include a hard fork, a radical change to the protocols of a blockchain network, that splits a single cryptocurrency into two. This allows the Council to propose breaking changes in the Libra protocol or resolve a situation where compromised validator nodes have resulted in many signed versions of the Libra blockchain. These and other powers are listed in Libra's White Paper on Governance, which was published in June 2019. In broad terms, the Council functions as the supervisory board, and the Libra Association Board, as the managing board along the lines of a typical Continental two-tier system of corporate governance. But in a number of ways, it is different. With a "supermajority" of two-thirds of the members voting, the Council has the power to change the Association's guiding principles, such as the Founding Members eligibility criteria, the incentives distribution policy and reserve management policy, and the governance and assignment of roles. That could lead to substantial changes in the distribution of power in the structure of the governance of Libra.

Nevertheless, in his testimony to the Senate banking committee, David Marcus, head of Calibra claimed that "all decisions will be made dramatically and transparently. To ensure the Association includes a diverse membership, the Association will work to remove as many financial barriers as possible so that a significant number of nonprofit and multilateral organizations, social impact partners and universities can join". None of that has happened, and even if it did, the Council meets only bi-annually and would not necessarily have the expertise necessary to manage the complexities of maintaining the reserves.[12] Such restrictions would limit the ability of the Council to oversee the management of what Zuckerberg plans to be a global institution.

The White Paper states that Facebook's role in governance of the Association will be "equal to that of its peers" and subject to the voting cap of 1 per cent. In addition, "Facebook created Calibra, a regulated subsidiary, to ensure separation between social and financial data and to build and operate separation between the social and financial data and to build and operate services on its behalf on top of the Libra network".[13] Although, during the launch period through 2019, Facebook "is expected to take a leadership role".[14] Most commentators doubt that Facebook would step back. Visa and Mastercard joined perhaps partly to monitor Facebook's payment ambitions and also to benefit from its popularity should it take off, as the *Wall Street Journal* speculated at the time. But it could also be in their financial interests, as it is for Uber, for example, which pays over $800 million annually in credit card merchant fees.

Uber, Lyft and others could all offer discounts for paying in Libra. The $10 million down payment is a small amount to pay for the prospects of entering such a massive market. In November 2020, Visa had 340 million credit cards in circulation in the United States and a further 800 million outside the US. It is small wonder that they were interested in the project.

IMMEDIATE CRITICISMS OF THE JUNE WHITE PAPER

Reactions to the June White Paper were immediate. The chairwoman of the House Financial Services Committee, Maxine Waters wrote to Mark Zuckerberg, Sheryl Sandberg, chief operating officer and David Marcus, CEO of Calibra,

> to request that Facebook and its partners immediately agree to a moratorium on any movement forward on Libra – its proposed cryptocurrency and Calibra – its proposed digital wallet. It appears that these products may lend themselves to an entirely new global financial system that is based out of Switzerland and intended to rival US monetary policy and the dollar. This raises serious privacy, trading, and monetary policy concerns for not only Facebook's over two billion users, but also for investors, consumers and the broader global economy.[15]

The issues of potential misuse of Libra and privacy were raised by the Federal Reserve in its semi-annual report to Congress on 10 July 2019. Fed Chairman Jerome Powell stated that "Libra raises many serious concerns regarding privacy, money laundering, consumer protection and financial instability. These are concerns that should be publicly and thoroughly addressed before proceeding."[16]

In his evidence to the Senate Banking Committee, Chairman Powell pointed out that at present, the "privacy rules we apply to banks, we have no authority to apply to Facebook or Libra, or to Calibra or to the Libra Association".[17] This was in response to the Chairman, Mike Crappo's opening remarks at the Senate Banking, Housing and Urban Affairs Committee in which he stressed the implications of Facebook's cryptocurrency payments system for individuals' data privacy: "Given the significant amount of user information already held by the largest social media platforms and the prospect of holding even more information, Congress needs to act to give individuals real control over their data".[18]

It is doubtful that the testimony of David Marcus, head of Calibra, did much to allay the Senate Banking Committee's fears. In the course of his testimony, he stated that "Protecting consumers and ensuring people's privacy is one of Libra's top priorities" and, as part of that, "the Association cannot and will not monetize any data on the blockchain". With regard to Calibra, he claimed that "because the Libra blockchain will exist as an open-source ecosystem, businesses and developers around the world are free to build competitive services on top of it, and Facebook intends to be one of the many businesses to do so".[19] Ensuring people's privacy has not been one of Facebook's priorities in the past, but that aside, regulators and others are right to be concerned, given that Facebook has given no details about how, given the current state of the technology, it would, in fact, be possible to protect users' privacy.

David Marcus stated that only "transactions together with the sender's and receiver's public addresses, the transaction amount and the timestamp will be recorded on the blockchain and no other information will be visible".[20] But transaction information can reveal a great deal about consumers and it is data which Facebook could sell. The Senate Committee hearing cited Facebook's trackrecord, including in June 2018, the discovery that Facebook was sharing user data with 40 device makers, including Amazon, Microsoft and Samsung,[21] that Facebook "continues to change even the privacy rules without informing users"[22] and even that Marcus himself had headed up Facebook's messaging team when other companies such as Netflix, Spotify and the Royal Bank of Canada were able to access and read Facebook-users private messages.[23] Even the use of Zuckerberg's mantra, "Trust is primordial" failed to satisfy the Committee.[24]

The issue of privacy rapidly became a matter of widespread concern. On 5 August 2019 Privacy Commissioners across the world issued a joint statement expressing their concerns about the risks posed by the Libra digital currency and infrastructure: "These risks are not limited to financial privacy, since the involvement of Facebook Inc., and its expansive categories of data collection on hundreds of millions of users, raises additional concerns." They noted that while Facebook and Calibra have made broad public statements about privacy, they have failed to specifically address the information handling practices that will be in place to secure and protect personal information, expressing their surprise that this further detail is not yet available. Facebook has the potential to drive the take-up by consumers throughout the world, even in countries without data protection laws in place. This means that as soon as the network goes live, it could immediately become the custodian of millions of people's personal information.

They set out a series of questions for the Libra Network to answer. The first question is fairly comprehensive:

1. How can global data protection and enforcement authorities be confident that the Libra Network has robust measures to protect the personal information of network users? In particular, how will the Libra Network ensure that its participants will:

   (a) Provide clear information about how personal information will be used (including the use of profiling and algorithms, the sharing of personal information between members of the Libra Network and any third parties) to allow users to provide specific and informed consent where appropriate;

   (b) Create private-privacy default settings that do not use nudge techniques or "dark patterns" to encourage people to share personal data with third parties or their privacy protection;

   (c) Ensure that privacy control settings are prominent and easy to use;

   (d) Collect and process only the minimum amount of information necessary to achieve the identified purpose of the product or service, and to ensure the lawfulness of the processing;

   (e) Ensure that all the personal data is adequately protected;

   (f) Give people simple procedures for exercising their privacy rights, including deleting their accounts and honouring their requests in a timely way.

The Joint Statement was signed by the Privacy and Information Commissioners of Australia, Canada, the European Union, the United Kingdom and a Commissioner of the Federal Trade Commission of the United States. The response from Libra Network's Dante Disparte was devoid of any detailed engagement with the content of questions: "We appreciate these thoughtful questions and share the commitment to protecting any personal information. As much as Libra represents an opportunity for the world to make inroads on financial inclusion, we acknowledge the need to design an infrastructure that complies with global privacy requirements".[25] Such a response would obviously do little to deal with the detailed questions the Joint Statement raises. It also indicates that little thought had been given to the issue of privacy in the development of Libra. Given Facebook's past actions and reputation, it should have perhaps been obvious that this would be one of the issues to be raised.

THE INTERNATIONAL REGULATORY RESPONSE

At their meeting in Chantilly, France in July 2019, the G7 finance ministers and central bank governors agreed that stablecoins – in particular, projects with global and potentially systemic footprints – raised serious regulatory and systemic concerns. The G7 asked for a report from the Working Group on Stablecoins, including its recommendations for the IMF/World Bank annual meetings in October. At the same time, in response to the G20 leaders Osaka Declaration, the Financial Stability Board (FSB) issued its Note on the Regulatory Issues of Stablecoins, and the Bank for International Settlements released its own report, "Investigating the Impact of Global Stablecoins".

The Bank of England also made it clear that Libra had the potential to be a "systemically important" payment system and that it would be regulated as such. The Bank also raised concerns about the wallet providers, exchanges and other links in the chain that form the payments system: "The resilience of the proposed Libra system would rely on the stability of not just the core elements of the Libra Association and the Libra Reserve but also the associated critical activities conducted by the other firms in the Libra ecosystem, such as validators, exchanges or wallet providers". These underscore the "need to ensure end-to-end resilience".[26]

On 13 September 2019, the finance ministers of Germany and France issued a joint statement: "France and Germany reaffirm their willingness to tackle the challenges raised by cryptocurrency and so-called stablecoin projects ... [we] consider that the Libra project, as set out in Facebook's blueprint, fails to convince that those risks will be properly addressed. We believe that no private entity can claim monetary power, which is inherent in the Sovereignty of Nations."[27]

Similarly, the Reserve Bank of Australia in its submission to the Senate Select committee on Financial Technology and Regulatory Technology, referencing the G7 cautioning that private sector global stablecoin initiatives should not be permitted to launch until all risks and regulatory requirements have been addressed, stated:

> The Bank is supportive of this view ... The bank is working closely with relevant agencies domestically and internationally to understand recent proposals to ensure that they will be adequately regulated and supervised. In Australia, it is unclear that there will be strong demand for global stablecoins even if they do meet all regulatory requirements, particularly for domestic payments ... and a number of new non-bank digital have entered the market in recent years offering significantly cheaper and faster money transfer services.[28]

So, Libra found it had few friends throughout the world. Even some of its supporters who had already signed up for membership of the Association, such as PayPal, Stripe, Mastercard, Visa and eBay, left in the face of the governmental and regulatory onslaught and before the international standard-setting bodies had set out the proposed new standards for consultation (see Chapter 7).

THE SECOND WHITE PAPER

In the face of such opposition, Libra retreated. Prior to the publication of the second version of the White Paper changes were made to the Libra website. One of the most interesting changes involved the operation of the reserve itself. Reference to the payment of dividends to investors who provided capital to jump start the ecosystem (the Libra Association) was removed. The problem with paying dividends to investors is that it could lead to loading the reserve with risky investments to maximize the returns for investors.[29] That could lead to fluctuations in Libra which would undermine the stability of the coin, even perhaps to the extent of the reserve being insufficient to meet the demand from those who wish to exchange their stablecoins for US dollars.

The Second White Paper was published in April 2020, in the year in which Libra was due to be launched. This version replaced the previous versions published by the Association. Facebook makes it clear that supporting technical papers have been edited or retired as well as details of the project, and that the project itself may differ according to regulatory approvals and may also evolve over time. That proved to be an understatement.

In May 2020 Libra's wallet was renamed "Novi" and in December, the Libra Association was renamed the Diem Association. The second White Paper outlined a number of key changes. The first is the move away from offering a single global currency and instead the introduction of single currency stablecoins, such as Libra USD or Libra EUR. Each of these will be fully backed by cash or cash equivalents as well as short-term government securities denominated in that currency. The Libra (now Diem) Association intends to work with regulators, central banks and others to expand the number of stablecoins available on the Libra network. It is hard to see why they should work together for this aim. The Libra coin will also be a digital composite of some of the stablecoins available on the Libra network, defined in terms of fixed nominal weights. They will also build a digital composite of some of these coins, which will be available for cross-border transactions and in countries with no digital currency. Although the new version still allows for the development of a multicurrency Libra coin, it is still not clear which currencies might be included.[30] That would depend on the Association "working together" with central banks, regulators and international organization such as the IMF and FINMA to find the right composition. The exact composition would be defined in the smart contract and the changes in the "weights" or the additions of new stablecoins would be submitted for approval by the network validators.

Another key change concerns the composition of the Reserve. At least 80 per cent of the Reserve will consist of short-term government securities with a very low credit risk (e.g. A+ S&P rating and Moody's A1 rating or higher and at the time of writing only 37 countries have such a rating) and whose securities trade in highly liquid secondary securities markets. The real step forward, however, is for the Libra Reserve to be audited and that these should be made public. The Libra Association would publish on its website daily the current composition of the Libra Reserve and the current market value of the assets in it.

There will be four types of participants in the Libra ecosystem: (1) designated dealers, committed to making markets with tight spreads and able to accommodate high volumes of trading; (2) regulated virtual asset service providers (VASPs); (3) certified VASPs, including those that have completed a certification process approved by the Libra Association; and (4) unhosted wallets. Unhosted wallets, however, are a serious risk. They are called "unhosted" or "non-custodial" wallets because they are not controlled by an exchange and cannot be blocked or shut down by a third party. Unlike the wallets used by exchanges, there is no need to provide an ID to acquire them. They really are pseudonymous. They allow people to transact digitally without the need for a financial intermediary. This matters because it is then very easy to launder money through these wallets without the need to produce any ID or verification to acquire them. It is for this reason that unhosted wallets have been postponed due to regulatory concerns, but the door is still open.

In response to the serious regulatory concerns about a permissionless blockchain, the Libra Network will remain "permissioned". Remaining "permissioned" of course moves the whole project far away from the original ideals of a decentralized blockchain with its own cryptocurrency. Libra will not be popular in certain parts of the cryptocurrency community. The plan, however, is to move towards a "market-driven" network for validators and "proof of authority". That probably will not worry Facebook too much, since that is not the purpose of Libra.

Finally, the Second White Paper's hope is that "as central banks develop central bank digital currencies, these CBDCs could be directly integrated with the Libra Network, removing the need for Libra Networks to manage the associated Reserves, thus reducing credit and custody risks. As an example, if the central bank develops a digital representation of the US dollar ... the Association could replace the applicable single-currency stablecoin with the CBDC". However, it is far from clear why central banks or governments should wish to work with Diem and provide services such as custodian services to one private currency riding on the back of their own fiat currencies. Zuckerberg envisages that "single currency stablecoins will only be minted and burned in response to market demand for that coin"[31] but that will be independently assessed by whom? The investment backing the stablecoins includes cash, cash equivalents or very short-term government securities, but even so that will require skilled asset management to determine the portfolio composition of the reserves and rebalance the portfolio on a daily basis.

It is hard to see why any central bank would or should be directly integrated with the Libra Network. Indeed, why should a central bank give precedence to the Libra Network? Given the potential size of Diem and its Reserve, would that, in effect, lead to power-sharing with a private, profit-led organization and the attendant conflicts of interest? After all, both the blockchain and the computer language, Move, are still in the process of development and it is not at all clear how effective and above all, what level of cyber security will really apply to the Network. The Second Paper anticipates using WhatsApp and Messenger but these are both subject to not infrequent outages, but there is no mention of the need to improve the security of the system and its stability. What would be the point of offering a cheaper and faster payments system if users are unable to access it for several hours at a time?

So what should we make of the Second White Paper's scaled-down digital currency? Some argue: not very much. The original proposal was to turn the digital coin into a global currency to rival the dollar, but that whole project appears to have been abandoned. The Association will now vet any wallet that is launched on the Network and strengthen its own scrutiny of what happens. The *Financial Times* argued that Facebook's Libra "went from a game changer to just another PayPal".[32] But enough elements of the original plan remain for the project to be viewed with distrust. Facebook has increased its efforts to facilitate payments across its platforms, notably WhatsApp and Messenger, despite their current lack of security. Although care has been taken to accommodate, or at least, to appear to comply with the concerns of regulators and central banks, Binance Research, has concluded, and rightly so, that "one of the core elements for Libra/Diem to really become a global settlement system are unhosted wallets ... [Diem] has made it clear that they see unhosted wallets as a core element that is crucial to their mission and will find a way to balance regulatory compliance and intuitive product design".[33]

As we have noted, the question still remains about Facebook's digital wallet, Novi Financial (which replaces Calibra) as to whether it would be able to use data from the users' social media accounts. Facebook insists that those decisions will be in the hands of the Association, the governing body and that Facebook will not be able to control the Association. But the fact remains that Facebook will have a digital wallet subsidiary and that will offer services on the Libra platform (or perhaps suddenly withdraw them as Facebook have been known to do) and could have a significant presence. The original proposal claimed that operating costs could be funded from the profits from investments, but there is obviously a conflict between investing for a profit and investing to preserve the reserves, an important conflict which the regulators should carefully observe. The charges for transactions through Novi Financial are not clear either. Novi promises instant transactions and "no hidden fees" for cross-border or domestic fees, but it is unclear whether this means that there are no fees or that there will be fees but the company will be transparent about them.

The White Paper recognizes that there may not be any earnings from investments, even more so today given the possibility of negative interest rates. The Libra Network will have to cover the costs "through its other revenue streams (e.g. transaction and other fees)".[34] But it does not provide any details. The White Paper provides more information about the various intermediaries undertaking the burning and minting of coins, taking customer assets and facilitating transactions, but very few details about how they will be compensated or what the costs will be. The Governor of the Bank of England raised the issue in the Treasury Committee on 6 January 2021, "One of the issues is where is the business model in this thing? ... This would be private sector access to information. How do you make money off this thing? Is it actually via the access to information?"[35] The fact that Facebook clients have consented to the use of their data to Novi does not mean that they fully understand the implications of that or whether or not their privacy has been protected. Many have, after all, given their consent to the use of their data when they signed up to their Facebook accounts, not realizing the extent to which that can be used. Since Novi is a wholly owned subsidiary of Facebook would Facebook's digital wallet be able to use data from users' social media accounts?

Libra/Diem was registered in Switzerland and its application for approval had been made to the Swiss Financial Markets Supervisory Authority. In May 2021, however, Facebook abandoned Switzerland and relocated its operations in the United States, having scaled back its global ambitions. FINMA stated that it was still considering the application for a payments licence in April, but that "the outcome and duration of the procedure remained open". FINMA was also in consultation with the Swiss National Bank and over 20 supervisory authorities and central banks from around the world. To my mind, it was obvious that FINMA was never going to grant a licence to Diem. Presumably, Facebook realized this, although the company claimed that its move was because it was heading in a different direction: "The Diem is pleased to announce a partnership between its wholly owned subsidiary, Diem Networks US and Silvergate Capital Corporation. Silvergate Bank will become the exclusive issuer of the Diem USD stablecoin. The FINMA license is not required under this new model". Presumably in order to overcome issues about the feasibility of many aspects of the Diem proposal, the press release went on to state that "Silvergate will become the exclusive issuer of the Diem Payment Network (DPN), a permissioned block-chain based network that facilitates the real-time transfer of Diem stablecoins among approved participants ... Silvergate is a California state-chartered bank and a member of the Federal Reserve, and Diem Networks will register as a money services business with the US Department of Treasury's Financial Crimes Enforcement Network".[36] The fact that Diem will still be responsible for the payments network suggests that the problems implicit in the second White Paper have not yet been resolved.

Shortly after the announcement of partnership with Silvergate, Diem's chief economist, Christian Catalini is reported as saying at Consensus 2021 that the initial vision of Libra was "naïve" and that "what we're really suggesting is more of a public-private partnership. We see this as almost like a temporary exercise, where issuers like Silvergate in collaboration with Diem will be issuing a diem dollar, but the moment there is a CBDC ... We are the only issuers of a stablecoin, to my knowledge, that committed publicly to phasing out our own token and replacing it with a CBDC token". He claimed that Diem was still committed to serving the unbanked, but "we'll have to work over time to develop better identity standards. It's very difficult to differentiate a good user from a bad actor, so our work will take multiple years to unfold".[37] The future of Diem therefore depends on the development of a dollar CBDC, but as that is not likely in the immediate future, it will be interesting to see what, if anything, happens with Diem in the meantime.

CHAPTER 7

Reactions to stablecoins

The regulatory responses to stablecoins were at a national level in the first instance. But the advent of Libra triggered the intervention of the international standard setting bodies. Some crytpocurrency enthusiasts like to claim that national and international regulatory authorities are seeking to stifle innovation and are nervous about the potential threat to traditional fiat currencies. That is unfair. Regulatory authorities must clarify the nature of the business conducted by the stablecoin's ecosystem and apply the relevant existing regulations to the stablecoin arrangement on the principle: "same activities, same risks, same regulations".[1] That is entirely reasonable: if it is the same business, with the same risks, then there is no justification for exempting cryptocurrencies from the same rules.

The responses of individual jurisdictions have inevitably varied from one to another. Yet they are insufficient to handle the risks involved in the use of global stablecoins or smart contracts that apply across jurisdictions. Hence global international standard setting bodies have stepped in to establish standards for the challenges and risks for public policy, oversight and regulation. The first step, however, was to identify the risks from global stablecoins. This became an urgent issue after the publication of the Libra White Paper in June 2019.

THE COMMITTEE ON PAYMENTS AND MARKET INFRASTRUCTURE

The Committee on Payments and Market Infrastructure published its report in October 2019. It points out that recent stablecoin initiatives have highlighted weaknesses in cross-border payments and access to transaction accounts. Cross-border payments have remained slow, expensive and opaque. For stablecoins to do all they claim is only possible using their new technologies, they still have further requirements to meet. If the providers of the global stablecoins really do intend to serve the needs of the unbanked and underserved, then they must provide a safe store of value, and protection and legal certainty for their users, as well as being compliant with all the relevant regulations.

The Report sets out certain general principles to which the design of stablecoins should conform, whatever their design may be. The legal basis has to be well founded, clear and transparent in all jurisdictions for all stablecoin arrangements, no matter what scale is intended. This is so that people using the stablecoin know whether or not it is an equivalent to money or whether they have rights to the underlying asset against the issuer of the stablecoin: in other words, what exactly they have bought through an exchange or through their banks. If it is a question of relying on DLT to record and transfer monetary value, careful consideration must be given to the rights and obligations of all involved.

The governance structure must be clear and explained to all participating in the stablecoin's ecosystem before the stablecoin goes into operation. Achieving good governance is more difficult with permissionless DLT systems, a decentralized system with no responsible entity to carry out the oversight and regulatory requirements. Given the history of stablecoins to date, one of the most important issues is the custodianship of assets. If reserve assets are not clearly segregated from the equity of the stablecoin issuer, then the investment policy could result in the assets remaining in the hands of the issuers but the losses shared amongst the users.

Poorly designed and operated payment systems can lead to systemic risks to the economy as a whole. Individuals and firms need accessible and cost-effective means of payment. Such systems facilitate commercial activities and economic growth. Financial markets rely on dependable clearing and settlement arrangements to allocate capital and manage liquidity. It is because payment systems play this role in the economy that central banks and other regulatory authorities have the statutory obligation to ensure that the payment systems are run safely and securely at all times. This includes taking into account legal, governance and operational risk, including cyber security. These are all issues which have to be taken into account with payment systems and other parts of the financial markets infrastructure, such as clearing and settlement. For the latter, that includes credit and liquidity risk. Understanding credit and liquidity risk requires the relevant skills and the ability and training to understand why these are important. The relevant management skills are also essential.

One of the most important issues is that of market integrity. Stablecoins are designed to reduce the volatility of their prices in relation to the prices of fiat currencies. That means there are fewer opportunities to manipulate prices. However, it is still not clear how the prices of some stablecoins are to be determined. If a designated market maker is involved, then they may well have significant market power and ability to determine stablecoin prices. The stability of the stablecoin price in the secondary markets depends on the "level of trust that market participants place in the issuer's ability and willingness to exchange it for fiat at a value consistent with reasonable user expectations".[2]

In addition, there are some specific risks not found elsewhere, which arise from the nature of the stablecoin's ecosystem. There can, for example, be a conflict of interest in that to attract business they may inflate the number of customers and trading volume. Similarly, since the stablecoin's ecosystem often involves the issuer playing many different roles, such as market-maker, trading platform and custodial wallet, this opens up the way to market misconduct in ways which are not available in other markets.

Data protection is another significant issue highlighted by the Report. An issuer of stablecoins, especially global stablecoins, has to be trusted to maintain data privacy. The authorities will seek to "apply data privacy and protection rules to stablecoin operators, including how data will be used by the participants in the ecosystem and shared between participants and/or with third parties".[3] Stablecoin users should also have clear information about how their personal data is to be used by participants in the ecosystem and how they will be shared between participants or with third parties. Collecting different categories of data by the operators of stablecoins and the further processing of users' personal data might also raise other problems with data privacy. The Report recommended that at the very least, "consumers or investors should be given comprehensive and clear information about what stablecoins are, the rights associated with them and the risks they represent".[4] They also need to know, as part of the information provided, on what grounds they might find that their accounts have been closed. Facebook, for example, has closed people's accounts for political reasons, so clear guarantees should be given, that accounts will not be closed without good reason and that there is the ability to challenge the grounds for closure. But, as has been detailed in previous chapters, that is precisely what was conspicuous by its absence throughout the period of the ICOs.

Global stablecoins (GSC) simply magnify the risks described above. Some of them are far more complicated than might appear to anyone aspiring to provide a global payments system. For example, providing proper levels of consumer/investor protection across many jurisdictions, the GSC will become subject to a variety of regulatory frameworks in each one. A GSC should have ample contingency arrangements in place to ensure continuity of service, especially as it provides a larger attack surface for malicious actors to compromise the integrity, confidentiality and availability of the ledger. The organization behind the GSC could suddenly become the custodian of millions of users' personal information.

Finally, the Committee on Payments and Market Infrastructure considers the effects on monetary policy transmission, where the GSC is a major player in payments. It is highly unlikely that the commercial providers of GSCs will consider the effects on monetary policy, including the effects on any of the emerging and developing markets, whose economy they wish to help. If, the GSC was widely used as a store of value, it could weaken the effect of monetary policy on domestic interest rates and credit conditions, especially in countries whose currencies are not part of the reserve assets. It could increase cross border mobility and affect monetary policy transmission. The effects are especially important for countries in which the domestic currency is not included in the basket of currencies, which is true for most countries. The GSCs would become widely used as payments and savings, even if the GSCs paid no interest, so monetary policy would have a much reduced effect. This would have a similar impact as countries in which cash usage has declined due to dollarization. But the problems would not be subject to any kind of resolution in the same way, since classic dollarization allows for sovereign-to-sovereign discussions of the policy implications of such substitution. Indeed, it is highly unlikely that a commercial enterprise with a narrow focus would recognize the need for and engage in the search for solutions.

THE FINANCIAL STABILITY BOARD

The Financial Stability Board was mandated by the G20 in June 2019 to address these challenges and to set out high-level recommendations, aimed at privately issued stablecoins designed primarily for retail use, after a widespread consultation with its own members and others.[5] The responses the FSB retained are very much in line with the Committee on Payments and Market Infrastructure's (CPMI) investigations. The FSB's purpose is to set out the general standards to which GSCs should conform.

The FSB's ten recommendations address the major risks. These include the fact that without highly skilled risk management, global stablecoins are vulnerable to runs, if all the stablecoin holders decided to redeem them at reference value at the same time. Poor governance, such as the lack of segregated funds in the reserve, a lack of clarity about the legal obligations of the issuer, may mean and has already meant in many cases, that the stablecoin holders are unable to redeem their coins for the reference currency (or the basket of currencies in the case of Libra or other assets). A problem with global stablecoins is that their structure may be decentralized or centralized or permissioned, making it hard to assess whether the issuers of the GSCs actually have the necessary skills for handling market, credit and liquidity risk in order to maintain confidence in the coin's value. Some, but not all, stablecoin issuers hold their reserves in a bank and use a bank as a custodian, but the wrong choice of a bank in a weak jurisdiction can, and has, meant the loss of millions of dollars. Recommendations 6, 8 and 9 are designed to ensure that GSCs have sound governance structures and systems in place for safeguarding, collecting, storing and managing data, whilst maintaining privacy for their customers. Regulators must be able to access that information.

Similarly, stablecoin arrangements must be clear and transparent and provide all the information that customers or users of coins should have available to them. They should be able to find out very easily which operators or service providers are responsible for what, how the reserves are invested, what the safe custody arrangements are and how to register complaints and seek redress. In addition, the global coin issuer should make it clear what legal rights the user has to reserve assets, if at all, should the company become irrelevant. Users need to know what their rights are if they lose access to their e-wallet, for example, because of a cyber-attack. Where the stablecoin is used for purchases in another country, the users must have access to a transparent rate of exchange.

The FSB highlighted the risks involved in stablecoins which reach a global scale. A systemically important payments system such as Diem is likely to concentrate risks, so its "safety, efficiency and integrity" is paramount. It would be expected to have contingency plans in place to support continuity of service, an issue which neither of the White Papers emphasizes. Indeed, global stablecoins arrangements that "serve as a system for large value payments may pose additional credit and liquidity risks over central bank real-time gross settlement payment systems".[6]

The potential for Diem to grow quickly, given the network effects of Facebook (including Instagram and WhatsApp) with its 2.4 billion users and the fact that its sponsors have sufficient resources to support its launch, is a central issue. An interesting article published by a senior adviser to the European Central Bank (ECB) considers the scale of the Diem stablecoin arrangements in order to examine what its impact could be.[7] The article sets out three different scenarios for estimating its size. The first compares it with Paypal as a means of payment and its 286 million users with average holdings of €64. For Diem's use as a store of value, the figures are much higher. The ECB paper acknowledges that its estimates on scale are high, given the assumption that all of Facebook's 2.4 billion users would use the payments system and also invest in Diem. These range from €153 billion to €3 trillion. This gives some idea of the huge impact Diem could have on the global financial system.

The other issue raised is that the Libra Association plans to hold highly liquid assets such as short-term government bonds, bank deposits and cash in its reserves. This could result in the withdrawal of deposits from banks and a shortage of such assets in the eurozone as well as in the United States, and the establishment of a fund that would eclipse Europe's and perhaps the US's largest money-market fund, currently J. P. Morgan with over $100 billion in assets. If Diem is used as a store of value, then its sheer size could potentially overwhelm the US's total money market fund, which stood at $3.04 trillion in

2018. It could lead to a shortage of such assets for money-market funds and pension funds amongst others. The demands of managing such vast funds would require exceptional skills and experience. The White Paper 2.0 does not give any indication of the enormity of the task or of its implications in terms of market dominance or risk.

FINANCIAL ACTION TASK FORCE

Of course, there are many other issues are presented by global stablecoins, but these fall under the auspices of other international standard setters, most notably the Financial Action Task Force (FATF), which is a G7 mandated intergovernmental organization tasked with developing polices to tackle money laundering, terrorist financing, cyber-crime and the misdirection of government funds or international assistance. Shortly after the FSB reported, the Financial Action Task Force issued its own updated recommendations in October 2020. The stress is again placed on due diligence regarding both the customer and the transaction, especially when that customer is carrying out an occasional transaction and identifying the beneficial owner. The FATF recommendations specifically exclude any financial institution or in this case a GSC issuer from keeping anonymous accounts or accounts in obviously fictitious names. Facebook's Libra and its replacement, Diem make it clear that pseudonymous holders of stablecoins will be accepted. Each country should make sure that anyone providing money transfer services should be licensed or registered. That includes those providing virtual assets, who should be regulated for AML/CFT and subject to the effective systems for monitoring or ensuring compliance. All of the money laundering and counterterrorism funding recommendations, apply to virtual assets and virtual asset service providers (VASPs). They are required to identify, assess, and take effective action to mitigate their money laundering and terrorist financing risks. They must be licensed or registered in the jurisdiction where they are created or, if the VASP is a natural or legal person, in the jurisdiction where their business is located.[8]

THE INTERNATIONAL ORGANIZATION OF SECURITIES COMMISSIONS

The International Organization of Securities Commissions (IOSCO) is an association of national organizations that seek to regulate the world's securities market. In February 2020 they published a report that examined the risks involved in cryptoasset trading platforms (CTPs) that provide marketplaces where users can trade cryptocurrencies. The aim of the report is to offer a toolkit or the issues to be addressed when regulatory authorities are considering how to apply existing IOSCO principles to these trading platforms. These issues cover access to the platforms; safeguarding participants' assets; identifying and managing conflicts of interest; transparency of operations of the platforms; market integrity, including the rules governing trading on the cryptoasset trading platform, price discovery and technology. At each stage, there are risks involved, including, for example, the role of intermediaries in ensuring compliance, the know your customer (KYC) and AML/CFT regulations and suitability requirement for retail investors. But if there are no intermediaries, then who is responsible for onboarding investors and protecting investors' interests and how do they carry this out?

In advising regulatory authorities on what kind of regulations should be in place, IOSCO offers a checklist of questions which should be posed about crypto trading platforms already operating in their jurisdictions or potentially might be located there.

The first set of general questions are ones any investor would be advised to consider, and include: Who can access the CTP? How does the trading system operate and what are the rules of that system? Which cryptoassets are available for trading? What degree of transparency of trading is provided? How does the CTP seek to prevent market abuse? What clearance and settlement services exist? How are the participants assets held? What possible conflicts of interest exist? What cyber security and system resiliency controls are in place?

Further more detailed questions are provided, for example, for the issue about how the participants' assets are held, the following points are raised: What kinds of cryptoassets are held in custody by the CTP? What is the life-cycle and audit trail of the movement of funds and cryptoassets between the participant, the CTP, and any third parties and within the CTP, including in whose names those assets are stored online or offline? Who has access to the private keys for all CTP wallets and what backup arrangements are in place to avoid single points of access? Whether the funds and/or cryptoassets are segregated or pooled; What ownership rights and claims an investor has to their assets and how they are evidenced? How and under what conditions assets, cryptoassets or funds can be withdrawn from the CTP. What happens if assets are lost, due to theft, bankruptcy or insolvency of the CTP?

IOSCO's contribution is designed to inform and advise regulatory authorities about the considerations to be taken into account when they consider whether and how to apply its existing principles to new trading platforms. IOSCO then applied these considerations and the results of its surveys of its members to provide educational materials for would-be investors. IOSCO has not altered its Principles regarding trading platforms but has simply explained how they should be applied to cryptoasset trading platforms by posing relevant questions to their operators. If all of the above seems burdensome and tedious, then it is worth remembering that cryptocurrency platforms have failed at an alarming high rate, with customers losing hundreds of millions of dollars with little or no redress.

The Bank for International Settlements (BIS) published a Consultative Document on the Prudential Treatment of Cryptoasset Exposures in June 2021. BIS's focus is inevitably on the risks cryptoassets pose to banks in terms of liquidity, credit, market and operational (including fraud, money laundering and legal risks). The underlying principle is once more "same risk, same activity, same treatment" but the "prudential framework should apply the concept of 'technology neutrality' and not be designed in a way to explicitly advocate or discourage the use of specific technologies related to cryptoassets".[9]

The Consultative Document divides cryptoassets into two groups. The first group comprises those and only those which meet the criteria set out by Basel as as follows:

- The cryptoasset either is a tokenized traditional asset or has a stabilization mechanism that is effective at all times in linking its value to an underlying traditional asset or pool of traditional assets.
- All rights, obligations and interests arising from cryptoasset arrangements that meet the condition above are clearly defined and legally enforceable in jurisdictions where the asset is issued and redeemed.

In addition, the applicable legal framework(s) ensure(s) settlement finality.

- The functions of the cryptoasset and the network on which it operates, including the distributed ledger or similar technology on which it is based, are designed and operated to sufficiently mitigate and manage any material risks.
- Entities that execute redemptions, transfers or settlement finality of the cryptoasset are regulated or supervised.[10]

It will be interesting to see how many cryptoassets and related services actually meet these criteria. Without substantial reforms of their structures, many of the cryptoassets and associated services described in previous chapters would not. The Consultation Paper, however, places the responsibility for assessing a cryptoasset's compliance with these requirements on an on-going basis with supervisors who need to have the appropriate risk management policies, human and IT capabilities to evaluate the risks of engaging in cryptoassets and be able to implement these. Basel proposes increasing the minimum capital requirements according to the increased market and credit risks, as well as an operational risk charge within the Basel framework on the grounds that the cryptoassets and the technologies on which they are based are new and evolving: "there is an increased likelihood that they pose unanticipated operational risks".[11] These and other details of the capital requirements for market and credit risk are set out in more detail in section 2 of the Consultative Paper.

But the more significant requirements are for cryptoassets falling into the second group: those cryptoassets which fail to meet any of the criteria set out for Group 1, and as a consequence pose additional and higher risks. For these cryptoassets, Basel proposes a new capital requirement, consisting of a new risk weighted asset of 1250 per cent, calculated separately for each cryptoasset to which a bank is exposed. The capital required is designed to ensure that banks need to hold risk-based capital at least equivalent in value to their Group 2 cryptoasset exposures: "The capital will be sufficient to absorb a full write-off of the crypto-asset exposures without exposing depositors and other senior creditors of the bank to a loss".[12] BIS also sets out the details of how the 1250 per cent applies to cryptoasset derivatives, counterparty credit risk for derivative exposures with cryptoassets as the underlying exposure or that are priced in Group 2 and its application to short and long positions. Group 2 cryptoassets are not eligible forms of collateral for securities financing transactions.

The full technical details have not been set out in detail here. The main point is the application of capital requirements and the care with which they have been calculated. Headlines in the media have suggested that this is simply a case of the central banks "stepping up their attacks on cryptocurrencies arguing that bitcoin has 'few redeeming public interest attributes."[13] But given the litany of fraud, money laundering, Ponzi schemes and market manipulation, perhaps those involved in the cryptoasset market should focus on putting their own house in order, as some have sought to do. The requirement that the "same risks, same activity, same treatment" should apply to cryptoassets as well as other financial institutions, assets and markets is a reasonable requirement.

Regulation is not a matter of stifling innovation. If a stablecoin is to be used and trusted as an international currency, then it needs a regulatory framework in which the issuer has to operate. None of these requirements are unreasonable. Indeed these safeguards are exactly what people take for granted when transacting with their traditional banks or when investing in securities. These high-level requirements take time to be adopted by national jurisdictions, so they will come into force throughout 2021 and over the next three or four years.

CHAPTER 8

Central banks and central bank digital currencies

As the world of digital currencies continues to develop, so has the work of central banks and other institutions seeking a deeper understanding of the benefits and risks involved in digital currencies, particularly the use of DLT to provide a faster and more efficient means of payment that might benefit the public. A number of pilot test projects, or proof-of-concept projects, using a consortium of financial institutions under the auspices of the regulatory authority were instigated in 2016. One such project is Project Jasper launched back in 2016 by the Bank of Canada, the Toronto Stock Exchange and the R3 Group.

Project Jasper consisted of three phases: Phase I, from March to June 2016, was designed to investigate the use of central bank-issued receipts for deposited currency to support settlement on a DLT developed and built by the Project Jasper team. Phase II, from December 2016 to April 2017, was a private–public initiative to explore a wholesale payment system, using DLT, which found that a stand-alone payments system was not as useful as a centralized payments system in terms of core operating costs. Phase III was concerned with an integrated payments and securities infrastructure.[1] Project Jasper concluded that the proof-of-concept was too limited, since it did not apply to exchange-traded equities after novation and netting by the Canadian Depository for Securities. Instead, it created a loose integration of the large transfers system and the CDS for equities. Andrew McCormick, Vice President of Payments and Technology at Payments Canada, commented that "it is less about the technology ... it's more about the regulatory, the legal and the monetary issues".[2]

Project Ubin, set up by the Monetary Authority of Singapore (MAS), was a collaborative project in 2016 to explore the use of DLT for clearing and settlement of securities and payments. Its report concluded that the key technological issues had been resolved for clearing, settlements and payments processing for domestic payments and could become "more efficient, if only common standards and common platforms were in place". But a key challenge in achieving a common international platform for cross-border payments is the "question of governance and ownership". Central banks would be the natural choice but understandably "would not be comfortable with having their currencies – essentially their liability – freely issued and recorded by a third party outside their control".[3]

The European Central Bank along with the Bank of Japan embarked on Project Stella in 2016 and published its first report in 2018. Its purpose was to study the possible use of DLT for financial market infrastructures. The work was conducted at a conceptual level and practical experimentation with the technology but did not involve consideration of the legal issues. The first report in 2018 concluded that DLT offers a new approach for "delivery versus payment (DvP) even without connection between individual ledgers", but notes that depending on their specific design, cross-border DVP arrangements on DLT "may entail a certain complexity ... [and] requires several process steps and interactions between the seller and the buyer. This could give rise to additional risks".[4]

Project Stella's second report concludes that "only payment methods with an enforcement mechanism, either through the ledger itself or a third party, can ensure that the transacting parties who completely satisfy their responsibilities in the transaction process are not exposed to the risk of incurring a loss on the principal amount being transferred." The report adds that "further reflections on legal and compliance issues, the maturity of the technology and a cost benefit analysis would be required before a possible implementation of new methods could be considered".[5]

These are extremely important issues that raise serious questions about the use of DLT in clearing and settlement and the easy abandonment of transparency for the sake of speed and cost reductions. It is worth noting that the various proof-of-concept experiments conducted of clearing and settlement and payments systems are inevitably limited in scope compared with the size and efficiency of the current markets, often limited to domestic markets. In the United States, for example, the value of securities held by Fedwire Security Service is over $80 trillion, and with the New York Depository Trust Company holding about $50 trillion and Euroclear and Clearstream International SA each under $20 trillion. By value of deliveries, the most active central securities depository (CSD) and securities settlement system (SSS) is Euroclear Bank at over $600 trillion, an international service that facilitates the holding of securities across borders. In terms of deliveries relative to securities held, turnover is highest at Euroclear UK & Ireland, at about $60 trillion. Against that background should be set the figure of some $14–17 billion spent annually on trade servicing. This is the amount many in the industry hope would be saved by adopting DLT and eliminating intermediaries and central depositories.

But once again, costs and speed cannot be the overriding determinants. As the EU and the Bank of Japan have pointed out, legal and regulatory issues, which have not been part of the projects described here, are essential to the markets, if they are to function effectively and provide the protection that all market participants require. The emphasis on speed itself also involves risks, such as the fact that clients may not know their financing needs for a given day until trading has stopped. This is well illustrated in the White Paper issued by the US Deposit Trust and Clearing Corp (DTCC) in February 2021. The DTCC proposes to use DLT to speed up and integrate the clearing and settlement process to T+1 within two years, which would reduce industry costs but at the cost of the loss of the DTCC guarantee of payment. Investors would need complete confidence in their trading partner to make good on the transaction even though that entity would be anonymous to them. The DTCC expects to move to T+1, the shorter time in 2023 but with "market participant and regulator alignment".[6]

The projects, which have occupied the attention of central banks, regulatory authorities, markets and market participants and their service providers have not been concerned with "money" at all, but with the *delivery* of money in payment for securities and services. All of these pilot projects are focused almost entirely on the capital markets and the clearing and settlement of those markets and have materialized as a response to the excitement surrounding blockchain and have focused on one aspect of the challenge posed by cryptocurrencies, namely the speed of delivery of payments. For clearing and settlement, the attraction is not only speed, but also finality of payment. The problem is, as we have seen, that the changes in the experiments raise legal and regulatory issues that have not been resolved. Even the latest proposals put forward by the DTCC raise issues which have not yet been resolved but the DTCC has a further two years before its proposals are put into action, despite the years of work prior to the February announcement.

CRYPTOCURRENCIES AS MONEY

In the Chapter 1, we offered a simplistic view of money – one of notes and coins, debit and credit cards, since that is what springs to mind when we talk of "money". But the concept of money is, of course, much more complicated than that. Money must be invested in "some form of legality" otherwise a "money-like means of payment will not last very long".[7] That is to set out a necessary but not a sufficient condition of what purports to be a means of payment as money. It is helpful as a means of understanding "fiat" money, that is, state money. But there is more to it than that. To count as "money", as Professors Avgouleas and Blair have pointed out, cryptoassets or cryptocurrencies must serve as a means of exchange and payment at all times. They do not include a "debt promise", that is, they do not constitute a "legally enforceable debt".[8] Fiat money is established by order of law as "money" without any intrinsic value or any commodity backing, except that "the law orders that such banknotes and coins *have to* be accepted as satisfaction of debts and thus declares them as *legal tender* or compulsory tender".[9] Cryptocurrencies, on the other hand, do not constitute an acknowledgement of debt, nor do they incorporate any promise of payment. As instruments that "are not perceived to enjoy the protection of private and/or public law [they] will not be able to survive as durable means of exchange under conditions of stress".[10]

Avgouleas and Blair argue that these new forms of payment do actually fit into a common law context. They stress that although common law has not sought to define "money", on the basis of various historical court decisions, one is able to argue that "any one of the new instruments, whether a cryptocurrency or a stablecoin that is regularly used for a discharge of debt obligations and is accepted for the purchase of goods and services, could qualify as 'money' in common law." They quote with approval a point made by Joanna Perkins and Jennifer Enwezor that "virtual currencies which have achieved status as a medium of exchange within a significant user community have a good claim to be regarded as money".[11]

A problem, however, is how one uses the term "community". As an advertising technique it can be used to encourage a warm sense of "belonging" to purchasers of a company's goods and services. But a "community" is a social unit with a commonality such as norms, values, customs or identity. Communities may share a sense of place, geographically or virtually through common platforms, but if the "users" of a virtual currency such as Bitcoin do not know each other, still less communicate with each other, it is stretching the notion, especially given the mix of users with competing aims. Some will be libertarians, others criminals, and others just looking for the chance to become millionaires overnight. More importantly, however, Bitcoin fails the common law test as it does not provide a continuous use as a means of payment and a measure of value.

Avgouleas and Blair also argue that common law provides a more flexible analysis (not a definition) of the concept of money, which allows cryptoassets or currencies to count as money. They stress the importance of money as *property*, referencing a recent London Commercial Court decision, according to which cryptocurrencies are a form of property capable of being the subject of a proprietary injunction by "granting an injunction against both the unknown persons who had extracted a ransom in Bitcoin and the crypto exchange to which the Bitcoin had been tracked, the court sought to maximize the possibilities of recovery and preventing the coin being exchanged into fiat".[12] Despite the flexibility of the common law and the claim that money need not be legal tender to count as money, they stress the importance of the token retaining its function as a measure of value at all times.

Underlying the use of common law to explain the concept of money are the notions that the use of currency depends on a legal framework, and that a currency becomes money because the coins (or monetary instruments more widely) are struck with the insignia of sovereignty and the state is involved. Money is "ultimately bound up with the stable existence and fiscal functions of the government in any given area".[13] More than that, the value of money in a particular state is not arbitrarily assigned to any particular set of notes and coins or their e-money equivalents, but depends on the management of the economy as a whole not only for its value at any one time, but for its ability to act as a store of value. The whole framework of law, regulation, the extent to which the laws and regulations are upheld, such as the ability to ensure that contracts are upheld, that bills are settled and that the individual can retain his or her property rights, all of these elements turn a currency into money. A private system *could* become money, but to do so requires the kind of framework just outlined.

Before we examine CBDCs, it is worth setting out the role the central bank plays by providing money to the public through cash and to other financial companies through reserve and settlement accounts. A useful summary of the role of the central bank is provided by the report of the Bank for International Settlements (BIS) report:

> Money is fundamental to the functioning of market economies inasmuch as these are based on exchange and credit. In a market economy, any two economic agents are free to agree on the means of payment to be used to settle a transaction. Acceptance of any form of money will, however, depend on the receiver's confidence that, subsequently, a third party will accept that money in trade. Fiat money is worth nothing without the trust of the community behind it. Manifestation of this trust is exemplified by the use of banknotes being intrinsically useless pieces of paper (or increasingly polymer) that everyone accepts from a trader in exchange for valuable goods and services, banknotes testify to certain bonds of confidence that tie together the members of a society.
>
> Today, any widely used form of money is denominated in a given currency. By sharing a currency, the individuals have in common a measure of economic value, a means to store value and a set of instruments and procedures to store this value. However, since the value of money lies in trust, there can be no absolute guarantee that confidence in the currency can be preserved over time. It may be shaken by a monetary, economic or political crisis or by the malfunctioning of the payment system. As a result, maintaining trust in the currency, and facilitating its circulation, becomes a major public interest. The central bank is, in most countries, the institution designated to pursue this public interest.[14]

A majority of central banks are in the process of investigating CBDC and about half of these are engaged in pilot projects or have reported on the completion of those projects. Although the decision to offer a general CBDC is one for each country's government to decide, nevertheless, BIS argues that "domestic CBDCs would still have international implications. Cooperation and coordination are essential to prevent negative international spillovers and simultaneously ensure that much-needed improvements to cross-border payments are not overlooked" and that a CBDC is "different from balances in traditional reserve or settlement accounts".[15] The Bank of England, amongst others, have pointed out that CBDCs would only bring any benefits if households and businesses hold it and use it to make payments. For the Bank of England, this means that "they must switch some of their funds of banknotes and commercial bank deposits and into central bank money in the form of CBDC".[16] The Bank does recognize that this could have significant implications for the banking system, monetary policy and financial stability.[17]

Before turning to these issues, it is important to consider what benefits CBDC could bring. It is argued, in support of CBDC, that it will provide a secure, efficient system, while strengthening its resilience, and increasing availability of retail payments as well as opening up competition. CBDC could make the financial system safer by allowing individuals, private sector companies and non-bank financial institutions to settle directly with the central bank rather than deposits. It would reduce the concentration of liquidity and credit, and reduce the negative effects of the large banks, thereby ensuring financial stability. In emerging and developing countries such as in Latin America and the Caribbean, retail CBDC is regarded as a central bank policy designed to build an ecosystem that fills gaps in financial access. In its digital form it is regarded as simply a cash equivalent, which, if introduced on a wide basis, might support a more effective transmission of monetary policy, a significant issue to which we shall return.

The reason put forward for central bank electronic money acting to increase the stability of the financial system is that it would "discipline" commercial banks.[18] In order to attract deposits they would have to change their business model or increase interest rate payments for the additional risks they assume. If there is a loss of confidence, customers' money can be easily transferred to central bank money accounts. "To avoid this, banks must make their business models more secure by taking fewer risks or by holding more reserves and capital or pay higher interest rates." If this should lead to a run on the banks, then the central bank would have to provide the commercial banks with the necessary temporary liquidity by offering standing facilities where commercial banks can obtain central bank money against collateral very quickly.

Some also argue that only CBDC can provide the right to privacy in financial transactions: "This central bank digital currency could satisfy public policy goals, such as (i) financial inclusion (ii) security and consumer protection; and to provide what the private sector cannot: privacy in payments".[19] However, a working paper published by the Bank of Canada has argued that transaction privacy may no longer be available since the steadily growing shares of commercial payment platforms produce datasets with payment histories at the user level. These platforms can monetize user data in a variety of ways, such as sharing it with third parties who may combine it with data from other sources and use the data set for marketing or generating predictions about creditworthiness. Machine learning, increases in computational power and the scale and scope of data gathering are likely to increase the effectiveness and profitability of such methods. The report also argue that this could lead to price discrimination, presumably in access and costs of loans, although this is not specified.[20] In my view, this could indeed lead to price discrimination, since many individuals do not share the characteristics of the "group" to which they are assigned. The Covid-19 pandemic, for example, illustrated this very clearly, when "the elderly" (which could be anything from the over 60s to the over 80s) were routinely assumed to suffer from physical frailty and/or declining mental capacity. "Machine learning" will ultimately depend on the nature of the algorithms used to find patterns in massive amounts of data. The assumptions made in the algorithms will be crucial as well as the nature of the data under consideration. That is why the algorithms used should be open to public view as well as the anonymized data in which the patterns have been observed.

CENTRAL BANK MONEY AND COMMERCIAL BANK MONIES

Most people would be puzzled by the notion that there are two different kinds of money in circulation in their country and would wonder if it mattered which one they used. In fact, people use both in making payments as they have the same value and one is exchanged for the other without any loss to the person holding the money and making payments with it. An American dollar has the same value whether it is central bank money or commercial bank money, and that is true of pounds sterling and other currencies elsewhere. Central bank money, that is money *issued* by the central bank, has a key role in payment arrangements as it has proved safe and efficient to have a central reference of value with which all other forms of currency are convertible at par, that is, they have the same value. Commercial bank money, on the other hand, refers to *deposits* held at a commercial bank. The public uses various forms of money interchangeably so long as they are denominated in the same currency: one dollar is one dollar; one pound is one pound. Confidence in central bank money and therefore in commercial bank money depends on the ability of the central bank to maintain the value of the currency as a whole, which as noted above, is part of the central bank's role.

The Bank of England, the Bank of Canada and the Monetary Authority of Singapore published a Joint Report on Cross-Border Payments in November 2018. This is a comprehensive report, covering future state models for cross-border payments and settlements of which the variants involving banks include those using wholesale central bank digital currency.[21] The report concludes that the following concerns need to be addressed:

- the necessary cross-jurisdictional governance framework required to ensure harmonized standards – both in definition and in implementation.
- the impact on monetary policy and the degree to which central banks will continue to exercise control over it.
- legislative changes required to recognize CBDC as legal tender for interbank payments and settlements.
- eligibility criteria for financial institutions and payment systems participants to become direct participants in these models, including coordination between central banks to align eligibility criteria.
- industry adoption of the selected model via incentives and regulatory changes.[22]

Perhaps the key question here concerns how the public's access to central bank money will be arranged and what would be the implications. Currently access to central bank money is restricted to a relatively small group of financial institutions in most jurisdictions. The Bank of England currently only allows banks, building societies, broker-dealers supervised by the Prudential Regulatory Authority and central counterparties to hold central bank money in the form of reserves. In addition, some non-bank Payment Service Providers and other Financial Market Infrastructures hold settlement accounts at the Bank of England. Similarly, the Federal Reserve Bank is responsible for the provision of central bank money in the form of bank notes. As of 31 March 2020, about $1.8 trillion in Federal Reserve bank notes were in circulation with some estimates suggesting that about half of these were held outside the United States. Eligible financial institutions are able to deposit funds at the central bank. Currently these include "depository institutions", defined as commercial banks, savings banks, saving and loan associations, credit unions, US branches and agencies of foreign banks (depending on the size of their deposits), Edge Act corporations and agreement corporations. It is worth noting that during the Covid-19 crisis, these relationships have been suspended. On 26 March 2020, the Board of Governors of the Federal Reserve reduced the reserve requirements to zero, eliminating them for all depository institutions, in order to enable banks to continue lending during the pandemic. Similarly, capital requirements have been relaxed at the European Central Bank in order to incentivize banks to continue lending.

These are examples of the actions central banks can take to deal with unprecedented emergencies. It is hard to see how a decentralized system could handle such issues.

What would a central bank need to do to make a CBDC work and available to the public? The discussion paper published by the Bank of England in March 2020 is one of the most detailed discussions of CBDC and is a good place to start.[23] Once again, CBDC is said to have all the advantages of cash and bank deposits as long as it is directly convertible into both of these. It could also be a more convenient means of payment for both households and businesses, especially for electronic and remote payments. The discussion paper sets out the design principles: reliability, efficiency, speed and open to competition. It must also be available 24/7. These requirements should also be scalable, that is, able to handle increased volumes if the demand increases and compliant with regulations and AML/CFT – and private. The use of CBDC should require a minimum number of steps and a minimum level of technical literacy. CBDC should be open to competition and interoperable, that is, no closed loop systems in which users can only make payments through the same payments provider. It should be possible to make CBDC payments between users of different providers and between users of CBDC and users of deposit accounts. The private sector partners should also be able to add additional services on the CBDC platform.

How might a CBDC balance the need to protect the individual's privacy and data with compliance with AML/CFT regulations, which require knowing your customer, including the source of their finances? One way might be to set up the core platform so that it only stores pseudonymous accounts and balances but each account is linked to a Payment Interface Provider (PIP) which knows the identity of each user. They would be responsible for applying AML/CFT checks to users and for reporting suspicious transactions to the authorities. That seems to be a simple solution but in terms of the European Data Protection Directive (95/46 EC), although it is uncertain whether pseudonymous identifiers, which conceal users' identities but allow them to be recognized on any subsequent occasion are inherently "personal" data or not. The use of pseudonyms would have to be carefully defined in terms of both the legal requirements and the way in which the pseudonym and the real identity are linked.

Any CBDC system would have to be compatible with privacy regulations, such as the 2018 General Data Protection Regulation (GDPR), which would apply to the Bank of England, PIPs and any other firms providing CBDC-related services. But the discussion paper also states that the "appropriate degree of anonymity in a CBDC system is a political and social question, rather than a narrow technical question ... however, CBDC *could* [italics mine] be designed to protect privacy and give users control over who they share data with, even if CBDC payments are not truly anonymous (or secret)".[24] That is the key issue. It will inevitably be a matter of deep interest to a central bank to gather even more "big data" than is already available and perhaps without too much difficulty who is spending how much on what. Given that a central bank's concern is with financial stability and monetary policy then more information about retail consumers' behaviour is valuable and, of course, can lead to the temptation to seek to alter personal choices.

IMPACT ON MONETARY AND FINANCIAL STABILITY

Central bank money, whether cash or CBDC is a liability on the bank, is a liability on the bank's balance sheet, backed by "assets" held by the bank, government bonds, loans to the banking sector through schemes like the Term Funding Scheme, as well as the bank's routine liquidity facilities. Commercial bank deposits are issued by commercial banks and are an important part of their funding. A commercial bank's deposits are recorded as liabilities on its balance sheet and are backed by its assets, consisting of central bank reserves, bonds, loans such as mortgages and other financial assets.

The Bank of England (BoE) recognizes, as other central banks do, that such benefits as there are in the introduction of CBDC, will only happen if households adopt and use it. That will depend partly on the form it takes: an account or a token? The BoE's description of a household transferring money from a bank deposit account to CBDC involves the notion that the retail customers have a CBDC account, an account held by the central bank. How quickly that happens will depend, in part, on whether the central bank pays interest on the account or not and what competing interest rates the commercial banks can offer. If it appears that CBDC is taking too much away from deposits at commercial banks, then the central bank could fix this by limiting the amount of CBDC each individual or business could hold. This would make it clear that the central bank account is supposed to be used for payments, not for large savings. There are indeed endless practical problems about this solution, such as the unrecognised fact that so many households only have modest incomes and find that paying bills and other running expenses absorb almost all of their monthly income, leaving little to keep in a commercial bank deposit account. This hard limit could be replaced by a "soft" limit, that is, tiered interest rates, so that balances above a certain level pay a lower interest rate or no interest at all. The Bank of England has not yet published its reply to the responses to its consultation paper of March 2020. Its Financial Stability Report, December 2020 only states that "the FPC ... is considering the potential effects on financial stability, if stablecoins were to be adopted widely. A discussion paper on these issues will be published in due course by the Bank. That paper will also address issues that may arise in connection with the concept of a Central Bank Digital Currency – an electronic form of central bank money that could be used by households and businesses to make payments."[25]

According to the BoE discussion paper, an account-based system would record the state of the system as a list of accounts, each of which has a corresponding balance. To initiate a transfer of funds, the holder of the account is required to demonstrate their authority to do so, through a password or private key which only the account holder knows. Setting up an account in the first place requires, of course, a clear knowledge of the account holder, according to the "know your customer" requirements. Another way in which CBDC could be approached is through a token-based system, which records the state of the system as a list of individual assets or tokens each of which has an "owner" who controls the asset. The tokens themselves have a specific value which does not change. To initiate a transfer, the holder of the token has to prove that they own it, usually by signing a payment instruction with the private key linked to that token. Change cannot be given, so the token being transferred is generally "destroyed" and replaced with two smaller tokens adding up to the same amount, one of which goes to the recipient and the other goes to the sender as "change". This does sound more complicated than receiving change from a cash payment or paying the precise amount required with a debit or credit card. It is not clear whether individual denominations – pound coins, fifty pence coins– and so on will be produced as tokens. In the account-based system, the amounts credited or debited will go through the operator and in the token-based system, any change in ownership of tokens has to be recorded on the register to prevent double-spending. In neither case is complete anonymity possible.

One claim made is that CBDC would open up the way for negative interest rates. This is an odd claim, since a number of central banks, the European Central Bank, and the central banks of Denmark, Japan, Sweden and Switzerland have already introduced negative interest rates, which essentially makes banks pay to park their excess cash at the central bank, rather than receiving positive interest income. Negative interest rates are often introduced to encourage people, businesses and institutions to spend or lend money, when they are inclined to hoard money. The aim is to encourage banks to lend out the funds in their deposit accounts. This method was used to counter the weak growth that persisted after the 2008 global financial crisis.

The Bank of Japan adopted a negative rate in January 2016, as a way of fending off an unwelcome spike in the yen, which was hurting the Japanese export market. It charges 0.1 per cent interest on a portion of excess reserves financial institutions park with the BoJ. The Swiss National Bank introduced negative interest rates of −75 bp in mid-January 2015. Denmark was one of the first to introduce negative interest rates in September 2012. At that time, the krone was outperforming the euro and Denmark wanted to weaken its currency so that investors would not hoard. By September 2019, Denmark's Jyske Bank began charging wealthy individuals for deposits instead of paying interest, shortly after launching the world's first negative interest rate mortgage, in effect paying customers 0.5 per cent to borrow money for 10 years. The interest rate was set at 0.6 per cent for clients depositing more than 7.5 million kroner ($1.1 million). Danske Bank and other Danish banks followed suit. But by September 2020, Danske Bank, Denmark's largest bank increased its deposits during the first half of 2020 to 1.271 trillion kroner from 1.117 trillion kroner and the total net loans to 2.122 trillion from 2.027 trillion. During the pandemic, customers want to increase their liquidity. The same applies to other Danish banks.

In June 2014, The ECB was the first major central bank to lower one of its key interest rates – the deposit facility rate was lowered over the years to -0.5 per cent in September 2019. The idea then was to "trigger a repricing of the expected future path of short-term interest rates by 'breaking through' the zero lower bound and to encourage banks to provide more credit to the economy".[26] Banks are generally reluctant to pass on negative interest rates to their retail clients, the funding conditions for deposit takers typically decline in tandem with the decline in interest rates. Analysis of bank behaviour suggests that the negative interest rates do not affect banks' retail customers to any great extent, but it has affected the pass-through to corporate deposit rates, which intensifies over time, inducing firms to decrease their cash holdings through investments. But counterbalancing that is the ECB's targeted longer-term refinancing operations providing refinancing operations at highly favourable rates provided they extend sufficient credit to the real economy. Schnaber concludes that side effects, such as the possible encouragement of risk-taking behaviour on the part of banks may become more relevant over time. Clearly care has to be taken in the way in which negative interest rates are employed and other policies, such as the ECB's targeted longer-term refinancing operations, to get the economy going again.

Whether or not negative interest rates are an effective policy tool is not the point. The only relevant point here is that all of these central banks introduced negative interest rates and have operated them from 2012 onwards. The general concern with negative interest rates is that they would encourage savers to move money out of deposits into holding cash. It has been argued that the effective lower bound on interest rates of zero has prevented the real interest from falling to the equilibrium negative level required to deal with the persistent shortfall in aggregate demand. The problem is that depositors can withdraw interest bearing assets and hold cash thereby avoiding negative rates. These costs in terms of holding cash against security risks and the difficulty in making large payments have to be weighed against the cost or negative yield of holding cash generates the lower bound on negative interest rates. It is argued that replacing cash with a CBDC would remove the effective lower bound on interest rate policy.

That negative interest rates have been applied for a number of years suggests that the lower effective bound has not affected the ability to apply negative interest rates by a number of central banks and over a long period of time. In fact, to take one example, even charging wealthy depositors in Denmark does not appear to have led to a flight to cash. Or to put it another way, for those central banks which have not yet applied negative interest rates, it should be a relief to know that these can be applied without a switch to CBDC.

Let's return to the form CBDC should take: tokens or accounts? In an earlier report, the BIS had provided a taxonomy of money – the then more widely used Venn diagram called the "money flower" – based around four key properties: the issuer (central bank or other); form (digital or physical); accessibility (widely or distributed) and technology (account or token-based).[27] Money can be based on one of two basic kinds of technology: tokens of stored value or accounts. A key distinction between token-based and account-based money is the form of verification required when it is exchanged. Token-based money, it is argued, depends on the ability of the payee to verify the validity of the payment object. In the case of cash, the concern is counterfeiting, although it should be noted that changes in design and technology undertaken in many countries, have reduced the possibility of counterfeiting, such as in the UK the replacement of the old pound coin with a new 12-sided coin in 2017 and the introduction of polymer-based notes. With the digital token, the concern is whether the "token" is genuine or not and whether it has already been spent. That is of course the issue which Nakamoto sought to resolve with the "miners" and the immutable entries on blockchain.

Those countries with the more advanced projects for providing retail access to the central bank money have settled for an account-based approach, although in the case of Sweden, this might include some element of token-based access with tiered accounts. However, the central banks first survey of CBDC in October 2020 found that a token-based model with the currency stored in a digital wallet, to be more popular among its respondents. In the view of one of the respondents, they wanted the CBDC to resemble cash rather than a bank deposit. Despite that support, the major central banks are focused on account based CBDC.

The Bank of England's own discussion paper sets out a model in which CBDC would serve as a payments platform on which the private sector could innovate. The BoE would provide the core ledger, which would record CBDC and process payments and private sector PIPs would handle the interaction with end-users of CBDC and provide additional payments functionality through additional services. The illustrative model of CBDC as a public-private payments platform reflects similar approaches taken elsewhere.[28] The core ledger or database records the CBDC itself and processes the transactions made using CBDC. It could provide payments initiated by the third party, PIPs to securely send payment instructions and ask for updates from the ledger. The PIPs would be regulated and would have the responsibility of applying KYC protocols and then registering one or more accounts in the core ledger. These would be pseudonymous on the ledger but the PIP would record the identity of the user on its own system and would know which pseudonymous account(s) the user holds at the Bank. However, although the Bank of England was expected to publish its response to the consultation in February 2020, at the time of writing, that has not happened.

Any CBDC system would have to be compatible with privacy regulations, such as the 2018 General Data Protection Regulation (GDPR), which would apply to PIPs and any other firms providing CBDC-related services. This means that users should have control over how their data is used and with whom it is shared. But, as already mentioned, "the appropriate degree of anonymity in a CBDC is a political and social question".[29] That is exactly the point. Privacy becomes a key issue, especially when one of the benefits is that CBDCs can bring more economic activity into the effective tax base, limiting tax evasion, boosting tax revenues and reducing the use of CBDC for illicit purposes. These are all proper and understandable aims for governments to have, but at what price?

The BoE's discussion paper and other proof-of-concept projects refer to this issue but generally spend little time on explaining how privacy can be maintained in terms of the technological options for the design they have set out. Before any decision to introduce CBDC is taken, the various technological possibilities for both disclosure and anonymity should be examined and set out in full before the political and social decision to issue CBDC is taken. Andrew Bailey's speech at the Brookings seminar in September 2020, emphasizes this issue:

> Privacy and data protection issues are also a key question. Digital currencies, depending on their design, could provide considerable information on how people spend their money, and we cannot compromise on the protection of our privacy ... Digital payments could entail greater data on users' identities and transactions being centrally visible. The data generated could have huge opportunities for the detection and prevention of financial crime, but this must be balanced with the risk of surveillance into private financial matters.[30]

Hopefully, the Governor's caution will be reflected in the work of the CBDC Task Force to coordinate the exploration of a potential UK CBDC, "which would exist alongside cash and bank deposits, rather than replacing them," announced on 21 April 2021. Amongst its other objectives, the Task Force will "support a rigorous, coherence and comprehensive assessment of the overall case for CBDC".[31]

PRIVACY AND TECHNOLOGY

Preserving privacy for CBDC transactions whilst also conforming to AML/CFT requirements is not an easy task, given its conflict in aims. Hence it is important to understand the various technical tools which could provide payments privacy and to be able to evaluate them. The system the BoE proposes, as do others, consists of holdings and transactions, where the holder has an owner, a balance, a transaction has a payer, a payee, and an amount, but with an intermediary, a PIP, and possibly other government institutions. Fulfilling the obligations of transparency, enabling validators to ascertain the correctness of transactions and their compliance with financial regulations with the ability to keep transactions private with regard to the sender, the recipient and the amount.

It would be possible for the central bank to hold all accounts and require users to place their trust in the central bank to protect clients from each other. But as the Brookings Institution report points out, "a single bulk data breach of just one replica of a permissioned ledger or an associated sensitive data base can expose the identities and financial histories at once, as the Equifax breach affecting nearly half the US adult population amply demonstrated".[32] This, however, is to miss the point. It is privacy in relation to the central bank (as well as other players) which is the chief matter for concern. Most people would prefer not to have the central bank or any other government agency have access to all their personal expenditure. That opens up the way for governments to intrude into their personal spending or even, in the worst case, seek to control it.

The Brookings report, drawing from technical developments, examines the issues of privacy and transparency with blockchains and cryptoassets, bearing in mind that a middle ground between full transparency and privacy has to be found. This ranges from pseudonymity, which is open to attack through an IP address, or proxy services to smart contracts. The authors of the report note that "there are no cryptocurrencies or privacy features today that make it impossible for attackers to learn information about the identity of senders and recipients in the network".[33] The report considers identity management delegated to several, perhaps more, commercial PIPs, what they refer to as "trust dispersal". Here it is possible that threshold signing, one of the applications of threshold cryptography, could help to reconcile the necessity for user identity privacy and the need for law enforcement to be able to investigate. Even where projects and technologies use blockchain to secure sensitive private data, it is the security of the device (mobile device, a cloud service, or a hardware security module), which may be compromised. That can easily lead to the leak of private data to others without it ever being recorded on the blockchain.[34]

The BoE proposed delegation of account and identity management to a PIP makes it possible to give users a limited form of accountable anonymity for identity privacy. The central bank treats all account holders as pseudonymous public keys. Only the PIPs have the responsibility for verifying and recording the association identity information, then individuals are pseudonymous with respect to the central bank and the ledger transactions it processes. As with the banks and existing payment providers, PIPs have a duty to protect this information. The identity can, however, be disclosed to the central bank or other regulatory authorities for fraud and AML/CFT reasons. Both the central bank and the PIPs are responsible for the protection of privacy of their clients, a shared responsibility. However, building a system, which the central bank would have to provide, that provides fully operational secure systems, allowing for both the privacy of the account and access to it when there is suspicious activity, is "challenging" to say the least. The development of such a system would have to fulfil the obligations laid on banks and other financial institutions to provide the highest levels of cyber security for their customers and data protection. The central bank might be subject to the same financial labilities for any malfunction of the system underlying the digital currency that could cause loss and damage to individual users.

The ECB's approach to the introduction of a digital euro alongside cash is to offer a range of designs, since it is "too early" to commit to a specific design, whilst at the same time, ensuring that it meets with a number of principles and requirements, including accessibility, robustness, safety, efficiency and privacy and complies with the relevant legislation. Theirs is a matter of being ready to introduce a digital euro should the need arise, rather than a commitment to introducing it. The ECB's initial report in October 2020 raises the following issues, such as whether a digital euro should be accessible by households and firms directly or indirectly through intermediaries, whether it should be remunerated or unremunerated and whether digital euro holdings should be limited or unlimited. The ECB argues that it might mitigate the effects on financial stability and the transmission of monetary policy by remunerating digital euro holdings at a variable rate over time, perhaps by using a tiered system or by limiting the amount of digital euros that users can hold or transact.[35]

It is hard to see, in practical terms how the latter limit would be applied. Is it an arbitrary limit for all users or related to the income the individual has, say per annum? What if there is a temporary inflow of cash into the digital account, say from the sale of a property whilst the individual is deciding whether or what to purchase next? The ECB states that to ensure that a user can always receive a payment in digital euro and no information is disclosed on current individual holdings, a "waterfall" approach would be activated whereby any incoming digital euros in excess of the holding limit would be automatically transferred to the payee's account in private money. This, of course, requires all payees to have a bank account.[36] Many individual households have insufficient monthly income to run both a digital and a cash bank account, so care would have to be taken over setting the limit. If it is too low, it would mean that low-to medium income households might not have access to a digital euro account, as their income may be too low to have two accounts, so they may settle for the digital account, but if they exceeded that limit, say, by €50 in one or two months, they would not have a bank account as well. Such incomes may fluctuate, perhaps due to overtime or a bonus. A low limit could mean the excess is only available in a bank account. Even free bank accounts may not help with this problem.

The requirement in the report is that the ECB should be able to control the amount of digital euros in circulation at any one time. The alternative is to control the demand for a digital euro through incentive schemes under which less attractive interest rates or service fees are applied when individual holdings are above an agreed threshold. But then incentive schemes based on tiered and variable remuneration of holdings would have to be in force, which would make offline payments more difficult.

Then there is another problem. In the current situation, it does not seem possible to "offer unlimited holdings of digital euro to corporate entities at zero interest rates. In line with the current monetary stance of the ECB, the nominal remuneration rate of risk-free euro investments achievable by corporate entities and domestic and international investors is currently below 0.5%. Unconstrained access of these entities to a digital euro could not be offered currently at more attractive rates without disrupting financial flows and the monetary policy stance."[37] This is why the ECB sees tiered interest rates as necessary to be able to provide digital euros on the same basis as bank notes (i.e. interest rates not below zero), granting others access to digital euros without quantity constraints and without limiting access to digital euros to EU citizens. This problem will not exist when nominal interest rates rise.

The interest remuneration of digital currency could be fixed or variable. If fixed, it would be zero, if variable, it could be linked to other central bank rates, or independent of them. It could also be tiered, allowing the Eurosystem to pay less attractive rates on large holdings of digital euros or on holdings by foreign investors to discourage the excessive use of the digital euro as an investment. Nothing has been decided, but the report plainly highlights all the issues to be taken into account in designing a digital euro, many of which are extremely difficult to resolve.

The Report assumes an account based digital euro open to use by retail customers and businesses. Users could access the digital euro either directly or indirectly through supervised intermediaries, which is the preferred route for the ECB. That leaves the intermediaries providing the end-user customer support, and identification of the customer. The regulations which currently apply to electronic payments must also apply to digital euros as well. However, the ECB's report adds that "anonymity may have to be ruled out, not only because of the legal obligations relating to money laundering and terrorist financing, but also to limit the scope of the users of digital currency when necessary – for example, to exclude some non-euro area users and to prevent excessive capital flows or to avoid excessive use of the digital euro as a form of investment".[38] The Report does suggest that the approach to privacy could be selective, such as strengthening trust in the privacy model of the underlying digital euro system could be reinforced through auditing by third parties. That is an interesting proposition but it is unclear what could actually be audited. Then digital euro transactions could be fully transparent to the operator of the infrastructure, who would guarantee the data protection as already required. It is interesting that, given the alternatives for the use of the digital euro, little has been said about the problems with the use of digital wallets or cryptographic signatures.

The Report makes it clear that the Eurosystem will "solicit the views of other public authorities, financial institutions, and society at large to assess the need, feasibility and actual business cases for a digital euro, without pre-empting a decision on issuance". It would indeed be a challenging and complex issue to present for public discussion, in which a range of issues need to be presented, including the issue of privacy, access to really "big data" as well as the point of its introduction.

The Bank for International Settlements published its report in October 2020, based on collaboration with a group of central banks,[39] and set out three basic principles for CBDCs:

- Do no harm. Any new form of money should not conflict with a central bank's ability to carry out its mandate for monetary and financial stability.

CBDC should maintain and reinforce the uniformity of a currency, so that the public can use the different forms of money interchangeably.

- Coexistence. These different forms of money, CBDC, cash, reserve and settlement accounts should complement each other and coexist with robust private money, for example, commercial bank accounts and central banks should continue to supply cash as long as there is sufficient public demand for it.
- Innovation and efficiency. Speed and efficiency of the payments system is key, otherwise the fear is that consumers may turn to other less safe payment methods or "currencies". However, there is a role for the public and private sectors in the supply of payment services to create a safe, efficient and accessible system, leaving private agents to choose which means of payment they will use to conduct financial transactions.

The BIS also sets out 14 core features, most of which we have already discussed, such as convenience, ease of use, scalable, resilience to operational failures, disruptions and cyber-attacks. To date, the problem is that the CBDC pilot projects have been limited in scope and have not been tested at anything like the scale needed, including involving the public, to test ease of use and acceptability. Some of the questions arise from the design of the ledger. For example, is it possible to select a centralized or a decentralized ledger? A centralized ledger might only record the total CBDC issued with individual balances stored on a smartphone or card, with an intermediary to manage and transfer liabilities, making anti-fraud and security features easier to incorporate. The ECB however, takes the role of a centralized ledger much further than that. A decentralized ledger could have the potential to make peer-to-peer and offline payments easier. But peer-to-peer requires "honest" nodes to be used, which again raises the problem of identifying honest nodes prior to transactions. Payment authentication designs, for example, identity-based, token-based or multifactor, will determine how it will integrate with others for "know your customer" or transaction monitoring requirements in addition to the level of privacy allowed to users of the system. All of these issues would have to be addressed in a new rule book setting out the roles and responsibilities of the operators, participants and possibly other service providers and stakeholders. But it is the role of the central bank which will be crucial. What powers would the central bank have to change elements of the system?

How would data-sharing and privacy be structured and any interoperability arrangements be organized? These are obviously important questions.

But there are more fundamental issues that are only touched on in much of the research, pilot projects and reports, such as those of the ECB and the BIS that we have discussed: the potential to give central banks the power to apply monetary policy more effectively and immediately. CBDC can be set up in such a way that central banks have access to the patterns of expenditure for retail customers and even details of their personal accounts. These are the vital issues we shall explore in Chapter 10, once we have considered other important drivers of the introduction to CBDC.

CHAPTER 9

The decline of cash

This review of the decade or more of cryptocurrencies has demonstrated that the dramatic "revolution" promised with the emergence of Bitcoin has not occurred, nor is it likely to occur. Bitcoin continues to exist as a rather dubious investment for the foolhardy, a useful means of conveying value, mainly for nefarious actors. In spite of the limitations of Bitcoin, its emergence and along with the whole panoply of stablecoins, continues to reverberate with central banks, particularly in the provision of cross-border payments, which remain slow, expensive and opaque. This is said to be especially burdensome for the 1.7 billion people globally without a bank account or with very limited financial services. It was at first assumed that cryptoassets and the technological innovations they embodied would overcome the problems. But as we have seen the original cryptoassets were too volatile for these purposes. Stablecoins were introduced to provide "stability" by linking the price of the "coin" to a specific currency or to a basket of assets. But, if stablecoins could ever fulfil the role of a reliable means of exchange, especially for cross-border payments, then a series of significant risks would have to be overcome. Generally, stablecoins have been unable to handle the risks involved, or have been unwilling to do so. The "wild west" era of initial coin offerings did not help. Nor, on the other hand, did Libra, but from an entirely different angle. Indeed, some see Facebook's formal introduction of Libra to the world on 18 June 2019 as a key moment, marking a threat to central banks monetary authority and their role as providers of fiat currency and prompting their interest in central bank digital currencies.

The response to Libra was indeed a "tipping point", and the reasons for the reaction to Libra will be explored more fully in the following chapter. The focus of this chapter will be on the role of cash (notes and coins). Many central banks are concerned about cash: either the costs of its production and distribution in some locations or the decline in its use. If the use of cash is in decline, then the case for introducing CBDC is stronger than it might otherwise be. But the decline in the use of cash is less straightforward than it might otherwise appear.

It is difficult to determine the extent to which the use of cash is declining. The BIS's Committee on Payments and Market Infrastructure (CPMI) publishes the Red Book, providing an overview of all the transactions through payment, clearing and settlement systems. This includes the value of cash in circulation, the number and value of card payments, point-of-sale terminals and ATMs. Its analysis of the 2018 data, published in 2019, shows that payment systems continue to innovate and develop fuelled by changes in consumer preferences, new systems, and new players. Systems offering near instant person-to-person retail payments are in operation in 45 jurisdictions across the world but that is likely to rise to 60 very soon. The value of card payments relative to GDP is increasing in most countries, whilst the value of small denomination notes and coins is either remaining constant or declining in most places. It is still interesting to note the variation between one country and another, which of course does not emerge in average figures; for example, the value of card payments (relative to GDP) for CPMI members is only 10 per cent in Germany, Japan and Mexico but is over 40 per cent in Korea, Saudi Arabia and the UK. The picture in the United States seems to follow the general trend, according to the latest triennial Federal Reserve Payments Study, as well as the US survey of consumer payments. The Federal Reserve Payments study found that the value and use of all kinds of non-cash payments (credit cards, prepaid and non-prepaid debit cards, the automated clearing house system, ACH, and cheques) increased by 6.7 per cent, compared with 5.1 per cent from 2012–15 as they have "retained their ability to be used in traditional ways even as they are adapted for use in innovative, non-traditional ways ... as many of alternative payment methods and services, such as smart-phone or internet services, ultimately involve payments processed through the general-purpose card networks or the ACH system".[1] But that does not mean that cash has disappeared, although its use is declining: down to 26 per cent of transactions in

2018 from 30 per cent in 2017. Indeed, it continues to be used for 49 per cent of all transactions under $10 and contrary to expectations, the share of cash use by individuals is highest among the under 25s and then by the over 65s.[2]

Customers want convenience. The availability of contactless cards per person has increased rapidly in both advanced and emerging market economies such as France, Switzerland, the Netherlands, Russia and even in Indonesia and Turkey, though to a lesser extent. In addition, the use of credit or debit cards when travelling internationally continues to increase, although not as much as it could have owing to expensive credit card fees for the merchant and currency conversion fees for the user. Cross border card payments have grown twice as quickly as domestic payments since 2012. These increases in usage have arisen partly because the point-of-sales terminals have been replaced by mobile terminals or lower cost smart phone or tablet-based terminals have emerged.

But despite all these developments, the demand for cash in circulation is often used as a proxy for cash demand. On that basis, the demand for cash is up from 7 per cent to 9 per cent on average amongst the CPMI members and in a number of countries that report cash in circulation to the IMF. This is the case in a wide range of countries, including Denmark, Norway, Uruguay, Israel, Indonesia, Malaysia and Nigeria. According to Bech, the increase in cash in circulation was largely due to an increase in economic activity in advanced economies following the financial crisis, with the largest increases in Hong Kong and Japan. The demand for cash varies from one country to another, even where the countries have similar economies and social characteristics. In about 2000, Iceland's cash-to-GDP ratio was 1.2 per cent but for Denmark, Sweden and Norway, the ratio remained at about 3–4 per cent. Since then, the demand for cash has remained about the same in Denmark, but not for Sweden and Norway, where the decline has continued. Unsurprisingly, Iceland's cash demand overall has more than doubled given the near collapse of its banking system in 2008.

There are wide variations even within the eurozone. In Germany, for example, the ratio of cash in circulation to GDP has remained fairly constant over the past ten years at about 8 per cent, but it rose to 9 per cent in 2018 and 9.4 per cent in 2020. Cash is still highly relevant, accounting for 74 per cent of all retail payments in Germany, but mostly in small amounts. Card use is growing but is behind other member states. Despite Germany's traditional devotion to cash, there has been a steady decline of 1–2 per cent of cash usage across all age groups, leading to an increased usage of card and digital payments.[3] "Cash is king" has long been the mantra for German consumers and small business owners. Card payments are primarily debit cards. The majority of German credit cards do not accrue long-term debt but deduct the balance in full from the user's bank account the following month. In 2017, the Bundesbank noted a slow but steady change in payments, but still that 88 per cent of people surveyed wanted to continue paying in cash in the future. It is not just a matter of culture: a study carried out by the Bundesbank together with the EHI Retail Institute found that "cash is still the quickest and most cost effective form of payment at the point of sale". German retailers settle approximately €20 billion per year with three out of four payments at the point of sale being settled in cash. It also ranked first in terms of the share of turnover, accounting for 51 per cent of the €410 billion total retail turnover in 2018.

It was not until 2018 that card payments in Germany edged ahead of cash payments for the first time (48.6 per cent for card payments and 48.3 per cent for cash). The monthly Bundesbank Report noted that debit card payments (Girocards issued by banks and payment institutions) rose by 20 per cent in 2019 on 2018 figures. The strong growth seen in previous years continued with the use of debit cards climbing more substantially than all cashless payment instruments. Credit card payments rose by 14 per cent and credit transfers and direct debits by 3 per cent. The Bundesbank notes that the coronavirus pandemic "heralded a rise in the number of contactless payments" so continued strong growth in debit card use is expected in 2020.[4] Since the onset of the pandemic, Germans have turned away from cash and contactless cards have become more popular, especially with the limit raised to €50. Georg Hauer, General Manager of Switzerland, Germany and Austria, at N 26 a start-up digital bank, "Covid-19 has probably changed German payment behaviour faster than any technology ever has".[5] On that basis, Germany is less likely to return to the predominant use of cash after the pandemic, but that remains to be seen.

There is evidence that the pandemic has actually increased the cash in circulation in some countries, with a surge in demand for cash and bank deposits. Goodhart and Ashworth examined "a reasonable amount of data available" in May 2020[6] and noted that this trend was especially notable in the US, Canada, Italy, Spain, Germany, France, Australia, Brazil, Mexico, India and Russia. In the US, cash in circulation increased 0.9 per cent in the week to the 23 March, the third largest increase on record after the surges in late December 1999 and January 2000 prompted by YK2 bug fears. Canadian weekly currency in circulation has accelerated from around 3 per cent towards the end of February 2020 to about 12 per cent. Goodhart and Ashworth conclude that so far, "economic shutdowns in most countries and increased use of online retailing have clearly diminished, at least temporarily, one of cash's main traditional functions, namely, as a medium of exchange".[7] But that the surge in cash in circulation in a number of countries affected by Covid-19 "likely affects the use of cash for one of its other traditional functions – panic driven hoarding".[8] Only time will tell what the effect of Covid-19 will be or how permanent an effect.

LARGE VALUE NOTES

Bech and others have shown that the issuance of large value notes has increased over the past decade, since the global financial crisis. What constitutes "large" notes varies from one country to another: for example, the most valuable notes issued by CPMI members are Switzerland's CHF 1,000 note (about US$1,060) and the Singaporean 1,000 dollar note (about US$760) and the relative share of large notes in the total cash in circulation also varies widely among CPMI member countries. In Mexico and Sweden large denomination notes are less than 10 per cent of the outstanding stock whereas in Hong Kong, Japan and Saudi Arabia, these notes are more than 75 per cent of the total. Bech's analysis of the CPMI membership suggests that the demand for cash increases when the opportunity cost decreases. He concludes that the impact of opportunity cost is statistically significant for total demand, and for large value notes, but not for small ones. The major variables are the monetary policy rate and macroeconomic uncertainty.[9] Large value notes could also be used as a store of value as a result of concerns about the safety of bank deposits in the immediate aftermath of the financial crisis. Macroeconomic concerns may also lead to the hoarding of cash, especially when interest rates move into negative territory, so that account holders are effectively paying the bank to deposit cash, and accompanied by low inflation. Then, keeping large amounts of cash in the house becomes a more attractive proposition.

There are different patterns of the use of cash as well as cash hoarding between advanced and emerging countries. This is shown by an examination of the cash demand in 22 economies, classified as advanced or emerging economies, where a decline in the use of cash may mean that access to the banking system has improved. The economies with a rising trend include the eurozone, Japan, Korea, Singapore, the UK and the US; economies with a broadly stable trend include Australia and Canada.

Research by Shirai has looked at the use of high value notes in emerging economies and identifies three groups: those with a rising ratio of high value notes include Mexico, the Philippines, Poland, Thailand and Turkey, where the rising trend started in the early 2000s. Those economies with a stable ratio include Brazil, Indonesia, Malaysia and Russia as well as India (apart from in 2016). And China was the only economy with a secular declining trend since the early 2000s. Professor Shirai concludes, along with her colleagues, that the high value notes are used for cash hoarding mainly in times of stress. In the case of Japan, demand for the ¥10,000 note, especially since 2013, increased at the same time as the Bank of Japan increased quantitative easing. Her empirical research found that the two most significant factors in the demand for cash was the central bank policy rate and the proportion of elderly people in the population, because they have the habit of using cash. However, income level is likely to be as significant as age in the use of cash or credit and debit cards. Retired people over 65 may not have access to a bank account and can only use cash or run on very tight margins because their income is low. Without a bank account, they may not have access to credit and debit cards, and may fear that they will end up with more debt than they can manage.[10] Others with medium to high levels of income use their credit and debit cards most of the time. As with many other age groups, credit cards are safer, since in the event of theft or fraudulent use, the use of the credit card can quickly be stopped and refunds can be made.

The continuing demand for large denomination bills in some countries would no doubt concern Kenneth Rogoff, whose book, *The Curse of Cash: How Large-Denomination Bills Aid Crime and Tax Evasion* has been much discussed, but the decision by the European Central Bank to stop issuing €500 banknotes from 17 January 2019 would no doubt have been welcomed. Their concerns over the high denomination note facilitating illicit activities was mitigated by their introduction at the same time, of the €100 and €200 banknotes. Their statement added that "in view of the international role of the euro and the widespread trust in its banknotes, the €500 will remain legal tender and can therefore be used as a means of payment and a store of value. The Eurosystem ... will take steps to ensure that the remaining denominations are available in sufficient quantities".[11] The highest value of notes currently in production in the US is the $100 bill.[12] In developed countries Rogoff would phase out all large denomination notes. In the US, he would phase out over a decade or more, first the $100 bills and $50 bills, followed by $20 and then perhaps $10 bills. For small transactions, he recommends leaving smaller notes in circulation, although he even considers replacing these with "equivalent-denomination coins of substantial weight". That is, of course, very much an American view of the world. Other developed countries already have higher denomination coins. The UK introduced pound coins in 1983 and two-pound coins in 1998. One and two-euro coins are part of the whole system of euro cash. Neither set of coins are particularly convenient to carry around in any quantity.[13]

A less successful ban on large value notes took place in India in 2016, when the Reserve Bank of India declared that all INR 500 and 1000 bank notes would no longer be valid. Together the two notes amounted to 86 per cent of the total value of currency in circulation in India at the time, worth about US$320 billion. The measure did nothing to bring in the cash hidden by tax evaders. In addition, the government claimed the plan would help to counteract corruption and counterfeiting. The attempt was a major economic shock. Two years later, the black money problem has not disappeared, large financial losses were incurred, and the poor, who were least able to withstand such shocks, suffered. Almost all the demonetized notes (99.3 per cent) were in fact returned to the Reserve Bank of India. The Indian press reported that the wealthy sold the currency at a discount to money-laundering intermediaries, who then deposited the money in banks through the accounts of low-income Indians. The government immediately introduced a Rs 2000 note, which seems to defeat the whole purpose of the exercise. The economic effects were disastrous for an overwhelmingly cash economy.

It does not seem that the inconvenience of coins has played a part in the reduction of the use of cash, but rather the growing use of credit and debit cards. The Bank of England reports notes to the value of £70 billion in circulation, now being printed on polymer, not paper. Although payments by debit cards overtook cash as the most frequently used payment method, many people continue to use cash in their daily lives. As we have seen, the decline of cash in the eurozone varies from country to country.[14]

Others have pointed out that Rogoff's figures do not accord with other estimates. As at the end of 2015, Rogoff concludes that, not counting US currency held in bank vaults, a large amount remains in circulation, amounting to $4,200 in cash per person with 80 per cent of that cash being held in $100 bills. Rogoff estimates that about 45–60 per cent of that cash is held abroad. But his figures are quite different from those estimated by the Federal Reserve and others. The diary surveys conducted by Federal Reserve banks suggest that only one in 20 adult consumers hold $100 bills. Ruth Judson, an economist at the Federal Board of Governors, estimates that at the end of 2016, US currency in circulation totalled $1.5 trillion of which nearly $1.2 trillion (almost 80 per cent) was in the form of $100 bills. She notes the "strong correlation between international demand for U.S. dollars and indexes of economic and political uncertainty between 2000 and 2014".[15] She continues, "We think that the significance of the demand is unique to the US dollar … overseas demand for the US dollars is likely driven by its status as a safe asset. Cash demand from other countries, increases in times of political and financial crisis".[16] Judson estimates that as much as 70 per cent of US dollars are held abroad and as much as 60 per cent of $100 bills are held by foreigners.

Rogoff gives a number of reasons for wishing to eliminate cash. He claims that the $100 bills are mainly used by those involved in criminal activities, such as drug dealing, bribery and corruption and human trafficking. Eliminating cash would curb these activities, but would only have a trivial effect on terrorism and counterfeiting, partly because these are minor concerns to begin with. But the large denomination notes are not the only means that drug dealers and others engaged in criminal activities, have to hide their ill-gotten gains. In part this depends on the level of activity. Drug dealers selling drugs on the streets to their clients use the cash for rent, food and clothing, on daily living in fact. It is only the wealthy criminals who would need to use $100 bills. But the aim is to launder the money by, for example, purchasing property or cryptoassets. Large bills are probably the very kind of bills those engaged in criminal activities wish to avoid as these would attract unwelcome attention. It is much better to deposit small bills in a number of bank accounts through the process known as "layering" and then using that bank account to invest in companies or equity or purchasing property or transferring it to a safe haven. It is odd to view large bills as the key means of hiding the profits from criminal activities, since cryptoassets continue to provide a useful means of laundering money, as they have done almost from the birth of Bitcoin.

Why do people still want cash? Cash is often used for small value payments, as it is easier, cheaper and universally available. Those with access to both credit and debit cards may still use cash for small items and for other exchanges, such as gifts for children or tipping. For those on low incomes, the costs of opening and maintaining a bank account can be too high in some countries, such as the United States. Many are also excluded from debit and credit cards as a means of payment, or access to cash through ATMs or cash back at stores. Assessing the amount of cash in circulation is therefore achieved through disentangling large and small value notes. The former is taken to be a store of value and the latter as a means of payment. It is worth noting that what constitutes "large" notes varies greatly from one country to another.

Before concluding our discussion of cash, it is worth noting the case of Sweden. In Sweden, the value of cash in circulation decreased by 45 per cent between 2007 and 2018, but the amount of banknotes and coins in circulation rose by 7 per cent to 62.2 billion krona ($6.5 billion) in 2018. The ratio of currency in circulation to GDP in Sweden fell from 2.9 per cent in 2010 to 1.3 per cent in 2017 and remained at that level until 2019.[17] The decline of cash in Sweden has been assisted by a range of public and private policies. Since the 1960s, Sweden has encouraged the use digital bank transfers, charged for cheques and invested heavily in card payment systems. Swedish banks worked together to produce one single automated clearing house, Bankgirot, and launched a popular mobile payments app, Swish. As the amount of cash in circulation declined, in 2017, the Riksbank announced the commencement of a project to examine the scope for the bank to issue a central bank digital currency, e-krona. In the first report on the project, the Riksbank argued that the failure to act on the bank's part would leave the general public entirely dependent on private payment solutions, which may make it more difficult for the Riksbank to promote a safe and efficient payments system. The concern is based not only on the decline of the amount of cash in circulation (until that was halted in 2017), but the decline in the use of cash, which according to the Riksbank surveys, was down from 39 per cent in 2010 to 13 per cent in 2017. The fear is that as more consumers turn to electronic payments, it will no longer be profitable for retailers to accept cash. It is easy for customers to turn to cards as even children from the age of 12 upwards have a charge card which they can use for spending on small items, drawn from their parents' bank accounts. Notes and coins are still the only legal tender in Sweden, yet shops and restaurants are allowed to refuse to accept cash and insist on cards or Swish payments. They can only do so by clearly stating at the entrance to the shop or restaurant that cash is not acceptable.

The survey published by BIS in January 2020 showed that central banks are undertaking extensive work on central bank digital currencies. Their survey showed that most central banks are working out the implications for their jurisdictions and that a significant minority are likely to issue a CBDC very soon. Some emerging markets report stronger motivations and a higher likelihood of introducing CBDCs. Domestic payments efficiency, payments security, and financial inclusion were all given as reasons by emerging market economies for considering the introduction of a general purpose CBDC. For advanced economies, as for central banks generally, motivations are more to do with reducing costs, improving KYC/CFT arrangements, and most importantly, increasing efficiency in cross-border payments.

What counts as legal tender has also to be taken into account. Central banks of course need to be given the authority to introduce new forms of legal tender by their governments. The BIS survey indicates that about a quarter of central banks have or will soon have the authority to do so with a third not yet having the authority.[18] The survey also investigated the likelihood of central banks issuing a CBDC, whether general purpose or wholesale in the short-term (three years) or the medium term (up to six years). About 70 per cent of the respondents said that they are unlikely to issue any kind of CBDC in the foreseeable future, with 10 per cent in the short term and 20 per cent in the medium term.[19]

Research published in the BIS quarterly journal suggests that most central banks are considering a range of CBDC architectures. Only one central bank is considering conventional technology, but five central banks are looking at DLT. Of those looking at the issue of currency, there is an even split between those looking at access based on digital tokens and those looking at access through accounts.

Some central banks have already rejected CBDC. Denmark's central bank issued a statement in December 2017 that CBDC would present challenges to financial stability and would not provide any new opportunities for monetary policy. That is interesting as other central banks see that as a clear advantage. The Danish Central Bank added that in the Danish context the central bank digital currency would not be able to contribute beyond what is already covered by the current payment solutions.

In December 2019 Switzerland ruled out the possibility of a retail central bank-issued digital franc for the general public in the foreseeable future. The Swiss Federal Council's Report concluded that "central bank digital currency cannot meet these expectations, or only partly" of making payments more efficient and help tackle money laundering. Such a move could bring "newly arising risks to monetary policy and financial stability." It is not, however, a final decision, as the report leaves open the possibility that rapid technological developments, changing payment behaviour and needs and the experience of other countries "may lead to a reassessment of the opportunities and risks of CBDC for the general public for the future".[20]

In July 2020 the Banque de France announced a series of experiments, exploring new ways of exchanging financial instruments (excluding cryptoassets) and testing the settlement in CBDC in order to improve execution for cross-border payments and revising arrangements for making CBDC available. These experiments will directly contribute to the Eurosystem's assessment of the value of CBDC. The aim of the experiments is to integrate a wholesale CBDC into innovative procedures for exchanging and settling tokenized financial assets. In a speech in September 2020, the Governor of the Banque de France said "we cannot lag behind on CBDC".

The road to a central bank digital currency is still uncertain. The decline of cash does appear to be one motivation, but statistics can hide the continued importance of cash for small everyday purchases for many and the functions of larger notes during a crisis. As we shall see in the next chapter, there are more fundamental reasons for rejecting the move to CBDC, especially if it means the abolition of cash. The decline of cash in advanced economies alone does not seem to provide a sufficient reason. That reason itself is undermined by the declaration on the part of some central banks that CBDC is not intended to replace cash.

CHAPTER 10

Credit and trust

In previous chapters, we have explored some of the major motivations for central banks considering the introduction of CBDC. One such consideration was financial inclusion, making banking services available to the unbanked. In the United States approximately 7.1 million households were unbanked in 2019. There are, however, much simpler ways of providing bank account access to those on low incomes than via a CBDC and it is something many other countries have been addressing. The UK, for example, introduced in the mid-1990s by agreement with some of the leading banks what were then called "basic bank accounts". These were (and still are in the newer version) a simplified form of a current account, providing direct debit facilities, a debit card, access to ATMs, and over-the-counter (OTC) banking, but no overdraft facilities. These accounts do not attract any charges. In 2014, the EU Directive extended the provision of fee-free bank accounts to each member state (which applied to the UK then as well), which led to the expansion of such provision in the UK, following its implementation.[1] By the middle of 2016, 4 million new bank accounts had been opened in addition to the 3 million existing "basic bank accounts". By September 2020, the number of the unbanked had fallen to 1.2 million. The remaining the lack of take-up is thought to be due to language barriers and, lack of ID for the KYC requirements. Provision for the unbanked does not require the introduction of CBDC accounts, but the introduction of "free banking" for those on low incomes.

The other motivation for CBDC is faster payments. In a recent article, Sir Jon Cunliffe, Chair of the Committee on Payments and Market Infrastructure, explained that it can still take as long as ten days to transfer money to some destinations at a cost off 10 per cent of the transaction, if it has to pass through correspondent banks and through a number of currencies for certain jurisdictions.[2] However, not all international transfers take as long as that. The Society for Worldwide Interbank Financial Telecommunications' (SWIFT) timeline for international transfers is one to four business days. SWIFT handled about 31 million messages daily in 2018, up 11 per cent from 2017, reflecting its investment in its GPI (global payment initiative). It is used to send more than $300 billion per day. "Fixing the plumbing" would face a number of significant challenges, not least the sheer number of international transfers per day.

The FSB published its first report on payment systems in April 2020, outlining the challenges to increasing the speed and efficiency of international payments. "Faster, cheaper, more transparent and more inclusive cross-border payment services, including remittances, would have widespread benefits for citizens and economies worldwide, supporting economic growth, international trade, global development and financial inclusion".[3] This brief report lists a formidable set of "frictions", including fragmented data standards or lack of interoperability, complexities in meeting compliance requirements, including for AML/CFT and data protection, different operating hours across different time zones and outdated legacy platforms. These frictions increase the need for intermediaries in cross-border payments to hold funds in many currencies against failures in the system. The decline in the number of correspondent banks (about 22 per cent since 2011 and by 3 per cent since 2018) does not help.

In October 2020, the FSB proposed a "roadmap" with five focus areas set out in a high-level plan. The first sets out the commitment to change, includes quantitative targets at a global level for addressing the challenges of cost, speed, transparency and access, as well as a framework for more detailed service-level agreements. The second focus is on the alignment of regulatory, supervisory and oversight frameworks across jurisdictions, where appropriate on the "same business, same risks and same rules" basis. The aim will be to promote a more consistent application of AML/CFT standards, better cross-border flows and information-sharing, and better digital identity frameworks. The next focus area is designed to strengthen links between payment systems through measures such as facilitating payment-versus-payments, improving access to systems, and extending and aligning operating hours between systems. Finally, the FSB will focus on increasing data quality and straight through processing by improving data and market practices. This will be achieved by harmonizing technical standards and providing a unique global identifier linking account information in payment transactions. The plan is also to explore new technology and the possibility that this will provide the answers to the challenges of cross-border payments. This is not just idle rhetoric on the part of the FSB. There is a clear timetable to complete the task. Changes in international payment systems are taking place rapidly with many existing payment services speeding up and reducing the costs of their services. SWIFT, for example, announced that the global banking community have collaborated to put in a new standard for handling cross-border payments, which will ensure that "international payments meet industry's needs for speed, traceability and transparency ... it enables banks to provide their customers with a transformed payments, experience, enabled through easy to use and simple to set up digital tools".[4] Other new international payment services providing cheap, fast, international payment services already exist. None of them require a new "currency" or dubious stablecoins.

The FSB's work to improve the speed, efficiency and costs of international payment systems covers all kinds of international transfers, not just using bank to bank transfers through correspondent banks. These include person-to-person (P2P), person-to-business (P2B) and business to business (B2B). These can use a variety of methods, such as international payment cards, pre-paid cards, initiating payments from existing bank accounts through a mobile application or a digital wallet without the need for the user to have an account through the FinTech overlay provider. Open banking allows a number of PSPs to focus their business models by providing payment services instead of end-to-end banking.

Facebook's argument in favour of Libra was that it was designed to solve two problems: the unbanked and remittances. Some emerging and developing countries have found other ways of providing banking services. Others are providing cheap, fast and efficient international payment services. The FSB's work at an international level will undoubtedly lead to a more efficient international payment systems, despite the differences in interpretations of AML/CFT and issues of ownership. Libra is no longer necessary as an alternative to existing payment systems or the new ones on the scene.

The issues Facebook raised in marketing the Libra project and its latest version (Diem) are indeed extremely important issues, and neglected issues. Not surprisingly, it has led to action by international bodies and encouraged the development of many companies to provide such services. Diem, if and when launched, would face intense competition from banks offering similar services or other companies offering fast and efficient payment services from bank accounts. Although with the resources Facebook has available, it could buy out some of the competition, but would still face more competition now than in early 2019. That competition would most likely come from what they would probably consider an old-fashioned source: SWIFT. On 1 December 2020, SWIFT and the Lloyds Banking Group announced the use of GPI (genuine progress indicator) so that banks can provide 24/7 faster speeds, clarity on feeds and predictability on when an end beneficiary's account will be credited.[5] SWIFT's detailed traffic report for November 2020, shows that there were 40 million messages handled daily with about $20 trillion per day, up from $5 trillion in 2004.[6] In addition, there are a number of companies providing cheap and speedy international transfers, providing competition for Libra's (Diem) proposals.

Facebook is by no means the only way in which greater financial inclusion or faster, efficient and less expensive international payments can be brought about. Another element in Libra's Second White Paper may also create concerns with regulators and central banks. Libra "can be used as an efficient cross-border settlement coin as well as a neutral low-volatility option in countries that do not have a single-currency stablecoin on the network yet. This approach has the added benefit of allowing the network to support a wider range of domestic use cases and of *providing a clear path for seamlessly integrating central bank digital currencies as they become available*" (italics mine).[7]

A defining feature of a central bank is that it has the monopoly on final means of payment (in a particular currency). It works in two tiers: the central bank balance sheet contains cash and commercial bank deposits (reserves) and the provision of commercial cash by the banks. The constant clearing takes place on the central bank's balance sheet, making it responsible for the final settlement of both wholesale and retail payment systems. The fact that a payment is final means that the person who receives a payment can use received funds for further payments. It is because central banks have this monopoly that they are charged with safeguarding price stability and an efficient and stable payments system. At the same time, by creating this settlement medium on demand (by generating intraday settlement liquidity, typically on a collateralized basis) it ensures that the payment system works without interruption. Facebook's stress on this "clear path" is unlikely to endear Diem to those central banks, which may decide to introduce CBDC in the medium term, if indeed, the demands of the central bank's role in the payment system are understood by the Association.

The supposed advantages of introducing various digital currencies, and stablecoins in particular, I believe, do not hold water. They have, however, triggered action on improving international payments and continuing to seek ways of lowering the costs. Action taken by governments to increase access to bank accounts is a significant step forward. It is vital if the supposed advantages of cryptocurrencies are to be met. At the same time as developments in cryptocurrencies have taken place, as we have seen, central banks have begun to experiment with blockchain in a series of projects usually limited to wholesale transactions and clearing and settlement. At the time of writing, the Bank of England has yet to report on its responses to the consultation process on its own discussion paper, Central Bank Digital Currency published in March 2020.

Firstly, we need to be clear about what is meant by CBDC. The Bank for International Settlements defines it as a "digital payment instrument, denominated in the national unit of account, that is, a direct liability of the central bank". The CPMI provides a somewhat different emphasis by referring to CBDC as a "digital form of money that is different from balances in traditional reserves or settlement accounts." The BIS is at pains to distinguish between CBDC and what some have called a "synthetic" CBDC. A "synthetic" CBDC is not a direct claim on a central bank. It requires a different framework from a central bank providing retail digital currencies itself. The central bank would engage with private sector providers to issue liabilities in the form of digital currencies matched by funds held at the central bank. BIS points out that if the regulatory framework could guarantee that these providers would always be fully matched by funds at the central bank, they would lack some of the essential features of central bank money.[8]

SWEDEN AND E-KRONA

Sweden, as we have seen, began in spring 2017, to first examine the scope for the Riksbank to issue a central bank digital currency, a "digital complement to cash, so-called e-kronas, and whether such a complement could support the Riksbank in the task of promoting a safe and efficient payments system".[9] The e-krona would give the general public access to a digital complement to cash, where the state would guarantee the value of the money. In its second report, the Riksbank proposed that the project build a technical solution for a value-based e-krona that constitutes a pre-paid value (electronic money) without interest and with traceable transactions. The second report also suggested e-krona could be account-based, that is, with an account based at the Riksbank. E-krona would then be a deposit, and an application to open an account at the Riksbank "may need to be assessed based on established rules and conditions just as when an account is opened at a private bank".[10]

The introduction of e-krona, "would offer the general public continued access to central bank money, as cash has done but in digital form ... It would reduce the risk of the krona's position being reduced, weakened by competing currency alternatives".[11] The technical solution for the e-krona involves the use of DLT, a "technology to keep databases operated by independent parties synchronized. Each participant in the DLT network runs one or more nodes in the e-krona transactions." This technical solution will be evaluated in a "test environment in which participants and interactions with the existing infrastructure and settlement systems will be evaluated".[12] The second report on e-krona was published in October 2018. It notes that "Sweden is at the forefront in terms of technological development in the payment market, with solutions such as Bank ID and Swish being used by many".[13] Its payment system, based on transfers of digital claims on the Riksbank's between accounts in private banks (via RIX) functions well. Riksbank's role in final payments will not change as the Riksbank as the central bank in Sweden will continue to have a monopoly in final payments rather than two when cash is used through RIX.

In February 2020, the Riksbank announced that it was conducting a pilot project with Accenture aimed at developing a proposal for a technical solution for an e-krona. The objective is to create, in an isolated test environment, a digital krona that is simple and user-friendly. The technical solution will be based on DLT. The aim is to show how e-krona could be used by the general public. The pilot project runs until February 2021 with the option to extend and further develop the technical solution. With the inquiry due to last two years, it is not clear when and if a decision to introduce e-krona will be made.

The structure of the pilot project is interesting. Only the Riksbank will be able to issue and redeem e-krona. It will be a private network and only the Riksbank can approve and add new participants to the network. The participants in the network will be able to obtain/redeem e-krona against crediting or debiting of reserves held directly by the participants or via a representative in the Riksbank settlement system, RIX, the central payments system at the Riksbank in which transfers between accounts in different banks are handled. The consumer or merchant controls their e-krona with a digital wallet, installed as an app on a mobile phone or the merchant's register. All transactions in the e-krona network occur separately from existing payment networks, and as these are stand-alone systems, they provide added strength. However, this will require merchants to be willing to invest in new systems, unless customers in large numbers demand it, or if they are obliged to invest in a new system through legal tender requirements.

With regard to governance, the Riksbank controls this network. The contracts and flows between the participant nodes, their databases and participant nodes enforce the regulatory framework set by Riksbank for e-krona through both technical and legal rules, such as the signing of transactions and storage of e-krona transactions. The project has some interesting features, such as the intention to retain cash and also to transfer e-krona via private network to participants approved by the Riksbank, due largely to the fact that the abolition of cash met with stiff resistance in some quarters. To be able to use e-krona for payments, the digital wallet must first be activated at a participant connected to the e-krona network. After activation, the user can, for example, receive e-krona as payment from another user, pay a retailer with e-krona as payment from another user, pay a retailer with e-krona, make transfers from their bank account to the digital wallet (and vice versa) and check their e-krona balance.[14] This, however, is not a new feature. Sweden already has an extremely accessible, widely used and efficient payments system in Swish.

The critiques by Finansinspektionen (FI) and the Swedish Bankers Association of the detailed proposals set out in E-Krona 2 are interesting and significant. Firstly, picking up on Riksbank's notion of "modernizing the product cash"[15] they make the point that the decline of cash in Sweden is not simply because the public liked Swish, but also because "the Riksbank twenty years ago, decided to transfer large parts of the responsibility – and thus the costs – for cash operations to private operators, i.e. the banks and transport companies. The banks have subsequently gained from promoting their own payment solutions. This has reduced the use of cash, which at the same time has contributed to a more efficient payments system". The report judges – probably correctly – that this development cannot be reversed.

Secondly, the FI concludes that "a value-based e-krona cannot be justified by the fact that it would make the payments system more efficient. On the contrary, for companies and households it would be a disadvantage to have to handle two types of payment through an obligation to accept or use e-kronor. The system would also be expensive to operate."[16] This is in line with the BIS report on digital central bank currencies, as the FI acknowledges: "Most importantly, while situations differ, the benefits of a widely accessible CBDC may be limited if fast (even instant) and efficient private retail payment products are already in place or in development".[17] This was the most forthright criticism, echoed to a large extent by the Swedish Bankers Association (SBA). The SBA argued that it was not appropriate for the Riksbank to launch its own investigation of e-krona since issues such as crisis preparation affect many players and the FI also handles questions relating to financial stability. The SBA considers that the most important socio-economic benefit of an e-krona would be if it increases the robustness of the payment system. However, it also points out that "this requires investment in a parallel payments infrastructure, and it believes that the costs of that would be significant ... [but] the focus of the e-krona pilot *does not* seem to be on building a parallel infrastructure ... An e-krona that does not increase the robustness of the payment system would appear to be meaningless."[18]

The Swedish Bankers Association and the FI also question how the Riksbank would invest the funds it receives if it issues e-krona: "The funds that the public holds in e-krona accounts will also need to be invested in suitable assets. The Riksbank would also have to accept responsibility for issuing credit, either through lending to the public or by the Riksbank issuing loans to banks to replace the funds transferred from accounts held at the bank to e-krona accounts."[19] We shall discuss the issue of account held CBDC in more detail later, but it is worth noting that Sweden's regulatory authority expressed such concerns as well as the Swedish Banking Association.

Per Bolund, Sweden's minister for financial markets announced a review to study the possibility of introducing the e-krona in December 2020. The review will be chaired by Anna Kinberg Batra, a former chair of the Standing Committee on Finance of the Swedish Parliament. It is expected to complete its work by November 2022. The Commission has very extensive and useful terms of reference, raising significant issues which are too often overlooked in the narrowly-based technology tests and projects: "Analyze the advantages and disadvantages of digital central bank money, in particular the effects on the public, the effects on monetary policy and financial stability, the effects of credit institutions' operations and competition in the payment market, the effects on society's preparedness for crises and wars and the effects on countering money laundering and the financing of terrorism." But as we noted in Chapter 8, the Governor of the Riksbank has said that the Riksbank "has not yet taken a formal decision on whether or not to issue e-krona. A decision to issue an e-krona requires legal basis and political support".[20]

PRIVACY

In Chapter 8, the issue of privacy was described as largely a personal matter. People certainly would not want to share all their transactions with the central bank, even when all those transactions are entirely legitimate. The systems proposed by the Bank of England and the Swedish e-krona are both based on retail (i.e. personal and small/medium-sized businesses) and the provision of a core ledger, which would record CBDC and process payments. The PIP, selected by the central bank, would handle the interaction with the end-users of CBDC. Similarly, to be able to use the e-krona for payments, the digital wallet must first be activated at a participant connected to the e-krona network: "The e-krona network is private and only the Riksbank can approve and add new participants to the network."[21] The Bank of England consultation paper points out that any CBDC system must be compatible with privacy regulations such as the 2018 General Data Protection Act (GDPR), which would be applicable across the board for CBDC. This ensures that users should have control over how their data is used and with whom it is shared. Privacy should be considered carefully when designing CBDC. The Riksbank takes a similar line.

But the issue of privacy remains a key issue to be resolved. Since these are at the proposal stage, we do not know yet whether or not it is possible to ensure privacy and at the same time allow access to individual's accounts to meet AML/CFT requirements. The CBDC proposals potentially allows central banks much more access to "big data" than individual companies or other large organizations. The question then arises as to how such data is to be used in policy-making. It also gives the central bank enormous access to individual expenditure patterns, even when the expenditure is legitimate. It is vital that the design of CBDC allows for the retention of privacy. Not all of those who publish papers or comment of CBDC seem to understand that. They are fascinated by the technology and the need to keep up in this exciting world where they see countries like China forging ahead. It is important to focus on the context in which China is developing CBDC and to note that in a centralized authoritarian regime, such developments do not need to face an investigation initiated by a politically responsible minister that is likely to take two years!

The People's Bank of China is forging ahead with its CBDC project. It does not involve the abolition of cash, now some 7 per cent of GDP, as the Chinese government claims that cash will continue to exist alongside a digital currency for years to come. Why is China moving so fast? Certainly, to compete with the US and to provide its own payment solutions. The aim is to replace the anonymity of cash, the accumulation of which increased by 10 per cent in 2020. The fact that China already has an effective payments system is not the issue. For the Chinese government, the fact that it is operated by the duopoly of Alipay and Wechatpay is significant. The People's Bank of China has been concerned about the systemic importance of these two companies and has sought to reimpose control over them by the 100 per cent reserve requirement it imposed on them at the beginning of 2019. But the two companies are responsible for the majority of the country's transactions: in the last three months of 2019, Alibaba controlled 55.1 per cent of the market for mobile payments with Tencent controlling the other 38.9 per cent. They are also concerned that people put their money in digital wallets rather than bank accounts. The Governor of the PBoC has made it clear that these companies pose "challenges and financial risks".

China's aim is to establish a retail CBDC. To that end, it has conducted a series of experiments with CBDC beginning with the districts of Shenzhen in October 2020, then Suzhou, in December, followed by smaller experiments in Beijing and Shanghai in January 2021. In each case, participation in the project has been assisted by a lottery open to 100,000 people in which individuals apply for a wallet containing the equivalent of $30. They are offered a digital yuan wallet incorporated in a number of wearable devices, such as ultra-thin card wallets, badges, watches and bracelets. Despite such inducements, not everyone was impressed with the new currency. They were already used to Alipay and Wechatpay, with which they were both familiar and found them easy to use.

The new currency is known as "DCEP" (digital currency/electronic payment). The PBoC will issue the digital currency to commercial banks which will then provide DCEP to individuals. Its state-led economic model is of course another "asset". Four of the largest and most important commercial banks are state-owned and therefore hardly likely to dissent from Beijing's policy priorities.[22] But the proposed digital currency would also increase the government's capacity to monitor and control economic activity. When individuals use DCEP, real-time data about the transaction is available to the Chinese authorities, although Mr Mu claims that the central bank will limit how it tracks individuals by "controllable anonymity".[23] The justification for such information being available to the central bank is that it can help to combat money laundering and corruption. But of course there is much more to it than that: DCEP set up in this way, can enable the government to track behavioural information of all kinds, and then connect it to China's controversial social credit system, which monitors the "trustworthiness" of individuals and businesses and functions as a surveillance infrastructure, as Fan Liang writes, "a state-sponsored big data-enabled surveillance effort that is increasingly used by a state-power to govern and regulate the political, economic and social domains of the nation."[24]

Fan's research provides an interesting and comprehensive analysis of the types of data which will be collected and the agencies involved. But in the end the authors are obliged to conclude that "not every subject will be assigned to a black list or a red list." "If the subjects have good credit records, exhibit compliance with the Party's rules and political goals, and perform good social responsibility, they stand to receive rewards and incentives ... those on the blacklist stand to receive punishments and constraints affecting their social, political and economic activities".[25]

The point here is that as an authoritarian state with such powers and resources available to it, it is much easier for China to have a central bank currency established than it is in a democratic state, in which it is not a matter of technological development alone but how the access to personal information is to be used. Hence the commitment to privacy on the part of Sweden and the Bank of England is so important. What remains is to see how that commitment can be defined and implemented in the new world of the central bank digital currency.

The point is simply that it is easy to be fascinated with developing what is assumed to be new technology and fail to consider the wider ramifications. There is also the fear that China will be the first country to establish a CBDC and leverage that to establish the renminbi as the global reserve currency, thus ousting the dollar. It will take more than that to displace the dollar since China does not have the deep, liquid and open financial markets, and (until now) the ability to maintain its value in the form of limited inflation and depreciation. The use of the yuan in international trade has increased recently, but it is still only 2.4 per cent of the world market. Even given President Xi Jinping's determination to leave his mark on history, achieving that goal is a distant one. That discussion is beyond the scope of this book, except to point out that the management of such a reserve requires (among other things) trust. China's lack of transparency over a wide range of issues such as the management of its economy, the pandemic, its treatment of the Uigher minority should militate against that. For Europe, the UK and the United States the decision is both a legal and a political one.

The ECB published its public consultation on introducing a digital euro on 12 October 2020 which went out to all interested parties, not just to financial institutions. On 13 January 2021, the ECB press release reported that it had received over 8,000 responses to its online survey. The ECB reports that their initial analysis of the raw data showed that privacy of payment ranked highest among the requested features of a potential digital euro, followed by security and a pan-European reach: "A digital euro would be an electronic form of central bank money accessible to all citizens and firms – like banknotes, but in a digital form – to make their daily payments in a fast easy and secure way. It would complement cash, not replace it. The Eurosystem would continue to issue cash in any case ... The protection of privacy would be a key priority, so that the digital euro can help maintain trust in payments in the digital age."[26] At the time of writing, the ECB has not yet announced a decision to introduce a digital euro, and even if the decision is taken within the next few months, it is not expected to launch for a further four or five years. When and if Europe, Sweden and the UK provide details of the way in which the introduction of CBDC will work in practice, the proposals must be analysed in great detail to see just how the privacy of accounts and the use of digital currencies will be protected as well as any redress those using such accounts would have if their personal data was not protected. The details will matter. But there are other important considerations as well, of which the foremost is the role of banks if the introduction of digital currency involves retail accounts at the central banks. The retail accounts are envisaged to include personal, and small-to-medium sized business accounts, currently held at credit institutions.

CREDIT

Some of the assumptions made by the proponents of digital currencies are unrealistic; namely, that individuals and households are able and willing to have two transaction accounts; one with the central bank and the other with their current bank. For those on low to medium incomes, maintaining two separate accounts would be difficult, since if the central bank account is used for paying bills, then there would be little or anything left from monthly salaries to keep in a commercial bank account. This is just one aspect of the way in which a central bank account would undermine the existence of commercial banks. Banks take in deposits, which are either available on demand or longer-term savings and time deposits, used to make long-term loans. The funding for loans is partly through deposits or funding on the wholesale markets either by directly borrowing, issuing securities, lending securities they own to other institutions for cash, and securitization. Bonds are issued in the financial markets for cash both to strengthen its reserves and also to invest, so a bank can maintain adequate liquidity reserves at all times, face withdrawals and settlements, and avoid a liquidity crisis, as required by regulations. Some of the deposits are therefore retained on deposit with central banks, such as the Riksbank, the Bank of England, the US Federal Reserve or the European Central Bank.

The rest of the deposits or monies raised in the wholesale markets is used to provide loans. Deposits are therefore a source of funding for banks. If these end up at the central bank, banks will be underfunded and must attract funding from other sources. This is the way in which banks create money, which is then used to purchase goods and services and may end up in the banking system as a deposit in another bank. The increased deposits will not fully back new loans, even though the bank lends to other borrowers, whilst holding in reserve an amount equal to a fraction of that bank's deposit liabilities. This process can be repeated frequently. Individuals, businesses and governments all need to deposit and borrow money at one time or another and repay loans. That is the process, endlessly repeated, by which commercial banks create money.

If central banks offer CBDC accounts to retail customers, this could have major consequences for the financial system. If households were able to convert commercial bank deposits into a CBDC at a 1:1 rate, they might well find it more attractive to hold a risk-free CBDC rather than bank deposits. That is highly likely to reduce the level of deposits with commercial banks and restrict their ability to lend. If that happens to any great extent, then since credit plays such an essential role in economic development, the central bank will have to allocate credit and the risks involved. That will require both the development of new skills (or hiring commercial bank staff as its own employees!). Central banks might welcome that, as it provides a more effective tool than the use of interest rates in the implementation of monetary policy. Credit would be restricted more directly, by refusing credit to individuals and businesses, when the central bank deemed it necessary.

So far central banks have chosen not to provide retail access to central bank money, despite the fact that technology for an account-based CBDC is already available. Fundamentally it is just a regular transactions account. In a speech by Yves Mersch of the ECB, he outlined some of the outcomes if the central bank were to take retail deposits, "it might also have to provide loans with all the ensuing consequences. The central bank would need to launch customer-facing business lines. Deposit and lending facilities would also require the central bank to take on the burden of regulatory compliance in areas such as anti-money laundering, consumer protection and confidentiality." The title of the speech ("An ECB digital currency? A flight of fancy?") does perhaps indicate the real underlying concern as to whether this should be a serious proposition for central banks to devote such a great deal of time.[27] It is inevitable that central banks have to discuss the issue, given the fact that cryptocurrencies of all kinds have attracted too much public attention as opening up new exciting possibilities. But in the post-pandemic world, when central banks will have a significant role to play in revitalizing seriously damaged economies, it is perhaps a "flight of fancy".

That is especially so given their potential powers over the supply of credit and the selection of the recipients of that credit, which could particularly impact on business start-ups, since those whose experience has been with the security of a large bureaucracy will find it particularly difficult to assess the risks involved in starting up a new business and the likely success or failure of the enterprise. Agustin Carstens in a recent speech suggested that "central banks could do without a lending operation if it sends customer deposits to commercial banks by opening central bank deposits at commercial banks".[28] But that would also create difficulties. Which commercial banks? How many retail deposits would each bank receive? Would the retail customer be able to choose which bank? Would the commercial bank only receive deposits if the central bank approved of its lending policy and recipients?

Mersch adds that "disintermediation would be economically inefficient and legally untenable. The EU Treaty provides for the ECB to operate in an open market economy, essentially reflecting a policy choice in favour of decentralized market decisions on the optimal allocation of resources."[29] That approach is true of the advanced economies. The record of central banks (or governments) decisions on credit allocation is extremely poor even when governments in developed economies have taken such decisions.

Giving central banks the power to make loans has wider consequences than that. Paul Tucker points out that "the case for lending to an account holder who had run out of money would not rest, as now, on the social costs to third parties of not lending to temporarily illiquid but sound banking intermediaries … it would be driven by the political costs of neglecting private hardship. This is a world where the central bank becomes part of the redistributive state". It would be "the end of central banks' insulation from quotidian politics. This would be (or could be driven towards) 'state banking' not central banking as we know it."[30] The spectre of China's social credit system should also hang over any such decisions.

The flow of credit to an economy is vital to economic development and trade. Neither can develop or function without it – within the limits of whether or not the borrower can pay back the loan over time. The required safeguards on borrowing and lending should be in place and be upheld. The proper lesson to be learnt from the financial crisis is that lending was politically driven by the attempt to ensure that access to mortgages was made available to all regardless of the means to pay back the loan on reasonable terms.[31] That is part of the reason for not placing the allocation of credit in the hands of central banks, which might then find that their independence is ebbing away.

These points have been expressed even more forcibly by Alex Pollock in his submission to the hearing on "The Future of Money" back in 2018. With regard to the notion of central banking for all, that is, retail accounts at the central bank, he pointed out that that would mean the Federal Reserve,

> ... would be in direct competition with all private banks in such a scheme. It would certainly be a highly advantaged, government competitor. It could offer 'risk-free' accounts and pay a higher interest. Rate, if it liked, cross-subsidizing this business with the profits from its currency issuing monopoly ... there are about $12 trillion in domestic deposits. ... If the Federal Reserve took half of these, that would be $6 trillion, which would expand its balance sheet to $10 trillion ... the Federal Reserve would have to do something with the mountain of deposits – namely make loans and make investments. It would automatically become the overwhelming credit allocator of the financial system. Its credit allocation would automatically be highly politicized. It would become merely a government commercial bank, with taxpayers on the hook for its credit losses. The world's experience with such politicized lenders makes a sad history.[32]

The focus here has been on central banks and credit. This is because central bank accounts might be held to limit the commercial banks' ability to lend because of the decline in retail deposits. Bank deposits or bank money make up 97 per cent of the money in circulation. This system is sometimes called fractional banking, since banks do not have to hold capital to match the total amount in deposits and reserves to match the amounts lent or held on demand. They do have to meet an array of capital and liquidity regulations to ensure they are managed prudently, and the central bank controls commercial bank lending by setting interest rates.[33] It can be seen that the balance between the central banks and commercial banks is designed to determine the *amount* banks can lend at any one time. Disturbing that relationship would oblige the central bank to select the borrowers, which in China may be an aim but it is clearly not a desirable outcome.

There appears to be no good reason and serious risks involved, in central banks providing CBDC accounts, especially at this time, when the effects of the pandemic on the economy have to be handled with care. There is a growing recognition that the risks of disintermediation (investing directly in the securities market rather than through an intermediary like a bank) and the implications for monetary policy and financial stability are real. Some argue that central banks have to show that the market does not allocate resources efficiently and that central banks can compete with existing and ever faster and cheaper payment systems so that potential customers will reject these systems and instead go with the central banks. Having an account at a central bank might be more attractive because of its safety, but then developed countries provide deposit insurance schemes, and are unlikely to provide the range of services which commercial banks can provide. The authors, Bofinger and Haas, conclude that "if central banks stick to their current approach, the risk is high that CBDCs will become a gigantic flop".[34]

Others argue that a central bank that is open to all is "capable of delivering the socially optimal amount of maturity transformation,[35] liquidity insurance,[36] and reduction of bank runs" but only if certain conditions are fulfilled. Central banks currently lack the skills in identifying the productive or innovative projects and would have to recruit skilled personnel. Banks finance long-term projects not only with demand deposits but by borrowing short and lending long. So, it is argued, the central bank would have to rely on investment banks (and commercial banks in general) and allow for competition with commercial banks. But if the central bank's competition with commercial banks is skewed, for example, bringing about "some fiscal subsidization of central bank deposits", then the central bank could destroy maturity transformation. Depositors would become aware of that and shift deposits to the central bank. Interest paid on central bank accounts would have the same effect. The authors conclude that it "also gives unseen power to central banks. It is not unreasonable to be concerned about the abuse of such power".[37] An examination of the credit monopoly of the State Bank of the Soviet Union might come in useful and its credit allocation.

TRUST

The claim has often been made over the last decade or so that it is the lack of trust in central banks, fiat currencies, financial intermediaries such as banks, which has led to the introduction of cryptocurrencies. That of course was the reason for Nakamoto's introduction of Bitcoin without the need for intermediaries. Steve Hanke, "the lack of trust in central banks and national currencies set the stage for the arrival of private substitutes. While technology played its part in making cryptocurrencies feasible, it is the lack of trust in central banking for what might be a new spontaneous order".[38] More than a lack of trust in Venezuela, Zimbabwe and Lebanon would be entirely justified, but should just as equally be extended to the governments and other institutions of those nations. However, the creation and distribution of cryptocurrencies has not turned out to be trustworthy nor part of a "spontaneous" new order. Indeed, in an attempt to inspire trust, some have turned to the application of existing frameworks to their own ventures in order to establish trust. Trust does not exist in a vacuum. It requires a framework every aspect of which is designed to establish and maintain trust. The ready acceptance of various cryptocurrencies on the part of too many, driven partly by the fear of missing out, or dreams of profits to be made, has simply resulted in losses.

The basic pitch from the cryptocurrency community is that it is possible to eliminate the need for trust in third parties by making the currency independent of central banks and financial institutions. That applied not only to Bitcoin but all the altcoins and the stablecoins we have discussed in previous chapters, which appeared during the past decade or more. Cryptocurrencies turned out to be slow, expensive and difficult to scale. The aim was to replace trust with technology. The parties to any transaction on a blockchain trust it to facilitate the transfer, to ensure sender authenticity and to vouch for the validity of currency exchanged. That does not eliminate trust but merely transfers it to other parties, such as the reliability of the blockchain, that there is no collusion because the incentives to remain honest work, that markets are not being manipulated and that trading platforms are using the best security practices. That became more difficult as time went on and more examples of hacking exchanges occurred. Ironically, it is precisely for such reasons (as well as increasing regulatory pressures in order to protect users of exchanges) that some trading platforms registered with the regulatory authorities and are subject to the same regulations as anyone else.

The promoters of cryptocurrencies of all kinds continue to make the same claims that you don't need to trust anyone else, the banks, intermediaries, merchants and payment processors, all of whom require fees. But the many scandals involving cryptocurrencies, wallets and exchanges, the thefts, hacks, hard and soft forks and false claims described in this book, show that had you trusted very many of the cryptocurrencies, you would either have lost your money or found you were facing extremely high and unexpected fees. As far as stablecoins are concerned, these had to turn to dependence on existing currencies in order to gain any kind of acceptance. Parasites rather than a "new spontaneous order". Indeed, the term "fiat currency" is itself a misnomer. "Fiat", which denotes "command", suggests an arbitrary creation or perhaps imposition. "Fiduciary" implies "trust". That is the reason why bits of paper and metal, or more likely, electronic entries on statements of all kinds are accepted as payments. The fact that such items are legal tender and the legal and regulatory frameworks surrounding their use is what justifies and inspires trust. Without such well-established frameworks or "ecosystems," a currency will not become money.

APPENDIX
Smart contracts

In simple terms a smart contract is a self-executing contract with the terms of the contract between the buyer and the seller being directly written in lines of code. The code and the implied agreements run on a blockchain platform and cannot be changed. These contracts were first proposed by Nick Szabo in two articles in 1996 and 1997. In his first article, he stated that "new institutions and new ways to formalize the relationships that make up these institutions, are now made possible by the digital revolution ... I call these new contracts 'smart' because they are more functional than their inanimate paper-based ancestors. No use of artificial intelligence is implied. A smart contract is a set of promises, specified in digital form, including the protocols within which the parties perform on those promises." The contract itself is a software programme written in one of the new languages, such as Solidity. The code itself can be either the sole expression of an agreement between two parties or it might be in addition to a traditional written contract, implementing certain elements.

In his second article, Szabo described smart contracts as combining protocols with user interfaces to formalize and secure relationships over computer networks. The objectives and principles for the design of these systems would be derived from legal principles, economic theory and theories of reliable and secure protocols. He claimed that by using cryptographics and other security measures, it would be possible to secure many algorithmically specifiable relationships from breaches by principals, eaves dropping or malicious interference by third parties. This would reduce the "mental and computational transaction costs imposed by the principals, third parties or their tools". His comments about the use of the word, "smart" together with the rejection of artificial intelligence is important, since it makes it clear that they are only "smarter" than traditional paper-based contracts because they can automatically execute certain preprogrammed steps. Smart contracts at present are fairly basic, because they have to be absolutely specific – if x, then y – and unalterable. Szabo's typical analogy of a smart contract is a vending machine. Once the buyer has fulfilled the terms of the "contract" and put the coins into the machine, then the machine automatically fulfils the terms of the unwritten agreement and delivers the bar of chocolate.

Szabo saw smart contracts as replacing not just traditional paper-based contracts but a means of replacing all those involved in writing the contract, determining when all the conditions are fulfilled and enforcement. Expensive "middlemen" will no longer be required. Smart contracts gained in popularity with the introduction of Ethereum, which uses the Solidity language to programme the contracts. Due to the fact that Ethereum is open-sourced, the self-executing contract runs when all the involved parties have signed the transaction or when the 30-day limit has passed, or whatever other conditions are contained in the contract. So it looks as though these contracts are ideal in many circumstances for all the advantages they seem to offer: immutable, swift settlement, the contract code is known in advance so that it cannot be changed or altered by malicious actors.

The possibility of using smart contracts and blockchain for clearing and settlement of exchange-traded and OTC securities, central counterparties, central securities depositories and trade finance documentation has been explored over the last few years. A number of projects have been conducted in order to assess whether or not smart contracts and blockchain might fulfil these hopes.

One of these was the Canadian Project Jasper, which we discussed in Chapter 8, the proof-of-concept experiment designed to test a blockchain wholesale interbank payments system. It also included an open source DLT platform, Corda, designed to record, manage and automate legal agreements between businesses. The assessment of the Project highlighted continued back-up and security needs. It was only the use of the Corda platform and the notarial function of the Bank of Canada that provided an element of irrevocability, but concerns over settlement risk remained. The role of the Bank of Canada also created a single point of failure. What is also important to note both here and in some of the other projects is that the proof-of-concept excluded many governance and legal considerations of traditional wholesale payment systems, including money laundering requirements. These would certainly have made the system much more complicated. Whether or not the DLT and smart contracts can handle such issues is unclear. The focus of these test projects has been on the efficiency and cost of this system.

Project Ubin, undertaken by the Monetary Authority of Singapore together with the state investment firm, Temasek and J. P. Morgan, launched in 2016 its blockchain-based multi-currency payments network, and has proved its commercial potential after tests with more than 40 companies. The final report on the Project concluded that the "key challenge in achieving a common international platform for cross-border payments relates to the questions of governance and ownership". There are a large number of projects and relatively small-scale initiatives using blockchain but some major issues remain, such as scale issues of the underlying DLT, cost/time savings, and comptational power.

Other problems with smart contracts relate to external information and the judgement, which is often required to determine whether or not A has really met the required conditions for the contract to be fulfilled so that B can receive the payment due. The external data required is not published on the blockchain and so the smart contract cannot be activated. So-called "oracles" have been introduced, which could, in theory, provide the required information, but that is not a straightforward matter. Disputes could and do continue as regards the nature of the "facts" and how these are to be interpreted remain. That is why the reference to the automatic response of the vending machine is so misleading: the "oracles" are really an attempt to replace dispute resolution or the courts.

Immutability also presents a serious problem, since it requires that the terms of the contract are met perfectly every time. But there's the rub. A couple of examples will suffice. In June 2015, a Deutsche Bank trader mistakenly sent $6 billion, based on the gross instead of the net figure, resulting in a trade with "too many zeros". Also in 2015, it was thought that a "fat finger" trade was responsible for such a sharp fall in energy prices that trading in energy stocks was suspended for several minutes. It was possible to reverse both these errors with the agreement of the parties concerned.

It may well be that some of the difficulties are insurmountable. For example, moving to a blockchain T+0 sytem in securities lending would mean that the loaned security would have to be returned to the investor in real time, whereas the current systems of T+2 in Europe and T+3 in the US allows the custodian or investor to return the securities over 2 or 3 days. There are other specific difficulties with trades usually carried out by institutional investors, now dominating the American and UK stock markets, for example, traders normally aggregate orders in the same security by different portfolio managers in the same institution. DLT makes this difficult because it is a record of legal ownership and the legal entity is technically not the institution but the single fund they manage.

The issues that remain unresolved are some of the familiar ones both of scale and cyber security. In the projects examined here and others besides, the focus has been on the technology and how this can be adapted. Compliance has not been built into the system, owing to the complexities involved. The goal remains of substantial savings if clearing and settlement of securities, bonds, derivatives and lending can use DLT and smart contracts. Some sources claim that is will save billions of dollars in transactions and transaction-related "middlemen" fees, but the realization of blockchain's potential for optimizing both speed and security of securities transactions at low cost remain unclear. That is why research has focused on permissioned networks, since the complexities around trust, privacy and scalability are better resolved with a consortium of known parties. New issues have come to the fore, such as the tokenization of securities, tokens for digital securities and how these relate to smart contracts. "The capacity and resilience of applying DLT and smart contracts to clearing and settlement is also yet to be proven,"[1] but smart contracts are very unlikely to play a part on their own. They are not smart enough nor are they contracts.

Notes

PREFACE

1 Phil Champagne (ed.), *The Book of Satoshi: The Collected Writings of Bitcoin Creator* (London: E53 Publishing, 2014), 100.

CHAPTER 1

1 S. Nakamoto, *Bitcoin Manifesto: One CPU One Vote* (Antonio Tombolini Editore, 2014), 6. Nakamoto did not publish his initial work as a "Manifesto", but as "Bitcoin: a peer-to-peer electonic cash system" (available at https://downloads.coindesk.com/research/white papers/Bitcoin.pdf). "Manifesto" is the title given to Satoshi's work by the publisher.
2 *Bitcoin Manifesto*, 15.
3 "Bitcoin Open Source Implementation of P2P Currency", P2P Foundation, 10 February 2009, 6, and Champagne, *Book of Satoshi*, 100.
4 *Bitcoin Manifesto*, 5.
5 *Ibid.*, 15.
6 This is just one of the components Nakamoto used. Hashes, time stamps, transactions in blocks, links between blocks of data, and the use of hashes. What he did was innovative in the sense that all these elements were combined in a new way to provide a digital currency which provides a "proof-of-work" in finding a hash that meets a low probability condition.
7 A "nonce" is a number only used once, a number added to a hashed or encrypted block in a blockchain.
8 According to a paper by Campell Harvey, National Bureau of Economic Research, "Currently [in 2016], the network capacity for hashes is enormous. To match the hashing power of the network would cost at least $2 billion ... In order to hack the chain, you

need to match the capacity – which seems very unlikely – at least for the average hacker" (Harvey, "Cryptofinance", 4).

9 *Bitcoin Manifesto*, 10.

10 *Ibid.*, 11.

11 *Ibid.*, 21.

12 *Ibid.*, 30.

13 *Ibid.*, 35.

14 This idea was first proposed by J. Kroll and others in "The Economics of Bitcoin Mining or Bitcoin in the Presence of Adversaries", WEISS, June 2013.

15 J. Bonneau, "Hostile blockchain takeovers", 5, Financial Cryptography and Data Security-FC 2018 International Workshops, 2019, New York University.

16 R. Pass & E. Shi, "Fruitchains: a fair blockchain", Proceedings of the ACM Symposium on Principles of Distributed Computing, July 2017, 315–24.

17 "How many Bitcoins are there?", Buy Bitcoin Worldwide.

18 Nakamoto commented on this in various emails, "Nodes will eventually be compensated by transaction fees alone when the total coins created reach a predetermined ceiling", "When that runs out, the system can support transaction fees if needed. It's based on open market competition, and there will probably always be nodes willing to process transactions for free" (*Book of Satoshi*, 78 and 91). The editor considers that transaction fees "may become mandatory" (285).

19 *Bitcoin Manifesto*, 35.

20 *Ibid.*, 35.

21 *Ibid.*, 6–7.

22 *Ibid.*, 6.

23 See https://www.blockchain.com/charts/median-confirmation-time and https://blockchain.com/charts/n-transactions.

24 Visa Fact Sheet 2020, https://usa.visa.com.

25 "Putting pressure on Bitcoin's lightning network vulnerabilities will strengthen it", Coindesk, October 2020.

26 "China's blockchain dominance: can the US catch up?", 23 April 2019, Knowledge at Wharton, Finance.

27 As reported in the *Financial Times*, 20/21 June 2021.

28 Tesla's CEO Elon Musk announced that they would no longer accept payments in Bitcoin for vehicles because of the "rapidly increasing use of fossil fuels for Bitcoin mining and transaction, especially coal" (quoted by Reuters, 12 May 2021). Bitcoin plunged by 17 per cent in Asian trading, before rebounding to $50,000 there the following day. At the same time, Musk revealed that Tesla held $1.5 billion worth of Bitcoin purchased in February 2021.

29 Nakamoto takes a very relaxed view of energy consumption given that he anticipated the use of a personal computer in a home heated by electricity, so the additional cost would be negligible: "Bitcoin generation should end up where it is cheapest. Maybe that will be

in cold climates where there's electric heat, where it would be essentially free" (*Book of Satoshi*, 237).

30 *Bitcoin Manifesto*, 17.

31 "Once a miner discovers a nonce providing the correct hash output, the block is broadcasted, and other miners verify it, accept it. Who will be the lucky miner to find a nonce with the correct characteristics?" (*Book of Satoshi*, 23).

32 "Distribution of Bitcoin's network hash rate in the last 24 hours until 17 February 2021", Statista.

33 "Bitcoin node count falls to a three-year low, despite price surge", Coindesk, 6 May 2020.

34 "Bitcoin node count hits a new all-time high", Cointelegraph, 20 January 2021.

35 World Payments Report 2020, CapGemini.

36 "Crypto inferno, an interview with Nouriel Roubini", *Octavian Report* 5:2 (Spring 2019).

37 "Exploring cryptocurrency and the blockchain ecosystem". Roubini's contribution: "Crypto is the mother of all scams and (now busted) Bubbles while Blockchain is the most over-hyped technology ever, no better than a spreadsheet/database", October 2018.

38 "Jamie Dimon slams Bitcoin as a fraud", Bloomberg, 12 September 2017.

39 See Marina Pasquali, "Economy and Politics", 18 June 2021; https://www.statista.com.

40 "A global first: Bitcoin as a national currency", *Wall Street Journal*, 16 June 2021.

41 An idea put forward by the *Financial Times*' Seeking Alpha, 9 June 2021.

42 *Ibid.*, 105.

43 *Book of Satoshi*, 342. The editor specifically claims that Andresen was allegedly the last person to have had a private exchange with Nakamoto before his withdrawal from public life.

CHAPTER 2

1 "2017 was the year when everyone (finally) learned Bitcoin isn't controlled by miners", Forbes, 30 November 2017.

2 *Ibid.*

3 "2x or No 2x, that was the question", Cointelegraph, 14 November 2017.

4 "What is Ethereum: guide for beginners", Cointelegraph. For further details about Ethereum, see V. Buterin, "The Ethereum White Paper: a next generation smart contract and decentralised application platform" (2015), https://ethereum.org.

5 Ethereum has certain important similarities with Bitcoin. Both have a built-in cryptocurrency: Bitcoin and Ether respectively. Both have proof-of-work and payment to miners, but Ethereum is much faster than Bitcoin at 13 seconds per transaction. Ethereum differs from Bitcoin with its smart contracts, written in a programming language and run "inside" the Ethereum miner nodes, when they are "called" by "user" accounts or other smart contracts inside the system. Ethereum by design enables its infrastructure to be used to create cryptocurrencies other than Ether for stablecoins or for the latest non-fungible tokens. These are unique digital items, such as art, audio, visual and other forms of creative work.

6   "Ripple unlocks 500 million XRP as analysts point to immense weakness", Blockchain, 1
    June 2020.

7   Quoted in "What is Ripple XRP? A complete guide to the banking cryptocurrency",
    Coincentral 20 May 2020.

8   "Lawsuit alleging Ripple's XRP is unregistered security moves forward", Cointelegraph, 27
    February 2020.

9   "Garlinghouse: Ripple would still survive even if XRP were declared a security", Coin-
    telegraph, 26 November 2020.

10 "SEC charges Ripple and two executives with conducting $1.3 billion unregistered securi-
    ties offering", 2020-338, 22 December 2020, press release. Case 1:20 cv 10832, Document
    4, filed 12/22/20. Summary, 1.

11 The Supreme Court's decision of what counts as an investment in the case of *W. J. Howey
    v SEC* is used to determine whether certain transactions qualify as investment contracts:
    the so-called "Howey Test". A useful discussion of the application of this test is found in
    the SEC's Framework for 'Investment Contract' Analysis of Digital Assets, 3 April 2019.

12 SEC Release N081207, 25 July 2017, Report of DAO.

13 Cointelegraph, 27 December 2020.

14 "What is Litecoin?", https://Litecoin.org.

15 Quoted in "New Malta Government says it still wants to run a blockchain island",
    Cointelegraph, 29 February 2020.

16 Public statement, MFSA, 21 February 2020.

17 Coindesk's interview with Changpeng Zhao, 8 May 2020.

18 All of these quotations are drawn from "EOS proves yet again that decentralization is not
    its priority", Cointelegraph, 15 November 2018.

19 "Everyone's worst fears about EOS are proving true", Coindesk, 19 September 2020.

20 C. Hoskinson on YouTube, as reported on "The Daily Hodl", 7 June 2020.

21 Cardano roadmap, Shelley/Decentralization; https://roadmap.cardano.org/en/shelley/.

22 "Shelley is delivered", Cardano Foundation Team, Announcement, July 2020.

23 See "What's behind the meteoric rise in obscure currency, Cardano?", MoneyWeek, 16
    March 2021.

24 This Open Letter can be found at https://passtebin.com/CcGUBgDG. The letter was also
    published by Steemit Crypto Academy.

25 "Some miners generating invalid blocks", 4 July 2015, Bitcoin.org.

26 *Bitcoin Manifesto*, 5.

CHAPTER 3

1   G. Klumov, "Looking into the history of stablecoins to understand the future of money",
    Cointelegraph, 13 April 2020.

2   *Investigating the Impact of Global Stablecoins*, a report by the G7 Working Group on
    Stablecoins, Committee on Payments and Market Infrastructure, Bank for International
    Settlements, October 2019, executive summary, iii.

3 Coin Rivet, 21 February 2020; *Irish Times*, 21 February 2020.

4 A less sympathetic response to the loss of a private key was given by Nakamoto in 2010: "Lost coins only make every one else's coins worth slightly more. Think of it as a donation to everyone" (*Book of Satoshi*, 129).

5 Latin American Bitcoin Conference, 10 December 2020, as quoted on Decrypt; https:// decrypt.co/.

6 "What is the ERC-20 standard?", ERC-20 Ethereum tokens, 7 September 2018.

7 "Untethered: the history of stablecoin tether and how it has lost its $1 peg", Cointelegraph, 17 October 2018.

8 *James v. IFINEX Inc.*, 2020 NY Slip OP. 03880, 9 July 2020: 3.4–5.5.

9 *James v. IFINEX Inc.*, Section 8, n.2.

10 *James v. IFINEX Inc.*, Section 8, n.2.

11 Cointelegraph, 11 November 2020.

12 "Bitfinex to compete with DeFi on new borrowing service", Cointelegraph, 11 November 2020.

13 "NYAG's $850m probe of Bitfinex tether ends in an $18.5m settlement", Coindesk, 23 February 2021.

14 Moore Cayman, Independent Accountant's Report, Grand Cayman, 31 March 2021.

15 See https://tether.to>content>uploads>2021/05.

16 "Tether's first reserve breakdown shows token 49% backed by unspecified commercial paper", Coindesk, 13 May 2021.

17 It is not surprising that the Basel Committee on Banking Supervision launched its consultation paper of stricter capital requirements for banks' cryptoasset exposures, 10 June 2021, press release.

18 "The 5 fastest growing stablecoins in August 2020: an analysis", Hackernoon, 4 October 2020.

19 R. K. Lyons & G. Viswanath-Natraj, "What keeps stablecoins stable?", Working paper 27136, National Bureau of Economic Research, 2019, 1.

20 D. Arner, R. Auer & J. Frost, "Stablecoins: risks, potential and regulation", BIS, November 2020, 10.

21 See https://ethereumstackexchange.com.

22 See https://ethereumprice.org/gas/.

23 Directive 2000/46EC and Directive 2009/110/EC.

24 EU Directive 2018/843, Sections 9 and 17.

25 D. Bullman, J. K. Leam & A. Pinna, "In the search for stability in cryptoassets: are stablecoins the solution?", ECB Occasional Paper Series No. 230, August 2019, 40–41.

26 V. Akgiray, "Blockchain technology and corporate governance", OECD Directorate for Financial and Enterprise Affairs, Corporate Governance Committee, 6 June 2018, 11.

27 It appears that this is now the subject of much research, beginning with a 1996 research paper by Dan Herman, a marketing strategist. Now there are sites with tips on how to combat it!

28 "Bitcoin worth $1B leaves Coinbase as institutions FOMO buy", Analyst, 2 January 2021.

29 C. Russo, "What is decentralized finance? A deep dive by the defiant", CoinMarketCap, 29 September 2020.

30 "How to code a flash loan with Aave", Finematics, 12 October 2020.

31 Collateralized loans in DeFi, the DeFi rate.

32 A useful analysis of the risks involved in DeFi is provided by the TAC virtual currency subcommittee of the CFTC; https://www.cftc.gov.

33 K. Rapoza, "What's the big deal about DeFi and how do you invest in it?", Forbes, 21 March 2021.

34 R. Nyuyen, "Why privacy and interoperability will fuel exponential growth in Defi", 4 March 2021.

CHAPTER 4

1 "Telegram abandons Telegram Open Network and Gram Tokens", Cointelegraph, 1 May 2020.

2 For further details, see "EOS is launched but not yet live – why?", Coindesk, 12 June 2018.

3 "Everyone's worst fears about EOS are proving true", Coindesk, 19 September 2019.

4 The full, complex story of Tezos can be found at "The History of Tezos", Cointelegraph, 5 July 2018.

5 D. A. Zetzsche *et al.*, "The ICO gold rush", EBI Working Paper Series, 2018-18.

6 "'The money's gone': Wirecard collapses owing $4bn", Reuters, 25 June 2020.

7 CryptoNinjas, 12 January 2021.

8 *SEC v. PlexCorps, Dominic LaCroix and Sabrina Paradis-Royer*, Case No. 17-cv-7007 (CBA) (RML) (E.D.N.Y.), 17 March 2021.

9 EY Study, "Initial coin offerings (ICOs): the class of 2017 – one year later", October 2018.

10 M. Fromberger & L. Haffke, *ICO Market Report 2018/2019: Performance Analysis of 2018's Initial Coin Offerings*, 23.

11 "How to launch an ICO: a detailed guide", Cointelegraph.

12 Stephen O'Neal, "How will we remember the Year of the Dog? ICO market decline, trend towards compliance and other takeaways", Cointelegraph, 10 February 2019, section entitled, "Compliance became cool".

13 *Ibid*.

CHAPTER 5

1 7 U.S. Code para 1a. Definitions, Section 9 Commodities. For what it is worth, Nakamoto described Bitcoin as a commodity: "Bitcoins have no dividend or potential future dividend, therefore not like a stock. More like a collectible or a commodity" (*Book of Satoshi*, 284).

2 This is covered in examples 2 and 3 which allow for the delivery to be made to a depository under certain circumstances, Retail Commodity Transactions involving Certain Digital Assets, CFTC, Final Interpretative Guidance, 24 March 2020.

3 CFTC Final Interpretative Guidance on the Actual Delivery of Virtual Currency, 24 March 2020; http://www.cftc.gov.

4 "CFTC orders Coinbase Inc to pay $6.5m for false, misleading or inaccurate reporting and wash trading", 19 March 2021, press release. "Wash trading" is a process by which a trader acts as both a buyer and seller of the same asset or security, with the aim of feeding false information to the market. It is illegal under US law and the IRS bars taxpayers from deducting wash trades from their taxable income. They can be used to generate fake volumes and pump up the price.

5 Securities and Exchange Commission, Report of Investigation Pursuant to Section 21(a) of the Securities and Exchange Act of 1934: The DAO. Release number 81207, 25 July 2017.

6 SEC's Investigation into DAO, 1.

7 SEC Securities and Exchange Act, 1934, Release No 81207/July 25,2017. Report of the Investigation pursuant to Section 21(a) of the SEC Act, 1934, The DAO.

8 Framework for "Investment Contract". Analysis of Digital Assets, Securities and Exchange Commission, Sections I and II, 3 April 2019.

9 The SEC refers to *Williamson v. Tucker*, 645 F.2d 404 (5th Cir. 1981), 422–4.

10 SEC Release No. 81207/July 25, 2017. Report of Investigation Pursuant to Section 21(a) of the Securities Exchange Act of 1934: The DAO, 15.

11 *Supreme Court v. Securities and Exchange Commission v. W. J. Howey Co et al.*, No. 483, Argued 2 May 1946 and delivered 27 May 1946. Text helpfully provided by the Legal Information Institute, Cornell Law School.

12 Congressional Research Service, "Securities regulation and initial coin offerings: a legal primer"; https://fas.org/sgp/crs/misc/R45301.pdf.

13 A Framework for 'Investment Contract' Analysis of Digital Assets.

14 Gary Gensler, Testimony before the Subcommittee on Financial Services and General Government, US House Appropriations Committee, 26 May 2021.

15 Directive 2004/39/EU Q&As published by the EU Commission, 22 February 2007.

16 E-Money Directive 2009/110/EC, Article 2(2).

17 On a blockchain payment network, the transfer of a token can be regarded as e-money, if it is electronically stored, has a monetary value, represents a claim on the issuer, is issued on receipt of funds, is issued for the purposes of making payment transactions and is accepted by persons other than the issuer.

18 Scriptural money is the money available on the current accounts of households and businesses, which can be used at any time to make payments using credit and debit cards, cheques, bank transfer or electronic money.

19 European Commission, Consultation Document, On an EU Framework for Markets in Cryptoassets, 5 December 2019, Introduction, 3.

20 *Ibid.*, 5.

21 Proposal for a Regulation of the European Parliament and of the Council on Markets in Cryptoassets, Explanatory Memorandum, 1 Context of the Proposal.

22 Token Alliance, "Understanding digital tokens; market overviews and proposed guidelines for policy makers and practitioners", Chamber of Digital Commerce, 2018.

23 R. W. Greene & D. Lee Kuo Chuen, "Singapore's open digital token offering embrace: context and consequences", *Journal of British Blockchain Association*, June 2019, 1.

24 Nizam Ismail quoted in, "Why Singapore ranks as the third most favourable country for ICOs", *Singapore Business Review*, September 2018.

25 Statement by Ms Loo Siew Yee, MAS press release, 23 January 2020.

26 Monetary Authority of Singapore, Reply to Parliamentary Question on the CryptoAsset Market, Question number 869, 5 April 2021.

27 Digital Economy Parliamentary Secretary Silvio Shembri, press release, 16 February 2018.

28 Malta Digital Innovation Authority Act, June 2018, Part II Guiding Principles.

29 "An overview of the Malta Digital Authority Bill", Ganado Advocates, 6 June 2018, para 4.

30 Quoted in "Journalist's murder darkens the story of 'Blockchain Island'", Forbes, 24 December 2019. The quotation is from "Running Commentary" which her sons and husband continued after her death.

31 Warning to the Public Regarding unlicensed VFA companies-MFSA, 24 April 2020; https://www.mfsa.mt.

32 *The Nature and Art of Financial Supervision, Vol II, Virtual Financial Assets*, MFSA, 8–9; https://www.mfsa.mt/wp-content/uploads/2020/12/The-Nature-and-Art-of-Financial-Supervision-Volume-II-Virtual-Financial-Assets.pdf.

33 "$71bn in crypto has reportedly passed through 'blockchain island' Malta since 2017", Cointelegraph, 20 June 2021.

34 *Guide for Crypto Currency Users and Tax Professionals*, Government of Canada, Canada Revenue Agency.

35 An Act to Implement Certain Provisions of the Budget Tabled in Parliament on 11 February 2014 and Certain Other Measures.

36 Christine Duhaime, "Canada implements world's first national digital currency law: regulates new financial technology transactions", Duhaimelaw, 22 June 2014.

37 Regulations amending Certain Regulations Made under the Proceeds of Crime (Money Laundering) and Terrorist Financing Act 2019 1(4), Canada Gazette, Part II, Vol. 153, No. 14, 2.

38 *Ibid.*, Part II, Vol. 153, No. 14 and Vol. 154, No. 12.

39 The progress of the regulations governing cryptocurrencies as securities can be seen in the series of steps taken by the CSA to applying the full rigour of securities regulations to trading in cryptoassets: CSA Staff Notice SN 4-307, Crypto currency offerings, 2017; CSA Staff Notice 46-208, Securities Law Implications for the Offering of Tokens, 2018. This was followed by a consultation paper issued by the CSA and Investment Industry Regulatory Organization of Canada in 2019 and in 2020, Staff Notice, 21-327, Guidance on the Application of Securities Legislation to Entities Facilitating the Trading of Crypto Assets.

40 Federal Report on virtual currencies in response to Schwaab (13.3687) and Weibel (13.070) Postulates, 3.

41 The amendments to the laws are not currently available in English. The details provided here are a summary of the details provided by the Library of Congress, Global Legal

Monitor, "Switzerland: New Amending Law adapts Several Acts to Developments in Distributed Ledger Technology", 3 March 2021.

42 Payment Services Act 2016, Definitions, Article 2, Virtual currencies, 5 (i) and (ii).

43 Payment Services Act 2016, Chapter III.

CHAPTER 6

1 On 1 December 2020, the Libra Association was renamed the Diem Association. The report, that is, the first White Paper, dated 19 June 2019 was published before the Association updated its White Paper v.2 in April 2020, which included a number of key updates to the Libra payment system. Outdated links have been removed, but, otherwise the report has not been modified to incorporate the updates and should be read in that context. However, this outline of the Libra Reserve is drawn from "The Libra Reserve" (2019) by Christian Catalini *et al.*, all of whom worked at Calabria, a subsidiary of Facebook Inc. The description of the Libra Reserve is drawn from this document, as it is a clear summary of the first view of the Libra Reserve. It is included here because the aim of this chapter is in part to trace the developments in Libra up to the end of 2020. This is essential if the regulatory responses, described in more detail in Chapter 7 are to be understood.

2 The original 28 founding members of the "non-profit" association announced by Facebook included "for-profit" companies in the payments industry (Mastercard, Visa, Mercado Pago and Paypal), tech companies (Lyft, Uber, Spotify, eBay), blockchain operators (Anchorage, Coinbase), Vodaphone, some venture capital groups such as Andreessen Horowitz Breakthrough Initiatives, Ribbit Capital, Thrive Capital and Union Square Venture, and three non-profits, Kiva, Women's World Finance and MercyCorps (all involved in microfinance).

3 Libra White Paper, Section "What are the actual assets that will be backing each coin?".

4 White Paper, v.1 Section "The Libra Reserve", para. "How is the reserve being held?".

5 White Paper v.1 Section "The Libra Association", Section 05.

6 Not to every country, since China, United Arab Emirates, Iran, Syria, North Korea, and Cuba (perhaps because the costs on internet use are too high for most to use). In addition, Facebook Inc could be forced to sell WhatsApp and Instagram after the US Federal Trade Commission and nearly every US state filed law suits against the company for his "buy or bury" strategy in December 2020. The case is still ongoing at the time of writing (April 2021). In the meantime, Facebook completed the merger of Messenger and Instagram chats in September 2020.

7 "What is Libra, Facebook's new digital coin?", *Financial Times*, 18 June 2019.

8 Letter to Mark Zuckerberg from Maxime Waters, Chair of House Financial Services Committee and Patrick McHenry, Ranking Member, 2 July 2019.

9 White Paper, v.1. Section 0.5 "The Libra Association", para 6.

10 "Buried in Facebook's Libra White Paper, a digital identity bombshell", Coindesk, 26 June 2019.

11 H. Vescent & K. Young, *A Comprehensive Guide to Self-Sovereign Identity* (2019).

12 David Marcus, Head of Calibra, 17 July 2019, Testimony before the House Financial Services Committee.

13 Written answer to Q4 from Senator Reed, Member of the Senate Banking, Housing and Urban Affairs Committee, 16 July 2019.

14 White Papers v 1.0, Section 0.2 "Introducing Libra", para 10, 18 June 2019.

15 Letter to Mark Zuckerberg from Waters and McHenry.

16 House Financial Services Committee, Monetary Policy and the State of the Economy, 10 July 2019.

17 Senate Banking, Housing and Urban Development Committee, 11 July 2019, Monetary Policy and the State of the Economy.

18 Examining Facebook's Proposed Digital Currency and Data Protection Considerations, 16 July 2019, 2.

19 Prepared Statement of David A. Marcus, Head of Calibra, Facebook, Protecting the Privacy and Security of Personal Information, for the Senate hearing, 49.

20 *Ibid.*, 49.

21 *Ibid.*, 22.

22 *Ibid.*, 25.

23 Senate Committee Hearing, 16 July 2019, 9.

24 *Ibid.*, 40.

25 Quoted in full in The Hill, 5 August 2019.

26 Bank of England, Financial Policy Committee, Quarterly Report, 9 October 2019, 26, para. 86.

27 https://www.bundesfinanzminiterieum.de and https://www.gouvernement.fr.

28 Submission to the Senate Select Committee on Financial Technology and Regulatory Technology, December 2019.

29 "The Libra White Paper has been edited, with notable changes", Fintech Policy, 10 December 2019.

30 The claim that a multi-currency Diem coin will be like the Special Drawing Rights of the IMF (SDR). But the SDR is not a currency. It is a prospective claim against the freely usable currencies that belong to the IMF member states, i.e. widely used to make payments for international transactions and widely traded in the principal exchange markets. The SDR basket is reviewed every five years to ensure that the basket reflects the relative importance of the world's currencies in the world's trading and financial systems, and it is these which remain fixed for over the five year SDR valuation period. The SDR value in terms of the US dollar is determined daily based on the spot exchange rates observed around noon London time, and posted on the IMF website. The IMF published a fact sheet on SDR on 18 February 2021 from which this explanation is drawn.

31 White Paper v. 2.0, Section 4 "Economics and the Libra Reserve"; https://www.diem.com/en-us/white-paper/.

32 "How Facebook's Libra went from being a game changer to just another Paypal", 17 April 2020.

33 "Will Libra live up to its initial ambitions?", Binance Research, 22 April 2020.

34 Libra White Paper, v. 2.0, 12–13. The second White Paper says that the Reserve will consist of short-term, high quality liquid asset – 80 per cent in sovereign bonds of up to three months remaining maturity with at least an A+/A1 rating and 20 per cent in cash with overnight sweeps into money market invested in similar government securities. A fiat currency received for each single-currency stablecoin would be invested in the securities meeting the criteria that are denominated in that currency. That makes for a complicated investment strategy.

35 Andrew Bailey, Governor of the Bank of England, House of Commons, Treasury Committee, Oral Evidence, Bank of England Stability Report, HC 115, Q 32, 6 January 2021.

36 "Diem announces partnership with Silvergate and strategic shift to the United States", Diem.com, press release, 12 May 2021.

37 "Diem co-creator says original plan for stablecoin was naïve", Coindesk, 26 May 2021.

CHAPTER 7

1 This is a general principle, frequently cited in discussions of the regulations which should apply to cryptoassets of all kinds.

2 *Ibid.*, 9.

3 *Ibid.*, 9.

4 *Ibid.*, 10.

5 The FSB analysed the financial stability risks raised by global stablecoin (GSCs) arrangements and conducted a comprehensive survey of the approaches to GSCs amongst its members and non-members of the G20 as well as outreach meetings with representatives from regulated financial institutions, financial technology firms, academia and the legal field.

6 "Investigating the impact of global stablecoins", Financial Stability Board report, October 2019, 11.

7 M. Adachi *et al.* "A regulatory and financial stability perspective on global stablecoin" (with the caveat that this does not represent the views of the ECB), *Macroprudential Bulletin*, 5 May 2020, Section 4.

8 The principles proposed by the Financial Stability Board, the Financial Action Task Forces and the International Organization of Securities Commissions are set out in Appendix 1.

9 The Prudential Treatment of Cryptoassets, Issued for comment by 10 September 2021, June 2021, 2.

10 These criteria are explained in more detail on pages 4–5 of the Consultation Paper.

11 The Prudential Treatment of Cryptoassets, 7.

12 *Ibid.*, 14.

13 *The Times*, 23 June 2021.

CHAPTER 8

1   For further details see "Project Jasper: a Canadian experiment with DLT for domestic interbank settlement" (September 2017); https://www.payments.ca/sites/default/files/29-Sep-17/jasper_report_eng.pdf and "Jasper Phase III" report (October 2018); https://www.payments.ca/sites/default/files/jasper_phase_iii_whitepaper_final_0.pdf.

2   "Fintech regulation trips Canada's stock exchange blockchain test", *Financial Times*, 12 November 2018.

3   Project Ubin Phase 5, Enabling Broad Ecosystem Opportunities, 7.

4   Project Stella report, 27 March 2018.

5   Project Stella, June 2019. Since then, the Bundesbank, the Deutsche Borse and Germany's Finance Agency have announced that they have developed and successfully tested a settlement interface for electronic securities by establishing a technological bridge between blockchain technology and a conventional payments system to settle securities in central bank money without the need to create central bank digital currency. See "DLT-based securities settlement in central bank money successfully tested", Bundesbank, 24 March 2021.

6   "Advancing together: leading the industry to accelerated settlement", DTCC, February 2021.

7   E. Avgouleas & W. Blair, "The concept of money in the 4th Industrial Revolution: a legal and economic analysis", *Singapore Journal of Legal Studies* 1 (2020), 7.

8   A. Rahmatian, "Money as legally enforceable debt", *European Business Law Review* (2018), 205–36.

9   Avgouleas & Blair, "The concept of money", 13.

10 *Ibid.*, 26. This section also defines *lex monetae* as the sovereign right of the state, that is, the right to issue currency, notes and coins that are legal tender within its territory; the right to determine and change the value of that currency and the right to regulate its use of that currency, or any other currency, within its territory.

11 Rahmatian, "Money as legally enforceable debt", 33–4, Quoting Joanna Perkins and Jennifer Enwezor, "The legal aspects of virtual currency", *Butterworth's Journal of International Banking and Financial Law* (2016), 569.

12 Avgouleas & Blair, "The concept of money", 37.

13 C. A. E. Goodhart, "The two concepts of money: implications for the analysis of optimal currency areas", *European Journal of Political Economy* 14 (1998), 408, 418.

14 "The role of central banks in the payments system", Bank for International Settlements, August 2003, 1.

15 *Ibid.*, 2.

16 "Central bank digital currency: opportunities, challenges and design", Bank of England Discussion Paper, March 2020, 35.

17 The Bank of England's platform model of retail CBDC would provide a fast, highly secure and resilient technology infrastructure which would exist alongside the Bank's Real-Time Gross Settlement and provide the minimum necessary functionality for retail CBDC

payments. The private sector could connect with this platform to provide customer-facing CBDC payment services.

18 A. Berentson & Fabian Schar, "The case for central bank electronic money and the non-case for central bank cryptocurrencies", Economic Research, Federal Reserve Bank of New York, 2018.

19 Christine Lagarde, speech, 14 November 2018.

20 R. Garratt & M. R. C. van Oordt, "Privacy as a public good: a case for electronic cash", Bank of Canada, 2019.

21 Joint Report on Cross-Border Payments, 27.

22 Joint Report on Cross-Border Payments, 48.

23 "Central bank digital currency", Bank of England, Discussion Paper, March 2020.

24 *Ibid.*, 32.

25 Financial Stability Report, December 2020, Section 5, 28.

26 "Going negative: The ECB's experience", speech by Isabel Schnabel, member of the executive board of the ECB, at the Roundtable of Monetary Policy, Low Interest Rates and Risk Taking, 35th Congress of the European Economic Association, August 2020.

27 M. Bech & R. Garratt, "Central bank cryptocurrencies", *BIS Quarterly Review*, September 2017, 59–61. The "money flower", as a taxonomy of different kinds of money seems to have fallen out of use.

28 The BoE notes that similar approaches have been taken by the New Payments Platform in Australia and Payments Canada's Modernization Programme.

29 Central Bank Digital Currrency Option, 32.

30 "Reinventing the wheel (with more automation)", speech by Andrew Bailey given at the Brookings Institution, virtual event, 3 September 2020; https://www.bankofengland.co.uk/speech/2020/andrew-bailey-speech-on-the-future-of-cryptocurrencies-and-stablecoins.

31 The Bank of England statement on Central Bank Digital Currency; https://www.bankofengland.co.uk/news/2021/april/bank-of-england-statement-on-central-bank-digital-currency.

32 S. Allen *et al.*, "Design choices for central bank digital currency: policy and technical considerations", Brookings Institution, Working Paper 140, July 2020, 44.

33 *Ibid.*, 41.

34 *Ibid.*, 39–47.

35 See *Report on a Digital Euro*, European Central Bank, October 2020, 17; https://www.ecb.europa.eu/pub/pdf/other/Report_on_a_digital_euro~4d7268b458.en.pdf.

36 *Ibid.*, 28.

37 *Ibid.*, 28.

38 *Ibid.*, 27.

39 Bank of Canada, European Central Bank, Sveriges Riksbank, Swiss National Bank, Bank of England, Board of Governors Federal Reserve System.

CHAPTER 9

1   *The 2019 Federal Reserve Payments Study*; https://www.federalreserve.gov/payment systems/2019-December-The-Federal-Reserve-Payments-Study.htm (last updated 6 January 2020). The value of all such payments totalled $97.04 trillion in 2018.

2   R. Kumar & S. O'Brien, "2019 findings from the diary of consumer payment choice", Federal Reserve Bank of San Francisco; https://www.frbsf.org/cash/publications/fed-notes/2019/june/2019-findings-from-the-diary-of-consumer-payment-choice/.

3   "A perspective on German payments", McKinsey & Company, September 2019, 2; https://www.mckinsey.com/~/media/McKinsey/Industries/Financial%20Services/Our%20Insights/A%20perspective%20on%20German%20payments/A-perspective-on-German-payments-vF.ashx.

4   "Ever more payments being made by card", Deutsche Bundesbank, 11 September 2020; https://www.bundesbank.de/en/tasks/topics/ever-more-payments-being-made-by-card-843634.

5   Quoted in "Will the coronavirus change Germans' love of cash?", BBC Worklife, 20 May 2020.

6   C. A. E. Goodhart & J. Ashworth, "Coronavirus panic fuels a surge in cash demand", CEPR Discussion Paper, 17 July 2020.

7   *Ibid.*

8   *Ibid.*

9   M. Bech *et al.*, "Payments are a-changing but cash still rules", *BIS Quarterly Review*, March 2018.

10 S. Shirai & E. Sugandi, "The cash hoarding puzzle", CEPR, 16 October 2019; https://voxeu.org/article/cash-hoarding-puzzle-and-rising-global-demand-cash.

11 "ECB ends production and issuance of €500 banknote", ECB press release, 4 May 2016.

12 In the distant past, the Federal Reserve has issued $1,000, $5,000, $10,000 and even $100,000 bills. The $500 bill was introduced in in 1945 and discontinued in 1969, but it is still legal tender, as is the $1,000 bill. With only 165,372 of these in existence, now worth more than their face value. The $5,000 bill was issued to finance the Revolutionary War but was discontinued in 1969 for fear of use in money laundering. Less than 400 of these are believed to exist. The $10,000 bill was first issued in 1918 and was part of the purge of large denomination bills in 1969. The $100,000 bill featuring Woodrow Wilson was actually a gold certificate for conducting transactions between federal reserve banks, not for public use. Only 42,000 were ever issued and a few are found in various federal reserve banks or the Museum of American Finance.

13 In 2014, there were 1,533 million in circulation of which the Royal Mint estimated about 3 per cent were counterfeit, which was the main reason for replacing the original brass and nickel to the current 12-sided bimetallic coins in 2017. The old pound coins were not convenient to carry around. Fifty coins in your pocket or handbag would mean carrying half a kilo, spoiling the line of your suits, jackets or weighing down your handbag. The euro coins do not weigh as heavily as the British coins, but enough to be inconvenient: 50 one euro coins weigh almost half a kilo.

14 The UK left the European Union on 31 January 2020.

15 R. Judson, "The death of cash? Not so fast: demand for US currency at home and abroad, 1990–2016", International Cash Conference 2017 – War on Cash: Is there a Future for Cash? April 2017, Deutsche Bundesbank, 3. The same view was also expressed in her earlier paper, "Crisis and calm: demand for US currency at home and abroad from the fall of the Berlin Wall to 2011", International Finance Discussion Papers, Board of the Governors of the Federal Reserve System, No. 2012-1058, November.

16 Ruth Judson, quoted by Funds Society, "As much as 60% of all Benjamins are held by foreigners", 20 September 2018.

17 Statista.com. Derived from currency in circulation in national currency, IMF and nominal GDP in current prices and national currency from Eurostat.

18 "Impending arrival: a sequel to the survey on central bank digital currency", BIS Papers No. 107, January 2020.

19 R. Auer, G. Cornelli & J. Frost, "Taking stock: ongoing retail CBDC projects", *BIS Quarterly Review*, March 2020, 97–8.

20 *Central Bank Digital Currency*, Federal Council report in response to the Postulate 18.3159, Wermuth, of 14.06.2018, Swiss Federal Council, 13 December 2019.

CHAPTER 10

1 EU Payments Account Directive (2014/92/EU).

2 "Cross border payments have been neglected for far too long", *Financial Times*, 30 July 2020.

3 "FSB reports on its work to develop a roadmap to enhance global cross-border payments", FSB press release, 9 April 2020; https://www.fsb.org/2020/04/fsb-reports-on-its-work-to-develop-a-roadmap-to-enhance-global-cross-border-payments/.

4 "The digital transformation of cross-border payments"; https://www.swift.com/our-solutions/swift-gpi/about-swift-gpi.

5 "SWIFT enables instant 24/7 cross-border payments"; https://www.swift.com/news-events/news/swift-enables-instant-247-cross-border-payments.

6 SWIFT detailed traffic report, November 2020 and the Financial Crimes division of the Treasury, 2006.

7 Cover letter to the Second White Paper. This refers to the section on offering single currency coins in addition to the multi-currency coins. The multi-currency coin would be a digital composite of some of the single-currency coins available on the Libra network. It will be defined in terms of the fixed nominal weights such as the Special Drawing Rights maintained by the IMF. But this is based on a misunderstanding of the SDR. It is only a potential claim on the freely usable currencies of IMF members. It is a funding of last resort only to be used by the IMF to rebalance economies when debt or liquidity crises occur.

8 "Central bank digital currencies: foundational principles and core features", Joint Report, October 2020, 3–4; https://www.bis.org/publ/othp33.htm.

9   "E-krona project, report 1", Sveriges Riksbank, September 2017, 4; https://www.riksbank.se/en-gb/payments--cash/e-krona/e-krona-reports/e-krona-project-report-1/.

10 "E-krona project, report 2", Sveriges Riksbank, October 2018, 4; https://www.riksbank.se/en-gb/payments--cash/e-krona/e-krona-reports/e-krona-project-report-2/.

11 "The Riksbank's e-krona pilot", Sveriges Riksbank, February 2020, 3; https://www.riksbank.se/globalassets/media/rapporter/e-krona/2019/the-riksbanks-e-krona-pilot.pdf.

12 *Ibid.*, 4.

13 "E-krona project, report 2", 25.

14 The Riksbank's e-project, February 2020. This is a short description of the pilot undertaken with Accenture.

15 The Riksbank's e-krona project, October 2018, 12.

16 Finansinspektionen's response to the Consultation, 11.

17 "Central Bank Digital Currencies", Bank for International Settlements, March 2018, 1.

18 "What is happening with the Riksbank's e-krona?" Swedish Bankers Association, 16 April 2019; https://www.swedishbankers.se/en-us/the-swedish-bankers-association-in-english/e-krona/what-is-happening-with-the-riksbank-s-e-krona/.

19 Finansinspektionen's response, 4, using comments from the FI's response.

20 "E-krona or bust, says Sweden's chief central banker, trying to drag Swedish govt into digital age", Coindesk, 16 October 2020.

21 "The Riksbank's e-krona pilot", 5.

22 The top four Chinese banks are the Industrial and Commercial Bank of China, the China Construction Bank, the Agricultural Bank of China and the Bank of China. They are all majority-owned by the Chinese government. The People's Bank of China has the typical central bank responsibility for monetary policy and representing the country in an international forum. The PBoC also regulates lending, not just for the safety and stability of banks, but also which companies, start-ups and individuals can receive credit, which would exclude those on the blacklist.

23 J. Areddy, "China creates its own digital currency, a first for a major economy", *Wall Street Journal*, 5 April 2021.

24 Fan Liang *et al.*, "Constructing a data-driven society: China's social credit system as a state surveillance infrastructure", *Policy and Internet* 10:4 (2018), 426.

25 *Ibid.*, 433.

26 "ECB digital euro consultation ends with a record level of public feedback", ECB press release, 13 January 2021; https://www.ecb.europa.eu/press/pr/date/2021/html/ecb.pr210113~ec9929f446.en.html.

27 "An ECB digital currency – a flight of fancy?" Speech by Yves Mersch, member of the executive board of the ECB and vice-chair of the supervisory board of the ECB, 11 May 2020.

28 "The future of money and payments", speech by Agustin Carstens, General Manager of the BIS, Dublin, 22 March 2019, 6; https://www.bis.org/speeches/sp190322.htm.

29 Carstens, "Future of money and payments", 6.

30 Sir Paul Tucker, "The political economy of central banking in the digital age", in The Financial System of the Future, 44th Economics Conference, 2017 of the OeNB (National Bank of Austria) in cooperation with SUERF, 53.

31 That is the argument of my book, *Fannie Mae and Freddie Mac: Turning the American Dream into a Nightmare* (London: Bloomsbury Academic, 2012).

32 Testimony of Alex Pollock, to the Subcommittee on Monetary Policy and Trade of the Committee on Financial Services, Hearing on "The Future of Money: Digital Currency", 18 July 2018: 42.

33 M. McLeay *et al.*, "Money creation in the modern economy", *Bank of England Quarterly Bulletin*, Q1 2014: 14.

34 P. Bofinger & T. Haas, "Central bank digital currencies risk becoming a gigantic flop", CEPR, Vox EU, 1 February 2021.

35 The process by which banks invest in long-term, illiquid assets, such as mortgages, funded by short-term liabilities.

36 Central banks provide this insurance by acting as a backstop to the banking system as a whole or individual financial institutions which may suffer temporary liquidity shortages by providing banks with highly liquid assets in exchange for a wide range of collateral assets of good credit quality but less liquid for a relatively short period of time. This "insurance" is not intended to be a permanent prop even to a solvent bank with temporary liquidity problems.

37 J. Fernandez-Villaverde *et al.*, "Central bank digital currency: central banking for all", Federal Reserve Bank of Philadelphia, August 2020.

38 S. Hanke, "Lack of trust opens door for cryptocurrencies", OMFIF, 22 January 2021; https://www.omfif.org/2021/01/lack-of-trust-opens-door-for-cryptocurrencies/.

APPENDIX

1 M. Bech *et al.*, "On the future of securities settlement", *BIS Quarterly Review*, March 2020, 75.

Index